For Dori[

Dame Stephanie Shirley

Steve Shirley

LET IT GO

Written with Richard Askwith

Andrews UK Limited

Second edition published in 2013 by
Andrews UK Limited
The Hat Factory
65-67 Bute Street
Luton, LU1 2EY

www.andrewsuk.com

Cover photo by PS:Unlimited Photography

Contents

Let IT Go

Dame Stephanie Shirley

1: A Strange Journey

My earliest memory of England is of Liverpool Street station. It was a grey day in July, a few weeks before the outbreak of World War II. I'm not sure if it was raining as I stumbled from train to platform, or, indeed, what time of day it was. All I remember is the shadows, and the great cast iron pillars and walkways, and the pain in my foot.

I was five years old. My nine-year-old sister and I had been travelling for more than two days, on a grim, tearful journey from Vienna. We knew scarcely half a dozen words of English between us, and I, at least, had only the vaguest idea of where we were going and why.

There were about 1,000 of us on the train: all Jewish; all children – apart from two young women charged with looking after us all; and nearly all distraught. We had numbered tickets hanging around our necks as if we were lost property. In a sense, we were.

Two-and-a-half days earlier, we had all said goodbye to our parents (in my case, just my mother) for what was, for most of us, the last time. We were among the last – and I was almost the youngest – of around 10,000 child refugees who were saved from Hitler's terror by that great gamble of hope and despair that came to be known as the Kindertransport. For much of the previous year, millions of Jews in Germany and Austria (and, later, Czechoslovakia and Poland) had been struggling to come to terms with the once unthinkable truth that the civilized nations in which their lives were rooted had descended into deadly barbarism. Many resigned themselves to staying put and hoping for the best, but others calculated – correctly – that staying put was equivalent to signing their families' death warrants. Yet the rest of the world had largely closed its borders to refugees. So when a coalition of concerned groups in the UK formed the Movement for the Care of Children from Germany – later known as the Refugee Children's Movement – and gained official permission for up to 10,000 Jewish children to be admitted as refugees, some families, including mine, decided that they had no choice but to send their children away to Britain to be fostered.

It is almost impossible, from the comfort and safety of today, to imagine the mental agonies that such parents must have endured. Extraordinary leaps of faith and imagination would have been required

– faith in the kindness of unseen strangers but also imagination of what Nazism must ultimately lead to. Unbearable pangs of doubt and regret must have followed.

For us children, it was simpler. Our lives – as we had known them – were coming to an end when they had scarcely begun.

Not all of us realized the full awfulness of what was happening, as our families voluntarily dissolved themselves. I suspect that most of the parents had scarcely faced up to the full truth themselves, let alone spoken unambiguously about it to their children. But the sense of bereavement on the platform in Vienna had been overwhelming. There were enough wailing adults, never mind howling children, to make a mockery of those who were trying to put a brave face on it. Maybe there were a few of us who really believed that we were being sent off on a nice adventure. But it was hard not to see the truth in the grown-ups' eyes.

Perhaps I should have been grateful for the pain in my foot. Most of my fellow passengers had nothing to distract them from the pain of being sent away. But I was too miserable to be interested in anyone else. I had grazed a big toe a few days earlier, and the wound had somehow become infected. Now, with each passing hour, the dull, throbbing ache became more tormenting. Perhaps it masked the ache of separation, or perhaps the two aches have merged in my memory.

It is hard, after all these years, to be certain how many of the remembered details of the journey are real and how much I have added to my mental picture from other sources. Was the weather outside really grey? Or have I just seen too many black-and-white photographs of the Kindertransport? Did one boy keep getting out to be sick during the train's many unscheduled pauses? Or was that just a dream?

I am pretty certain that children slept on the floor as well as on the long wooden benches that lined the sides of the carriages; there were some large strips of corrugated cardboard that they used as mattresses. I presume that I slept too, although I cannot remember doing so. I think our parents had given us sandwiches for the journey; but, again, I may be wrong.

But I do know that they had given us presents (in my case, two tiny model dogs, joined together on a miniature leash) which we were forbidden to open until the train was moving – making us heartlessly eager for the journey to begin. I know, too, that I clung grimly for most of the journey to my favourite doll.

I remember many stops, and occasional frightening interruptions from uniformed guards. I recall vividly the cold, oily smell of the sea – an entirely new experience – when we eventually reached the Channel (presumably at the Hook of Holland); and I vaguely remember a nauseous crossing in a cabin below deck. I am certain that, at some point in the train journey, children slept on the long overhead luggage racks – although the scene in my mind's eye is quite different from the carriage interiors I have since seen in archive photographs. And I doubt that there is much wrong with my impression that there was scarcely a moment in those two-and-a-half days of travelling when our miseries were not exacerbated by the jarring sound of other people's crying.

But what about my sense that, when we finally arrived at Liverpool Street, the platform was silent? It seems somehow implausible, and perhaps I have merely projected the numbness of my emotions on to the past. None the less, that is how my mind has preserved it: we spilled out on to the platform, speechless and wide-eyed, as if in a dream. Most of us were wearing hats and overcoats. We were allowed to bring only as much luggage as we could carry, and so our parents – desperate that we should not go cold or ragged in the strange new world to which they were banishing us – had packed our little cases to bursting-point and then flung a few extra garments on to us for good measure. Our coats still bore the yellow stars we had been forced to have sewn on to them in Austria.

The slow river of exhausted, bewildered, tear-stained faces flowed noiselessly down the platform. Renate (my sister) and I found ourselves in a huge, high, cavernous hall – now long-since demolished – where, after a quick roll-call, we waited for our new families. There were piles of palliasses – big bags filled with straw – heaped up against one of the walls, and the air was sickly with the smell of unwashed children.

None of us had any idea what to expect. The RCM had simply advertised in various British newspapers for families who were willing to foster a refugee child or two, and Renate and I knew nothing about the couple who had volunteered to take us in beyond their names. Every now and then adults would hurry past and say things, and occasionally announcements were made, but the strange language meant nothing to us. Our father had, at the last minute, taught us a handful of English phrases, but they were bizarre and random things such as "windscreen wiper" and "slow combustion stove". I had no idea how to ask to go to the toilet, let alone how to understand strangers' explanations about what was going to happen to us.

The afternoon wore on. Renate and I sat on a palliasse at the back and watched as more and more children were led away, usually in ones or twos. No one seemed to protest when confronted with their new parents. Perhaps they were too tired and scared to do so. Or perhaps I was too absorbed in my own miseries to notice.

I don't know how long we sat there. Eventually, however, Renate and I were summoned. We were led outside by a serious-looking, gruff-voiced, middle-aged man in dark clothes. The streets seemed strange and dirty compared with Vienna. A big red Morris car was parked nearby, with a middle-aged lady, wearing lots of make-up, waiting in the passenger-seat.

We all got in, and drove off to our new life.

The journey, which lasted several hours, could not have been more miserable. We were tired, hungry and traumatised. Our new parents, who went by the name of Guy and Ruby Smith, spoke no German, so conversation was impossible. Meanwhile, it had just dawned on me that, in addition to my other woes, I had somehow managed to lose my precious doll. I am told that I howled my heart out for the entire journey.

Was it really the doll that bothered me? Or had its loss become a symbol of everything else we had lost? I cannot be certain: not after so much time. But I am sure of one thing. This was not really (as it seemed then) an ending. It was a beginning. This was the moment when, to all intents and purposes, my life began.

I have done more in the seven decades since that miserable day than I would ever have believed possible. I have achieved undreamt of riches – and given most of them away. I have built a global business empire, founded schools and institutes, dined with heads of state and exchanged ideas with some of the most brilliant minds of our time. I have been involved in pioneering achievements in business, science, medicine, academia and philanthropy. I have, I hope, changed many hundreds of lives – perhaps more – for the better. I have achieved fame and influence and am in the fortunate position of being able to do more or less what I like with my own life while also being able to make a difference to the wider life of the nation.

I have, in short, been extraordinarily lucky.

I have known failure and heartbreak as well as success, but I have never quite lost sight of two life-defining ideas – both of which I can trace back to my arrival in England all those years ago as a terrified, weeping child refugee.

The first is the conviction that even in the blackest moments of despair there is hope, if one can find the courage to pursue it. Sometimes the worst is less overwhelmingly awful than we fear; sometimes the right attitude can create good even from life's most terrible situations..

My second big idea is the matching conviction that, even though I ostensibly lost everything when my parents were forced to send me away, I was not just the victim of bigotry and cruelty. I was also the fortunate beneficiary of the unearned generosity of many people: the Jewish and Christian activists who set up the Kindertransport, the Quakers who kept the project going when it ran out of money, the ordinary people who chipped in with the various tedious administrative tasks that allowed the project to function, the Catholic nuns who helped to educate me, and the quiet, middle-aged, nominally Anglican couple who took me in.

Without my being fully aware of what was going on or why, a large number of good-natured strangers took it upon themselves to save my life. It took me some years to digest this fact and its implications. But, once I had, a simple resolution took root deep in my heart: I had to make sure that mine was a life that had been worth saving.

I may not always have succeeded in this aim. But I have at least learnt lessons along the way: about how to make things happen, how to deal with setbacks and how to turn the most improbable dreams into realities.

If I now presume to write this account of some of my life's defining episodes, it is because I believe that these lessons – the lessons life has taught me – are worth sharing.

It has, at any rate, been an unusual life.

2: My Lost World

My life wasn't supposed to be interesting. I began it in a respectable, well-off family in Dortmund, Germany. The four of us lived in a nice town-house in a fashionable part of the city, with two live-in servants, and Renate went to school with the children of other prosperous bourgeois families.

If all had gone according to plan I would have remained in that comfortable world indefinitely. I would have married a nice professional man and raised a similar family myself. It is unlikely that I would ever have had a meaningful job. But the shadows had been gathering since shortly before my birth, and my time as a member of the leisured Westphalian bourgeoisie turned out to be so short that today I can scarcely remember it.

My mother was beautiful but brittle: the younger daughter of a wealthy gentile family in Krems, in Austria, who had educated her to be a middle-class wife. She had never worked – beyond a little dress-making that she pursued more as a hobby than as a business – and put her energy instead into fussing about appearances. She was always immaculately turned-out, and so were we. Yet she usually seemed discontented, as if she had wanted something quite different from life.

My father was a high court judge: a brilliant but rather distant man. I think he was almost a genius – but maybe a bit autistic too. A coffee-importer's son, he was a gifted violinist who spoke seven languages and had the most extraordinary memory. He could recite railway timetables by heart – and, to our embarrassment, sometimes did.

But he was also charming and had a quality of absolute integrity: a single-minded devotion to principle that was slightly unworldly but also, sometimes, slightly inhuman. I have a vivid early memory of going for a family walk in some semi-rural setting – presumably one of Dortmund's famous parks – and stamping, for some reason, on a beetle. My father exploded into a blazing fury. "How would you like it if someone stamped on you?" he shouted. It was an extraordinary rage, really, to direct at a mere toddler. Yet he did get his point through to me.

I also remember him suffering occasional bouts of violent vomiting. I later learnt that these were connected with the ghastliest aspect of his job: like all German judges at the time, he was required to witness the execution of anyone he sentenced to death. I'm not sure if the sickness occurred before or after the events (which were mercifully rare); but the memory shows that he did not take his responsibility lightly.

I think he imagined that his incorruptibility would enable him to fight the evils of Nazism, but the tide of evil proved too strong. He had been a rising star of his profession, becoming a judge shortly after his thirtieth birthday (that is, in 1930). But by the time I was born – on 16 September 1933 – career doors were starting to be closed in his face, partly because of his Jewishness and partly because of his open contempt for National Socialism. Again and again, we were forced to move – from city to city and eventually from country to country – in search of work and security. By the time I was five we had lived in seven different European countries. Of these, I dimly remember Germany, Italy and Hungary; and Austria, where we eventually settled on the outskirts of Vienna.

We had a nice home there – a big, square town-house at the top of a hill in the leafy suburb of Perchtoldsdorf, near the Vienna Woods – and my father had work for a while. But the Nazi plague soon infected Austria as well – the Anschluss annexed Austria into the Third Reich on 12 March 1938 – and by my fifth birthday, a few weeks before Kristallnacht, the writing was on the wall for anyone who dared to read it: Jewish families who stayed in Central Europe faced catastrophe.

One of my clearest memories of Perchtoldsdorf is of walking to fetch my sister from school; I particularly remember a huge stone wall – like the side of a giant's castle – that lined part of our route. Years later, I discovered two things about this memory. First, the wall wasn't huge at all. (I learnt this when I revisited the city a few years after the war.) More importantly, there was a reason why we were going to collect my sister. It was because, even as a nine-year-old, she was beginning to suffer from the kind of violent anti-Semitism that was about to overwhelm us all. She was lucky enough to have a kind teacher, who used to let her out early so that that she could get home – under escort – without being stoned by her fellow pupils.

I imagine that it was my father – with his habit of interpreting the world with his head rather than his heart – who first faced up to the unthinkable reality that the once solid social framework in which our lives had been built had collapsed, leaving a choice between escape and eventual extinction.

It was 1939 by then, and country after country was closing its borders to refugees. But we had some remote family in America, and it seemed possible that, with their help, we might end up there. Time was running out, however, and my parents' immediate priority was to protect their children. When they heard about the Kindertransport, they decided that Renate and I should be sent to safety.

I was too young to suspect what this desperate decision must have meant to them. Later on, I would feel guilty about this – just as I would feel guilty about a lot of things that can hardly have been my fault. The fact was, these were troubled times, and ours was already a troubled family.

My mother had had high hopes of her life. Pretty, clever and well-educated, she had married well: my father was not only brilliant and handsome when she met him but cultured and well-connected – with a circle of sophisticated friends that would later include Georg Solti, the great conductor – and he had dazzling career prospects. I think she entertained visions of being a lady of leisure, hosting a glittering salon in which clever people played music and discussed philosophy. Instead, she found herself uprooted and persecuted, with a husband whose prospects diminished by the day. Not being Jewish herself, she blamed my father for her misfortunes. Yet their relationship had been in trouble even before the Nazis came to power: I was once told that I had been "the child to save the marriage". If this was true, it was not a role that I performed very successfully. I was largely brought up by nurses, and I have little memory of my mother being loving or maternal towards me. Instead, in my mental images of my early childhood, Mutti – as we called her – is always displeased with me.

But I must not be unfair. No one who has not been in such a position themselves can judge parents for their reactions to the intolerable pressures placed on them by a poisonous dictatorship. Perhaps, if we had stayed together, I would remember my parents with more affection. The fact that we did not was not their fault. On the contrary, it reflected their concern for our well-being.

The Kindertransport trains had been running for about six months when the decision was taken to send us away. Time and funds were running out. But it was not a simple matter. Forms had to be filled in, documents stamped, permits queued for at inconvenient times, guarantees provided. We spent several weeks in a children's home – of which I remember little beyond the fact that it had a large indoor swing on one of the landings – while my mother devoted herself full-time to grappling with the obstacles of Nazi and British bureaucracy.

Meanwhile, there was the scarcely less urgent problem to be addressed of finding a way for my parents to escape too – and, if possible, for the family to be reunited. The difficulty was identifying a place that would accept us. The Refugee Children's Movement had found Renate and me a foster family in England who were prepared to guarantee, with £50 of their own money, that we would not be a burden on the state. But with millions of would-be refugees seeking safe havens from Nazi Europe, and with the Nazis making it all but impossible for them to take any wealth with them, most adults had no choice but to remain where they were, irrespective of the dangers they faced.

Renate and I left Vienna eight weeks before the outbreak of war. A few weeks earlier, my father had escaped over the mountains to Switzerland on foot, like the von Trapp family in The Sound of Music. The Gestapo had visited our house a few days earlier, and he must have realised that he was in imminent danger of arrest; but I think the idea may also have been that, with him gone, my mother could be freed from the handicap of being considered Jewish or anti-Nazi.

If so, it was a good strategy. Unlike most of the parents who sent their children away on the Kindertransport, mine survived. While Renate and I were struggling to find our feet in our strange new world, our parents both managed their own desperate journeys to England. My father got there before us – I have a strange memory that he actually appeared for a few moments while we were being collected from Liverpool Street – but was soon interned as an enemy alien and in due course transported to Australia, where he remained until 1941, subsequently joining the Pioneer Corps in the UK and, much later, becoming attached to the US army in Germany.

My mother was able to escape by train – apparently on the basis that she was an ordinary Austrian with ordinary travelling rights. She was more inclined than my father to fit in, sometimes even wearing a swastika to avoid drawing attention to herself. None the less, she had no intention of staying behind without her family, and, when she fled, she had to leave behind everything that she possessed. When she eventually reached England she was penniless, homeless, jobless and stateless. It would be a long time before we heard from her again.

Meanwhile, in a small village in the English Midlands, Renate and I were already beginning to forget the wide avenues of the central European cities which had hitherto formed the backdrop to our world. Instead, we were absorbing the unfamiliar rhythms of a new culture and a new language – and, in effect, a whole new life.

Those early pre-English days now seem almost unreal to me, as if they belonged to someone else's memories. As an adult, on at least one occasion, I have given my date of birth on an official form as July 1939: an entirely subconscious slip with an obvious explanation.

Looking back today, from the other end of a life that has been exceptionally rich in nearly every sense, I can see that most of my subsequent achievements can be traced back to that unnatural separation. It marked the beginning of a narrative far more interesting than the one that had originally been scripted for me. But it also taught me, with the ending of my first life, a profound lesson: that few things in life are as solid as they seem; that tomorrow will not always resemble today; and that wholesale change, though often terrifying, is not necessarily synonymous with catastrophe.

3: England, My England

My new life in England began badly. Our foster parents, Guy and Ruby Smith, had no experience of child-raising and seemed to be as taken aback as we were by the gulf between our cultures. They were a middle-aged, conventional couple, set in their ways, who had read about our plight in a local newspaper. "Two sisters," the advertisement had said, under pictures of Renate and me, "brought up in a nice family. Will somebody give them a home?" You can imagine the horrified doubts they must have harboured during their first days as custodians of the real, flesh-and-blood sisters in question: two strange, bewildered children, one of whom – Renate – was becoming withdrawn and sullen while the other – me – scarcely stopped crying.

The Smiths lived in the West Midlands, in a village called Little Aston, now a prosperous suburb of Sutton Coldfield but in those days quite modest and rural. Their home, called Northways, was an unremarkable detached house, solid and relatively new – but also barer and colder than anything we were used to. There had obviously never been children in it.

Renate and I shared a small double room, with nothing in it apart from a double bed (which we would divide down the middle by a bolster); a dressing table (with a black ebony tray on it bearing matching hand-mirror, hairbrush and comb); and a rather unsettling portrait of Ruby's father on the wall. It was perfectly comfortable, but it was hard, on those first strange nights, not to fear that life in our nice new home was going to be a grim ordeal.

Yet things improved surprisingly quickly. Shortly after our arrival, Ruby, having failed to mollify me over the loss of my doll with soothing words that I could not understand, disappeared for an hour or two and returned with a gift: a rag doll. It was a pretty disastrous piece of needlework, to be honest: just a couple of dusters badly sewn together. But as a childcare tactic it must have worked, because I kept Kate – as I called her – for at least a decade and was devastated when she was eventually thrown away.

Not long afterwards, I developed measles. This was no laughing matter then, and death must have seemed a real possibility. But Ruby, horrified at the thought of losing one of the children who had been

11

*This formal portrait of Renate and I was done immediately
prior to our leaving Vienna on a Kindertransport.*

entrusted to her, nursed me assiduously, and, in due course, I pulled through. I don't know how effective her practical ministrations were, but her obvious, tearful concern and tireless attention helped to create a bond between us. Before long, I was settled quite happily in my new home.

Guy and Ruby could hardly have been more different from my own parents. Neither was very educated – Guy had left school at 14 – and there was nothing intellectual or cosmopolitan about them. They owned half-a-dozen records and a library of perhaps 20 books. Yet they were, in their stolid way, a lovely couple.

Guy was in his mid-forties, the managing director of a small light engineering firm in which he had started out, three decades earlier, as an apprentice. He was hard-working but wonderfully solid: firm, loving, consistent and calm. He had done well for himself but never talked about work when he came home – and never betrayed the slightest sign of any stress he might have been feeling. Instead, he went about his domestic duties in a patient, methodical way, radiating reassurance to those around him – especially children and animals.

Ruby was more of a flibbertigibbet: an impulsive, highly strung, romantic woman who had married Guy on the rebound and often told him so. There was something slightly ridiculous about her: she was brittle, self-centred, hopeless in the house, with a "mutton dressed as lamb" approach to clothes. She was also rather snobbish, with more interest in appearance than in substance. Yet there was a genuine warmth inside her that her foibles could not stifle. It had been her idea that they should take us in; and it was she, I think, who was first to love us.

Renate found it hard to love her back. I remember her getting desperately upset when Ruby insisted that she brush her hair in a different way from the one she was used to. Another time, there was a huge row involving Renate's use of butter. I never grasped the details – only the fact that, for Renate, it was a mortal affront to be forced to do things differently. Little physical foibles and habits are part of what defines families, and Renate – who had inhabited the world of our family for nearly twice as long as I had – felt almost violated by the requirement to adopt different habits. (In later life, when I learnt about the experiences of other Kindertransport children, I realised that she had been far from alone in this. Almost invariably, it was the older children who had found it hardest to settle.)

Despite the tears, however, we grew used to our new world. We called Guy and Ruby "Uncle" and "Auntie", which is how I have thought of them ever since. They in turn called me "Pickles". My actual name, I should add, was Vera: Vera Buchthal. (I adopted Stephanie, hitherto my middle name, when I was 18, along with the anglicised surname of Brook. The Steve and the Shirley came later, for reasons that will become clear in due course.) Renate was nicknamed "Bob" – a reference to her hairstyle – but never took to it and soon became Renate again.

Within a couple of months, we were deemed to have learnt enough English to be capable of being educated. So we were enrolled at the little village school, down Forge Lane. It was near enough for us to be able to walk there – just a few minutes across the fields – and near enough, too, for Ruby to observe through binoculars what went on in the playground. (When Renate learnt that she had been doing this, there was another furious row.)

The children at school were friendly enough, with none of the anti-Semitism that had blighted Renate's earlier schooldays. Outsiders were not uncommon in rural England: more than 800,000 schoolchildren had been evacuated to the countryside because of the risk of urban bombing. And, in any case, the headmistress, a formidable lady called Miss Proud, would never have tolerated bullying.

But although we enjoyed school, it was the atmosphere at home that I remember most vividly. Even with Renate's unhappiness, and Auntie's volatility, there was something very calm, and very nurturing, about that household. Auntie and Uncle had clear ideas as to how children should be brought up. Some of these, which I attribute to Auntie, were superficial: we were supposed to wear little gloves when we went out, for example, and she was very keen on table manners. But most of them involved traditional, almost Victorian values. We had to do the housework before we were allowed to go out and play, and Uncle was always quoting the kind of sayings that were commonplace among respectable people in those days, such as "Waste not, want not" or "If a job's worth doing, it's worth doing well." It may have been a rather clichéd outlook, but most of it sunk in – and I am glad that it did.

Both were patriotic – Uncle had fought in the Great War – and this rubbed off on me too. The handful of 78rpm gramophone records that they owned consisted largely of tunes such as "Pomp and Circumstance", "Rule Britannia", "Jerusalem" and Purcell's "Trumpet Voluntary" (tunes that still move me), and they believed strongly that everyone had a duty to their country. Sometimes they would have friends round to play whist, and, when they did, we would listen to their grown-up conversation. A recurrent theme was the abdication of Edward VIII in 1936. When I first had the story explained to me, I thought: how romantic, he gave up the throne for the woman he loved. But the grown-ups insisted that this wasn't the point. "Yes," Uncle would say, "but he didn't do his duty." He said it with such certainty that I was eventually persuaded. Even now, I can never quite shake off the idea that, somehow, you always have to do your duty – otherwise you are letting yourself down.

Auntie and Uncle were comfortably off, but our life was austere by modern standards, largely because of the war. Food was rationed, and we would never do anything like, say, buying clothes. (My mother, not wanting to put our foster family to any avoidable expense, had sent after us a trunk packed with clothes. Some were for me to wear straight away and some were for me to grow into; others, similarly, were for Renate to wear straight away or for her to grow into. Both of Renate's sets would then be handed down to me. By the time I had grown out of all four sets – all of which looked embarrassingly foreign – the war would be almost over.)

We spent a lot of time being cold. The boiler was switched on once a week, briefly, so that we could have a bath, and I have painful memories of the vividly mottled shins that resulted from standing too close to the fire – when we had one – trying to warm up.

It was a much more rural life than anything we had known before: walking to and from school through the fields, playing among the sweet-smelling bluebells in the woods, or helping Uncle in the vegetable garden he had made by digging up his long back lawn – these were all new and rather delightful experiences. Uncle used to push me around in a big wooden wheelbarrow, or just chat to me in his slow, matter-of-fact way as he dug up his root vegetables, in which he took great pride. (We ate a lot of beetroot.) I grew to love the reassuring smell of his pipe smoke, and the approaching purr of his car when he

Auntie and Uncle had not had children but brought us up as if we were their own. Renate did not settle easily but I am totally their child.

came back from work. Sometimes we would rush out on to the lane to meet him and ride the last few yards of his journey on his running board.

At Christmas, we went to stay with Uncle's parents – whom we called Large Uncle and Little Auntie – in a tiny cottage in Bromley Wood, near Abbots Bromley in east Staffordshire. This was truly rural. They had no gas, no electricity, no running water: just the patient, plodding power of their own incessant labour. To a child's eye it seemed idyllic: a magical pocket of ancient country life that had somehow survived into the 20th century. You could pump water from the yard, but the water from up in the village tasted nicer. I can still see today the image of Large Uncle going to collect water with a yoke over his shoulders, with a bucket on each end.

As 1940 unfolded, we became more aware of the war. The Germans began to bomb Birmingham, which was near enough for a decoy "factory" to have been built in a field not far from Little Aston. It looked like a mass of chicken huts on their sides, all lit up, and was supposed to look like the target factories in Birmingham. It only ever attracted one bomb. People joked that the German pilots knew all about it and used it simply as a landmark from which to take their bearings for the real Birmingham.

But air raids were taken seriously. Uncle, who was an Air Raid Protection warden, had dug a large shelter into the garden, big enough both for us and for the neighbours. There were plenty of alarms, and I have many memories – all blurred into one – of being lifted out of bed and carried half-sleeping down to the shelter. But I don't remember feeling frightened.

The other thing that was curiously absent – at least in my memory – was anxiety about what had become of my parents. As a five-year-old, one adapts and forgets quickly. But we did have reason to believe that they were both alive – and an early letter from my father in which he said that he had heard nothing from Mutti for a long time and assumed that she was "lost" was, I think, kept from us until later. The Red Cross ran a wonderful communication service that allowed people to send five-word telegrams across the war-torn continent. Every few months, one would arrive from our grandmother, who lived in the Netherlands. Most just said things such as: "Hope well. Be good. Granny." But she also tried to keep us – or our foster parents – abreast of what was happening, and I know that there was one, a few months into our stay, that said – with reference to my mother – "We think she's got out."

At some point, presumably in 1940, a letter arrived from Mutti herself. I don't think I was told about this straight away; in fact, for all I know there may have been more than one letter. But the gist of the message or messages was that she was in England but had no money, no fixed home and, for the time being, no way of coming to see us. There was no work available to her as a refugee, apart from domestic service or working in the fields. I think she tried both.

Eventually, she found a job in Oswestry, in Shropshire, working in a school kitchen. I think she had heard the town recommended by some other refugees from Germany. She had stayed briefly in the house of an émigré German professor called Dr Hachenberg, but now that she was working she had been able to find somewhere more permanent to live: rented rooms in the house of a family called Blythe.

Today one can drive from Little Aston to Oswestry in less than an hour and a half. In 1940, without motorways, or a car, or petrol, or money, for a "friendly enemy alien" who in any case was subject to travel restrictions and a curfew (and who – unlike Auntie and Uncle – did not have access to a telephone), we might as well have been on different planets. So it was a long time before we met up, and, when we did, the meeting was brief and stilted. Mutti visited us in Little Aston, where Auntie and Uncle gave her tea and everyone was on their best behaviour. Perhaps Mutti felt it necessary to "be brave" for our sakes; or perhaps, as it seemed to me, she just wasn't very pleased to see me. Either way, things took a turn for the worse when she said something about hoping that we would all be able to move to America before too long. I burst into tears and clung to Auntie's knees, wailing "I want to stay with Auntie!" – with predictable effects on my long-term relationship with both women.

Mutti then disappeared back to Oswestry – I presume that she would have been required to return there that same day. But the issue then arose of whether and how we could be reunited on a more long-term footing. This was, again, less straightforward than it might sound. Mutti had only a single bedroom – and scarcely enough money to feed herself. Logic – and the prevailing wartime consensus that doing what was best for children didn't necessarily involve keeping them with their parents – dictated that we should remain in our stable foster home. This prospect pleased me a great deal more than it pleased Renate.

I feel, in retrospect, huge sympathy for Renate. Not only had she lost her family: she had also had to look after her little sister for a year. It distressed her to have Ruby occupying the place in her life that had hitherto been occupied by our mother. And now she came under two additional pressures. Our school, recognising her talent, had begun to coach her with a view to getting a scholarship to a fee-paying school – but, they had told her, don't tell your foster parents as it will be a wonderful surprise for them. At the same time, she began to receive letters from our mother saying, in effect, I think I may have found a way for us to live together again – but don't tell anyone else for now. Those were huge secrets for a 10-year-old heart to carry around.

But both hopes were in due course realised. Renate won a scholarship to a girls' high school in Oswestry, and the Blythes agreed that Mutti could have one child – but not two – living there with her. So Renate left Little Aston to live in Oswestry, and I was left with Auntie and Uncle.

I hadn't exactly been thrilled when it had first seemed that there was prospect of leaving my foster parents to re-join Mutti – and no doubt Mutti had taken this into account. Yet when it sank in that, forced to choose only one of her daughters, she hadn't chosen me, I felt bitterly hurt.

The pain faded. Auntie and Uncle now pampered me like an only child, and I felt more loved than I ever had in my own family. It must have been around this time that they bought me a dog: a "spaniel" called Topsy. I put the word "spaniel" in quotation marks because, although she had been sold with all sorts of assurances about her pedigree, it soon became clear that, whatever else she was, she was not a spaniel. Eventually we took this long-legged mongrel back to the pet shop, where the manager, spotting me in the background, cleverly offered to take her back, no questions asked. Predictable floods of tears followed, and Topsy came home with us. (I see this now as an early lesson in the power of imaginative marketing.)

Meanwhile, Auntie and Uncle had become concerned that, at the village school, I was learning to speak in a Birmingham accent. So I was sent instead to a convent, St Paul's, just outside Sutton Coldfield, to which I travelled each day by bus. I was happy there. I enjoyed the

Mutti.
1947.

*Post-war my mother trained as a teacher – refusing to return to
Germany with my father. We were both naturalised British in 1951.
But Renate chose to remain stateless. When she emigrated to Australia,
she – almost immediately – applied for Australian citizenship.*

slightly more serious lessons, and the nuns who taught us were lovely: gentle and tolerant, not forcing their religion on us but, instead, quietly promoting such fundamental values as honesty and compassion. Perhaps as a result, my memories of that period are largely religious in flavour: the prettiness of the Masses I used to attend if I went to stay with my friend Christina at weekends; and the sense of calm by the grotto in the convent driveway, where the Catholic girls would stop and say a "Hail Mary" each time they passed while the rest of us would just stop for a moment in respectful silence.

My other vivid memory of that period is far from pretty. It is of going with Uncle in his car to Coventry on 15 November 1940 – the day after the notorious German bombing raid that reduced half the city to rubble. Uncle's light engineering business had a factory there, and it was, it turned out, among the 60,000 buildings that were damaged. I don't think I appreciated the full awfulness of what had happened (more than 500 people were killed), but I can still remember driving past the smoking ruins of what used to be the cathedral. We children might not have thought about it often, but there was, without doubt, a very nasty war going on.

For the most part, though, that war passed us by. The last significant bombing raid on Birmingham was in May 1941, and thereafter the main day-to-day signs of the conflict were rationing and the black-out, both of which we had long since taken for granted; and, to a lesser extent, travel restrictions. I mention these, because, from late 1941 onwards, I began to make relatively regular journeys, by train, to Oswestry. (I think that Auntie and Uncle must have paid.) Each time, as a "friendly enemy alien", I had to report my journey in advance to the local police station and then register at the Oswestry police station on arrival – so that there was, in effect, an official record of where I spent every single night of the war. Perhaps that seems excessive for an eight-year-old (as I then was). On the other hand, we children were at least spared the curfew to which the adults were subject. I can remember several days out in Oswestry – with my mother, Renate and one or two other refugee families – when the adults had to hurry home at sundown while we children carried on playing.

My visits to my mother rarely lasted more than a day. I think the Blythes, who were a kind, elderly couple, must occasionally have allowed me to sleep there, but for the most part these were just flying

*I enjoyed the lay teaching of the Roman Catholic
nuns who educated me in the 1940's.*

visits – facilitated by Auntie and Uncle (and, I suspect, my mother) largely out of a sense of duty. My main memories of these visits are of the house itself: a big Edwardian building on the edge of town with a large hall and central staircase; an Ascot "geyser" water-heater that emitted a terrifying roar when it fired up; and a living-room with a strange squiggly pattern on the wallpaper that made it look as though the wall was crawling with insects. I can remember sitting in the living-room at least once when my father was visiting as well, listening in complete silence to a concert on the radio.

He was wearing, by this stage, a British Army uniform, which he had acquired after a circuitous and painful journey. As a male adult German refugee he had been categorised as an "enemy alien" and briefly interned before being deported, in July 1940, to Australia. He went there on the transport ship HMT Dunera, along with around 2,000 other German Jewish refugees and more than 400 German and Italian prisoners-of-war. The conditions on the 57-day voyage were so appalling that – to Britain's everlasting credit – Parliament found time in the midst of the war to debate the scandal. Those deportees who survived the journey were interned in a camp in Hay, in New South Wales, where the largely middle-class inmates made the best of their plight, printing their own money, creating their own system of law-and-order (my father was a judge) and developing a remarkable educational and cultural programme – with lessons, concerts, discussions and much else. By May 1941, however, partly as a result of the outcry in Britain about the harshness of their treatment, a substantial number of these internees were released to join the Pioneer Corps, a relatively new auxiliary force that provided valuable back-up work for the conventional armed forces. My father was among them, and, at some point in 1941, he found himself based in the UK, at Bicester in Oxfordshire. Even then, however, I didn't see him more than once or twice a year, and I don't think my mother did either.

This strange approximation to family life continued for much of the war. I lived my generally contented, uneventful life with Auntie and Uncle, travelling to Oswestry as often as circumstances permitted. It was clear, even then, that there were issues of jealousy between Ruby and my mother, but Auntie and Uncle clearly considered that it was their duty not to come between us, and so the visits continued.

My father, on leave from the British army, with my mother in Oswestry.

At some point, my mother got a job as a cook in a hostel for girls attending the school that Renate was going to and – with help from a charity set up by the Quakers to support refugees – was able to rent a two-bedroom house of her own. It was called Llys Arfon (Arfon – as in Carnarvon – Court) and was, again, on the edge of town, with fields beyond its little garden. My visits became more frequent now – or, rather, less fleeting – and I was certainly staying there when Renate, who must have been about 15 by then, became alarmingly ill.

She had gone to bed the night before feeling fine. Then, in the morning, she was unable to move. This was the terrifying and – at the time – widely dreaded symptom of paralytic poliomyelitis. Likely outcomes ranged from permanent paralysis to death, but Renate was one of the lucky ones (roughly half of those who developed the disease) who eventually recovered, thanks in large part to my mother, who, even in her impoverished state, had somehow managed to pay a penny a week into an insurance fund. This meant that Renate now received the best possible treatment. There was a former military hospital nearby, at Gobowen, which specialised in such cases, and she spent nearly a year in a special ward, one wall of which was entirely open to the elements. (Fresh air was considered crucial to recovery, even if the beds were occasionally covered in snow.) For much of this time she was in an "iron lung". She was also treated with penicillin, which was still in its infancy and – as we were often reminded – hugely expensive. (Producing large stockpiles of penicillin was considered a vital part of Allied preparations for D-Day, so it was remarkable that any at all was spared for a young refugee from Germany.)

As a result of this frightening episode, Renate and I became much closer. Coming so near to losing her made me appreciate how much she had done for me, and how much she meant to me – perhaps especially when I had to go back to Little Aston and worry about her from afar. We had spent much of our childhood as rivals: she the sensible one, me the silly one; she good at arts and letters, me good with figures; she the first-born, me the baby. Being refugees had meant different things to each of us: largely painful for her, more positive for me. Yet it remained essentially a huge, life-changing, shared experience that only we two could entirely understand. Even when we were living at opposite ends of the Earth – as, for much of our later life, we did – I never lost the feeling that Renate in some way saw the world through the same eyes as me, in a way that no one else could. (My jaw does still drop, though, at the memory of one trick she played on me when we were still in Vienna. My parents noticed that I had suddenly become very sedentary and, after a few days of worrying, made inquiries. They discovered that Renate had persuaded me that I had an artificial heart, and that if I made any sudden movements it would break down.)

But Renate's illness did little for my relationship with my mother. Her desperate – and understandable – concern for her elder daughter made it all the more obvious, in my eyes, that she felt no such warmth for me. She always seemed to be finding fault with me: for my immaturity; for my clumsiness; and (less explicitly) for my attachment to Auntie and Uncle. "Vera is stupid" was the unmotherly refrain that has stuck in my mind through the years. I seemed to irritate her and she, in turn, seemed to me to be unfairly unappreciative of me. As my teenage years approached, the distance between us increased: no doubt as much through my fault as hers, but no less painfully for either of us.

Physically, however, events were bringing us closer together. The nuns at my convent in Sutton Coldfield had noticed that I was showing promise in mathematics – to such an extent that they didn't feel qualified to give me the tuition I needed. So they suggested that I should sit for a scholarship to go somewhere else. I did so, and in due course I won a place at a fee-paying school in Lichfield called The Friary.

I rather liked it there – partly because of the daily train journeys (paid for by my scholarship) that began and ended each day. But within a year I had been moved again: to Oswestry, where I was given a place at the same school as Renate. (The precise administrative mechanics of this escaped me, but I was told that my scholarship had been transferred from one school to the other.)

This was a big improvement in academic terms, but not in terms of domestic arrangements. I began, briefly, by living with my mother – which proved a fraught experience. I think it was around this time that I looked in my drawer one evening on returning from a visit to Little Aston to find that Kate, the rag doll that Auntie had made for me when I first arrived in England, had disappeared. I asked my mother about it. "What?" she said. "That disgusting thing? I threw it out." It seemed an apt symbol of the jealousy and mutual incomprehension that had poisoned our relationship. With the intolerance of youth, I resolved not to forgive her.

Then (presumably when Renate returned from hospital), I was boarded out to a nearby hostel, called Queen's Park, where I and other evacuees shared Spartan dormitories and were taught ladylike table-manners. I never entirely understood if I was sent there to save money, or to ease the overcrowding in my mother's house, or to ensure that I was brought up to be a proper young Englishwoman. Whatever the truth, it felt a lot less homely than Auntie and Uncle's house, and I was delighted that, in the holidays, I was able to go back to stay in Little Aston.

A little later, my mother got a job as cook in a new hostel, called Oakhurst, which had been set up for pupils of the same school. I was moved here – and, once again, slept in a dormitory and had a careful eye kept on my manners. But it was a lot more pleasant, both physically and in atmosphere. Oakhurst was a converted stately home, with plenty of space and small comfortable dormitories, and I remember a distinct sense that here, finally, we were becoming young adults. There was a large hall, a great big sweeping staircase and a big landscaped garden that had partly reverted to nature, and I think that at some level our surroundings encouraged us to think about life's possibilities in a less circumscribed way than we had been used to.

Oswestry was far from the war, and far from any urban smoke or bustle. We still carried gasmasks, but it never occurred to us that we might ever need to put them on. Like everyone, we spent much of our free time on the time-consuming mechanics of living – which in our case included lots of food-gathering: for example, picking blackberries or rosehips, or (as older children) helping with the potato harvest. But I also remember going for long walks – especially on a spectacular patch of grassland above the town known as The Racecourse, which had been a real racecourse in the 18th and 19th centuries, before the coming of the railways. I remember pausing on such walks and gazing out over the green, velvety hills of Wales, and feeling a sense of the wonder and potential of the world stirring in my heart.

I had more friends by now, including my two dormitory-mates – one of whom, a tall, kind-hearted bank manager's daughter from Derbyshire called Val Adams, remains a close friend today. The other was a troubled, highly strung character called Hazel who, I discovered later, had a schoolgirl crush (unrequited) on me. There were ups and downs in our shared lives, as there always are in adolescence: in my memory, I was always being told off because Hazel had been "upset" by one thing or another that I had done or said. But there are worse places for a teenager to grow up than in a quiet market town on the Welsh border. We had many happy walks in the countryside – often involving a certain amount of trespassing on the estates of the local aristocracy – or just met up after school to do nothing in particular in the town, browsing in the bookshop without ever buying anything, while catching occasional exotic glimpses of passing boys; or enjoying the atmosphere of market day, when all the old farmers came down from the hills, many of them speaking Welsh.

No doubt I have sentimentalised the memories, and filtered out the miseries of adolescence and family life. But when people ask me nowadays if I love my adopted country, the resounding "Yes" with which I invariably reply is prompted largely by idyllic memories of the two sleepy rural places – Little Aston and Oswestry – in which I was allowed to grow up in safety. My image of wartime England – or rather of Britain, because there is much about Oswestry that is Welsh – is of a quiet countryside, where even outsiders like me could be confident that those in authority would generally do their best to do the right thing by us. Civilisation might have been collapsing over most of the planet, but Britain remained committed to the values of peacetime.

But my main pre-occupation in those days was not what happened outside school but what happened in it. Even in my early teens, it was always important to me that I should do well in my education – not least because Renate continued to do well (eventually winning a scholarship to Oxford) and because my mother was never slow to criticise me if she felt I was underachieving. I also knew that we remained fundamentally poor. We couldn't, for example, afford to buy the sweets that we were allowed under rationing, but instead could only give away our sweets points as presents. Every Saturday I would accompany my mother to Lloyds Bank, where she would collect her small weekly charitable payment from the Quakers, to help her pay the rent. The staff always treated us very tactfully (and we vowed, as a result, that we would always bank with Lloyds in future). But we had no desire to remain dependent on charity any longer than was absolutely necessary. And it was clear to me that, if I wanted to escape from the frustrations of poverty, doing well at school was a pretty indispensable start.

But I also genuinely loved – and love – learning things. One of my greatest pleasures outside school was to go to Oswestry's wonderful library, where I could borrow any book under the sun without paying a penny. Light, serious, fiction, non-fiction, appropriate or wildly inappropriate – I read everything, voraciously, and learnt much as a result. (I might, however, have derived even more benefit had I taken the trouble to work out how the books were organised, rather than simply starting at A and trying to work my way through the alphabet.)

At school, meanwhile, I was taking huge pleasure in mathematics, which I found simultaneously easy and stimulating. I wasn't much good at a number of other things – French, for example, or sport. But anything involving maths or science seemed self-explanatory to me, and I used to look forward to lessons in such subjects with the glad expectation that, when they came, some gap in my understanding of the world would be satisfyingly filled.

The drawback was that, when the question of Higher Schools Certificate (roughly equivalent to today's A-levels) came up, and I expressed an interest in studying maths, it became clear that this school, too, wasn't really equipped to teach me. If that makes me sound like a genius, it shouldn't. The point was just that this was a girls-only school, and girls, in those days, weren't expected to study maths.

A certain amount of pressure was applied to persuade me to choose a different subject, such as Biology – the only science then available to my gender. But eventually the school consented to my undertaking some kind of psychometric test to see if I deserved to be treated as a special case. The psychologist asked me a variety of questions which I have long since forgotten – and was for some reason highly impressed by my ability to remember long sequences of numbers backwards as well as forwards. He subsequently lobbied enthusiastically for me to be given the tuition I needed.

The upshot was that from the age of 16 onwards I was taught maths at the nearby grammar school, which in those days was for boys only. There were drawbacks to this arrangement. The timetables of the two schools had little in common, and so I was always walking out in the middle of lessons and generally falling behind with other subjects. There was also the ordeal of walking into the boys' school:

the only young woman among hundreds of drooling young men. I never reconciled myself to the daily gauntlet of leering and catcalls. But the lessons themselves were enjoyable and absorbing, and the sexism was, in retrospect, invaluable preparation for the trials I would later encounter in the workplace.

It still had no idea what I was going to do with my life. But with Renate now at Oxford – reading English at St Hilda's – it was clear that high things were expected of me. I applied to myself to my studies with a passion that my male classmates must have found intimidating.

They might have been daydreaming about sport, or girls, or whatever it was that kept distracting their attention from beyond the classroom window.

I was dreaming about doing well in my exams.

4: Picking Up The Pieces

I have, of course, omitted one rather crucial episode. In 1945, the Second World War ended. Victory in Europe came in May, with victory in the Far East following three months later, shortly before my twelfth birthday.

I spent VE Day – fittingly, I think – with Auntie and Uncle. They took me up to London, where we somehow managed to see Buckingham Palace and the Tower of London before spending the night in a hotel near Marble Arch. I suppose this must have been the occasion when, in an incident that remained in my memory as a symbol of the good heart that lay beneath her snobbish exterior, Auntie reprimanded an American GI for trying to make a black woman give up her seat to him. "You're in England now, you can't do that," she insisted, before telling the woman: "Sit down, dear."

But it was the celebration of peace that defined that day. I can still remember the madness in the air. Years of repressed emotion had exploded in an anarchic half-riot of joy. By late afternoon, no one was paying fares on buses; complete strangers were kissing and hugging; and there was singing and dancing in Trafalgar Square. It was simultaneously exhilarating and rather frightening – especially in the company of this respectable couple who, deep down, probably didn't entirely approve. But I wouldn't have missed it for anything.

Thereafter, my life carried on much as before. The actual violence of the war had hardly affected us in Oswestry or Little Aston, while the general austerity resulting from the conflict continued for years after hostilities had ended. Yet for my parents there was one crucial difference: they were now free, in theory, to return to the homeland from which they had been driven six years earlier.

My father returned more or less immediately. Shortly before the German surrender he had managed to leave the Pioneer Corps and (after a spell running a mental hospital for prisoners-of-war in Talgarth in south Wales) transfer to the US Army, who needed educated German-speakers to help with the post-war administration of what remained of Germany.

He started out as a very minor jurist, but at least, from his point of view, it was a step back into a world he understood – especially when

*My Jewish father kept the dismissal letter he received in 1933
throughout his travels; around Europe, interned to Australia on the
HMT* **Dunera**, *back to England then, postwar, back to Germany.*

mechanisms began to be set up for putting Nazi war criminals on trial. But it would have been very difficult, in the short-term, for his family to have joined him in occupied Germany, and I don't think any of us felt much urge to do so. Renate and I were enjoying our education, while my mother was still so traumatised from having lost everything in the 1930s that she could hardly bear to hear the word "Germany" spoken, let alone start considering the feasibility of living there again. She had scarcely seen my father for the past six years, and any yearning she may have felt to be reunited with him had long since faded.

But we did, after a year or so, start making occasional visits, paid for out of my father's US army wages. These visits made a deep impression on me. Germany had entirely broken down. The contrast to the orderly societies of Oswestry or Little Aston couldn't have been stronger – or more nightmarish. There was no money, no gas, no electricity, no water – and no semblance of civil structure, apart from the crude military authority of the Americans. People were living in the cellars of ruined buildings, among rats and human remains, buying food on the black market to survive and using cigarettes as currency. There was no warmth in people's faces: just the blankness of hunger and fear. Sinister men loitered in alleyways, and there was no question of going out alone or at night.

I had lived through six years of the most devastating war in human history, but this was the first glimpse I had had of its utter, dehumanising horror and destruction. I sometimes wish that more people in Britain had seen such scenes: they might understand their fellow-Europeans better if they had.

The first time we visited, we stayed in a bed-and-breakfast while my father stayed in military quarters. The second time – which must have been in 1947 – we stayed in a hotel in Nuremberg, where my father was working on the military tribunal. There had been some failure of communication, and when we arrived he was not there. His colleagues, however, could not have been kinder or more solicitous to us during the 24 hours or so before he turned up. Only years later did the missing piece of the story become clear to me: he had gone away for the weekend (thinking we were in England) with the young woman who would later become his second wife, and his colleagues were embarrassed on our behalf.

But several things were clear already. By the standards of the rest of Germany, my father was doing quite well. Anyone connected with the US armed forces was by definition a "have", while ordinary Germans struggled to avoid starvation. There were special shops – called PX – where only Americans and their families could shop, and we had access to luxuries such as tinned fruit.

It was also clear that, by 1947, my father was beginning to prosper even by British standards – or at least by the standards that we were used to. He was still a relatively junior researcher, but it did not escape my mother's notice that, despite his cramped living conditions, he had plenty of cash in his pocket – none of which had been sent back to us in the UK. This did nothing to improve relations between them.

I watched a few sessions of the trial he was working on: the famous Justice Trial, in which 16 senior lawyers and officials of the Nazi ministry of justice (including Josef Altstoetter, Oswald Rothaug and Franz Schlegelberger) were charged with crimes against humanity. Most of the proceedings went over my 14-year-old head, but I could understand what was at stake. These had been some of the most senior figures in the German legal system – pillars of German society – and they were accused of, among other crimes, murder; persecution on political, racial, and religious grounds; deportation and enslavement; plunder of private property; and torture. All denied the charges (10 were ultimately found guilty), and every possible legal nicety was invoked to keep justice at bay. At one point my father was called to give expert evidence on the precise linguistic nuances of the phrase "Polnisches Untermenschen" – "Polish subhumanity" – and its use in German legal circles in the 1930s.

But there was nothing complicated about the message that sunk home for me: you cannot judge people by their appearance. These were respectable, well-dressed men; men who had occupied positions of authority and dignity; well-spoken and even charming men, with kindly eyes. Yet they were also monsters...

These post-war visits to the Continent – which also took me to Austria and the Netherlands – were always darkened by the shadow of Nazism. I remember paying a visit to the Kehlsteinhaus, Hitler's mountain-top retreat (also known as the Eagle's Nest), at Obersalzburg. There should have been beauty in the spectacular views over Austria – and yet all I could think of was the suffocating atmosphere of cvil.

And when, a lot later, we returned to Vienna, Renate could hardly contain her horror as we walked along the streets on which she had been persecuted as a child. She kept looking at the faces of passers-by, asking silently: "What did you do? Were you one of them?"

Another time, my mother took me to see a film – one of many such public information films that the Armies of Occupation were showing at the time – about Auschwitz. I fainted. Whether it was the thought that I might so easily have been among those victims, or some other form of "survivor guilt", or just simple empathetic horror at the suffering of all those human beings, I don't know. It was just more than I could bear. (It still is. Even now, I get nightmares after seeing pictures or footage of the concentration camps, and have to be careful about when and how I allow myself to dwell upon the subject.)

The other theme that dominated these visits – and that must have dominated most such visits by returning refugees – was the search for family and friends. We proved luckier than most. My grandmother – the one who had sent us the Red Cross telegrams – had survived the war in the Netherlands, hiding in the farmhouse of some kind strangers and coming out only at night. She had been arrested at one point, but had talked her way out of it. She was a remarkable woman, who had at one point been mayor of Dortmund – one of Germany's very first woman mayors. (Since 2007 there has been a street in Dortmund, Rosa Buchthal Strasse, named after her.) When she died, she left me her two sets of identity papers – one real, with a big J for Jew, and one fake and J-less – along with her yellow star; they are now in the Imperial War Museum.

My aunt Alice – my father's sister – had been kept safe in a convent. My mother's best Austrian friends had survived too, somehow; we tracked them down, with difficulty, near Vienna. On another, later occasion, we visited some of my father's cousins in the Netherlands – of whom I remember little except that they had a very buxom teenage daughter, Annaberte, who wore low-cut dresses and took me hitchhiking, at which she was extremely proficient. I also remember the haunting little plaques we kept seeing – on roadsides, in villages, on pieces of wasteland – commemorating the victims of Nazi atrocities.

I think this might have been the same trip from which I returned, unaccompanied, with three large trunks full of family possessions: mainly carpets and so forth but also some silver cutlery that had been buried in someone's garden for safekeeping during the war. I also had six daffodil bulbs, which I had bought as a present for Uncle. When I mentioned these bulbs at Customs, they threw a fit and confiscated them. It only occurred to me many years later that I should probably have mentioned the cutlery as well.

We also managed – eventually – to visit my mother's elder sister, Ilse, in Diessen, near Munich. She too had survived the war, along with her two children, Gerhardt and Gelinde, and her husband, Otto. It had clearly helped that Otto, who seemed a pleasant enough man, had been a minor Nazi. The subject caused some tension between the two sisters, and I can remember it being discussed. Otto said simply: "I kept my family fed."

He could have added "and alive".

I don't think Otto did anything too awful, although one can never be certain. But meeting him did bring home to me – again – just how lucky my family had been. Millions of parents just like mine had been murdered; countless children like me never got out; most of my fellow Kindertransport refugees lost most or all of their family and friends. And those who lived through the war years in central Europe – while I was enjoying my English idyll – knew fear and hunger and moral anguish far beyond my imagining. More than a year after the war's end, Gerhardt and Gelinde were still so tormented by fear of starvation that all food in Ilse's household had to be kept under lock and key.

Such comparisons – between the security of England and the unhealed wounds of Germany – would no doubt have passed through my mother's mind as she and my father debated (normally by post) the question of what they should do next. Each had a firm view. Sadly, their two views had nothing in common.

My father was desperate to rebuild his life in Germany. His legal career could not be revived anywhere else: he had neither the relevant training nor the relevant experience. Without his prowess as a jurist he was, as he saw it, nothing – just another refugee who could do odd jobs or, at best, be used as a translator; whereas in Germany he had a good chance of one day becoming a high-powered judge again. To move permanently to England would mean giving up the career dreams that defined him.

My mother saw it differently. She had had a world in Germany – a life of comfort, status and material security – and, bit by bit, it had been stolen from her. Perhaps some of her very identity had been stolen with it. Having escaped with her life and little else, she simply could not face the idea of entrusting herself again to the country that had nearly destroyed her. And while she was poor in England, and had incomparably less social status than she had had before she came there, she was not destitute, and at least she could trust the place. It was a stable, predictable society – in stark contrast to Germany. As far as she was concerned, it was unthinkable that her husband should do anything but build a new life from scratch in England, just as she had done.

The outcome was – to modern eyes – predictable. They decided to divorce. The bitterness and distrust that my mother felt towards Germany had become indistinguishable from the bitterness and distrust she felt towards my father, who had not only brought all this suffering upon her – by being Jewish – but had also been making scandalously little effort to alleviate it, now that he was in a position to do so. I don't know if she was aware at this stage that he had taken up with someone else – a younger version of herself called Maria; but, if she was, I imagine that she would by this stage have considered his infidelity entirely in character.

In later years, I found it easier to see all this from my father's point of view. ("The trouble with your mother," he told me towards the end of his life, "is that, whatever I did, she was never satisfied.") At the time, I shared my mother's view that his behaviour towards us had been disgraceful. But while I sympathised, my sympathy didn't extend to approving of the divorce. One or other of them, I felt, should have stuck with the other. Perhaps in other circumstances they would have done, but their relationship – like millions of others – lacked the strength to survive the cruel strains placed on it by the separation necessitated by war.

Back in England, I told no one about this. I'm not sure that my mother did either. This was 1950: no one divorced in those days. Or, if they did, it was a guilty secret. So we "packed up our troubles in our old kit-bag" and carried on with our lives. I continued to do well at school. Renate did well at Oxford. My mother started training to become a teacher, eventually spending a year at teacher training college in Speke in Liverpool (while I boarded at Oakhurst). If we suffered from my father's absence – as I am sure we must have – we gave it little conscious thought. We had other things on our mind.

I turned 18 in 1951, and was faced straightaway with a big choice: did I want to go to university? After much agonising, I decided against it – a decision I have regretted ever since. With no money coming in from my father, and my mother now training rather than earning, we were so short of funds that it was hard even to find the fee for sitting the scholarship exam, let alone to justify the prospect of still more years without an income. It seemed better to try to start earning money without delay.

But I have never regretted the other big decision I took that year. On 29 January 1951, my mother and I became British citizens. Renate considered joining us but chose not to: she had never really bonded with her adopted country. (Some years later, faced with a choice between naturalising and leaving, she moved to Australia – where she felt so at home that she was naturalised after just six months.) So it was just my mother and I who went to the local police station, paid £9 each, filled in various forms, and swore a solemn oath of allegiance.

We took the opportunity to change our name, as if closing a symbolic door on the past. Instead of Buchthal, we chose Brook, to mark our shared enthusiasm (one of the few things we had in common) for that most English of poets, Rupert Brooke. It seemed less pretentious without the "e". I also formally adopted my middle name, Stephanie, which I had increasingly been using for some time.

I was conscious that this was a turning-point in my life: a solemn and welcome one. I had been impressed with England and the English way of doing things ever since my arrival in 1939. Now, in formally committing myself to the country, I felt that I was also committing myself to repaying all the generosity that English people had shown me: to living a life that was worthy of their kindness.

I was, in other words, committing myself to making a success of my life as Stephanie Brook, Englishwoman.

5: The Awkward Age

Finding employment was surprisingly easy. Young, numerate people were in demand, as Britain's budding technology industries broadened their ambitions and their markets. Within weeks of leaving school, I had two interviews, both in north-west London, and, shortly afterwards, two job offers. Both involved being a junior research assistant. One was for the General Electric Company (GEC) in Wembley; the other was at the Post Office Research Station in Dollis Hill. GEC paid slightly better, but they said plainly that they had no interest in helping me to pursue further studies – whereas the Post Office research station was interested in my further development and was prepared to arrange my hours to allow further study. So I signed up with the Post Office and, shortly afterwards, enrolled for evening classes in applied mathematics – and, later, physics – at Sir John Cass College in Moorgate (now the Sir John Cass School of Science and Technology).

So began a strange period in my life: a time of development and turmoil in which I didn't really seem to go anywhere and yet in some important sense was metamorphosing into my true adult self. Now that I look back on them, those ostensibly becalmed years – in my late teens and early twenties – seem faintly surreal. Yet they were critical to the shaping of my career. I suspect that such directionless periods form part of most working lives: what determines our future is how we respond to the frustrations.

I began by living with my mother. Shortly after we were naturalised, she had bought a small house in Colindale, also in north-west London, borrowing the money for a deposit from some German émigré friends and taking in lodgers to help pay for it. (One of the lodgers had helped me to get my two job interviews.). She was now working as a teacher and, with her marriage behind her, was reclaiming control of her life. But we constantly rubbed each other up the wrong way, and so, as soon as I could, I began to rent a bedsit of my own, in Cricklewood.

It was an attic room in a tall Victorian house in a wide, tree-lined road called Walm Lane, with a bustling, bossy, very Jewish landlady called Mrs Cohen; five other lodgers; and a shared bathroom. Even by the standards of the day, it was far from luxurious, yet it felt wonderfully independent. I used to leave early, six mornings a week, to catch the bus to Dollis Hill (Saturday was a half-day) and often wouldn't get home until 10pm, if I had had an evening class, which generally happened three times a week. There was also studying to be done at weekends. So there wasn't much time to worry about my living conditions.

I learnt to look after myself; to cook (after a fashion, in an oven without a thermostat); to make and mend things; and, above all, to be organised. Long-term existence in a bedsit is tolerable when all the surfaces are clear, but the space closes in on you horribly if you let it get cluttered. Luckily, I didn't have many possessions to keep tidy.

My annual salary – £215 – seemed enough for my needs: I had grown used to living carefully. The monthly pay packet (about £14 after tax) included one crisp white £5 note, which I always tried, in vain, not to spend. Most of the money went on rent and travel, and – a stupid habit that I had for some reason decided to acquire – smoking. I was careful: I would walk part of the way to work rather than pay an extra stage of the bus fare. I often ran out of money before payday – and on one occasion I went without food for so long that I passed out. But I wasn't conscious of being poor in the way that we had been in Oswestry – not least because, for the first time in years, I wasn't dependent on anyone else's charity.

Cricklewood seemed a cheerful place, with lots of Jewish and Irish people and a few early Jamaicans. It felt lively but safe – unless you walked down Cricklewood Broadway at pub throwing-out time – and I was glad to live there. Compared with the rural England I had known thus far, north-west London buzzed with cosmopolitan sophistication.

My work at the Post Office was menial. As a research assistant, I was there to perform routine or tiresome tasks for proper researchers. A lot of it was mere arithmetic – drawing graphs, or slogging through repetitive calculations or tables to try out ideas, or banging figures through a comptometer (a kind of electromechanical adding machine that was effectively a primitive calculator) to make statistical inferences or to work out probabilities. The subject matter varied. One day we'd be helping some near-genius with pioneering work on, say, telephony; the next we'd be doing tedious sums connected with the postal service. I remember once having to analyse the number of strands in a piece of string from a ball found in a suspected thief's shed, to see if, statistically, there was a match with the string of a stolen parcel.

It was unexciting but strangely satisfying. You knew exactly what your work was, and whether or not it was done, and whether or not it had been done well (which it had to be). And I, at least, felt that there was some purpose to it.

There were four of us, all in our late teens, all working on similar tasks on the same little block of desks. For about a year we called each other "Miss Brook", "Miss French", "Mr Hodges", and so on. Then, daringly, someone suggested: "When nobody's here, shall we use first names?" So we did. But we never really became good friends: the nature of the work wasn't conducive to casual chat. One of the highest priorities was to have a completely clear desk at the end of each day. Apparently this was for security reasons.

Our immediate boss was very staid, buttoned-up Scotsman called Ettrick Thomson, who shared an office with three other senior people, one of whom was his boss: a bad-tempered, reclusive man called H J Josephs, who had a chip on his shoulder about being self-taught and who dealt with his insecurities by trying to make his junior employees cry. He never quite succeeded with me but came close several times. What saved me was the discovery that, as my evening classes expanded my mathematical education, I was beginning to understand many concepts better than he did – and could make him back off simply by speaking confidently about whatever subject he was picking us up on. Yet for all his unpleasantness he had a passion for his subject – a sense of its beauty – and a genuine yearning for excellence. It was hard not to be inspired by this, and, in a strange way, I think he was a good influence on me.

I also had a more distant boss – Mr Joseph's superior, Doc Jarvis – who was notable for having appalling handwriting, like a doctor's. No one dared go back and ask him what his scrawled memos meant, and so one of my tasks was to decipher them by sheer force of logic. (For example: "This must be a 'D', because he always starts with 'Dear', and so this must be a 'D' too... while that must be another 'e'..."; and so on.) In a sense this was fitting. Deciphering had an honoured place in Dollis Hill's intellectual traditions. Workers at the research station (which had opened in 1933) had built the world's first programmable electronic computer, the Colossus 1, in 1943. This was used, along with nine Colossus 2s built the following year, by the code-breaking team at Bletchley Park that cracked the Nazis' supposedly indecipherable

Enigma code – and it's even more opaque successor, the teleprinter code known as Lorenz or FISH.

There were people still working at Dollis Hill in the early 1950s – Tommy Flowers and Allen "Doc" Coombs were the most senior – who had played a pivotal role in the wartime work of Bletchley Park, which in turn had been crucial to the Allied victory. The Colossus 2, Tommy Flowers's brainchild, provided vital decrypt information on the eve of D-Day, days after its delivery from Dollis Hill to Bletchley Park.

No one spoke about this at the time. People still took the Official Secrets Acts very seriously. (Even Tommy Flowers's family didn't learn about his war work until 1970.) But I think we had a vague sense that this unassuming man had done something important. And, in the meantime, it was clear that his area of expertise – essentially, the development of very early computers into recognisably modern computers through the pioneering use of thermionic valves (tubes) rather than electro-mechanical switches – was close to some of the wildest frontiers of human knowledge.

The current aims were relatively mundane: developing the first electronic telephone exchanges for the Joint Electronic Research Council; or – something I would later be involved in – developing ERNIE, the Electronic Random Number Indicator Equipment used to pick Premium Bond numbers. But there was still an exciting sense of being at the forefront of new technology – especially at those points where our work edged into territory that would nowadays be known as computing.

At some stage, after a year or so of evening classes, it began to dawn on me that, while I loved the beauty of maths, and could master it to a fairly high level – and began to study for a bachelor's degree in mathematics as soon as I had obtained the matriculation requirements – I was never going to become the world's greatest mathematician. This might have been disillusioning had I not more or less simultaneously fallen in love with computers.

It was a good time to do so. On the one hand, some of the most brilliant minds of the day were developing the field. On the other, the technology was still sufficiently basic for a mind like mine – clever but not genius material – to be able to grasp the problems involved, if not to deduce the solutions. The mechanical calculator on which I churned out my boring calculations was so basic that it hardly deserves to be called a precursor of the modern computer. Yet even I could sense – intuitively – that, with sufficient brainpower, this simple concept could evolve into an unimaginably powerful computing device.

It was a bit like being in at the birth of, say, American democracy. First principles were being laid down and tested, as the twin streams of automated calculation and programming converged to make what had hitherto been a boffins' fantasy – high-powered artificial intelligence – a tantalisingly achievable possibility.

I had no idea how the next breakthroughs would be achieved, but the evolution of technologies to date – punched tape, punched cards, thermionic valves, transistors – was perfectly comprehensible to me, and I sensed, correctly, that when the history of computing came to be written, several of its early chapters would be set in Dollis Hill, in the early 1950s.

All this made my work seem rather less banal than many first jobs. I was growing used to the disciplines of work – doing things in an orderly, reliable way, keeping records, putting personal moods and problems to one side – and I could see the value of doing so. The calculations entrusted to me were growing gradually more challenging. And if I did sometimes balk at remaining an insignificant drone in the great scheme of things, well, I was also young, and there were other things in my life.

I might, however, have been pushed to say honestly what those other things were. Yes, there were my studies, in which I took a keen or arguably excessive interest (partly because they were inherently interesting but also because of a neurotic obsession with doing as well as I possibly could in exams). I enjoyed those early evening journeys across London, eagerly anticipating each evening class (although I never quite adjusted to the fact that some colleges had no women's toilets); and, heading back to Cricklewood later on, I would feel my eyes drooping with satisfied exhaustion.

But even the most serious-minded young woman cannot work all the time, and gradually, as London grew less strange, I became aware of empty spaces in my life. Some were filled simply with loneliness; others by staying in fairly frequent touch with Auntie and Uncle. I also made occasional weekend visits to some friends of my mother's, the Samsons, who had known my parents from Dortmund but had got out with their wealth intact in 1933. They lived in Edgware, and were kind in a very serious sort of way. Helen Samson was a dentist; I still have the gold fillings she gave me as birthday presents.

The Samsons introduced me to the refugee circles in which they moved, for which I should have been grateful; but I felt stiflingly bored in the company of people who talked only of what they had left behind. I also had a phase – also suggested by the Samsons, I think – of working as a volunteer serving drinks on a charity barge on the Regent's Canal: not from any altruistic motives but as a way of meeting people.

Then, as I developed a sense of myself as an independent adult, I began to feel that I was too grown-up for that sort of thing. The result was that I spent less time with the Samsons and their contacts, without meeting anyone else. Sometimes I went all the way from Saturday lunchtime to Monday morning without speaking to another human being.

At other times the emptiness was filled with a series of rather pointless love affairs with a succession of not very suitable young men – whom I had met, usually, via work or college. I look back today on this period of promiscuity with a combination of embarrassment – all those floorboard-creaking tiptoed departures late at night – and pity for my former self. I suppose it was a fairly predictable response to the lack of human warmth in my life – and a not uncommon way for an insecure young woman to create a sense of identity and self-worth. In a sense, I was discovering who I was. It is interesting, in this context, that on one occasion in this period my father sent me a letter using my old name. "Do you know anyone called Buchthal?" Mrs Cohen asked me when I came home. "No," I said – and had climbed two flights of stairs before I realised my mistake.

The cumulative effect of these experiences was neither escape nor self-confidence but, instead, increasing misery. I became jumpy and anxiety-prone, and I often felt paralysed with terror on my late-night walks back from the bus-stop. Such fears were not entirely unreasonable, especially in those impenetrable "pea-souper" autumn fogs that still plagued London before the 1956 Clean Air Act. There was almost an assumption, in those days, that an unaccompanied woman who bumped into a man in such conditions would be raped. I dealt with this by learning some basic self-defence skills, which boosted my confidence a little. (It's always reassuring to know how to knee a man in the groin.) But a broader, less specific anxiety continued to gnaw away at my life. Everyone else seemed to have roots, whereas I was just an exile, an outsider. The sound of Viennese music would reduce me to tears; but then so, increasingly, would all sorts of things, including the most mundane setbacks in everyday life. I began to fear that I would never be at peace again.

Eventually, I sought medical help. The doctor, a Jewish émigré, prescribed me dexamyl, the notorious amphetamine-based antidepressant better known (especially by US servicemen) as Purple Hearts. At first I would take one only when I felt especially bad; then, whenever I felt I needed help to get through a particularly difficult day; and then to get me through just about any day, in case it was difficult. Eventually I was taking them most evenings as well – just to get me through the night.

These were bleak times – and of course there was no question of sharing my troubles with either my colleagues or my family. At least once I seriously contemplated putting my head in the oven. If the oven hadn't been so filthy I think I might have gone through with it – but it seemed ridiculous to clean the oven just in order to commit suicide.

Instead, I finally told a little of what I was going through to one of my ex-lovers, who was perceptive enough to suggest that there was an underlying cause to all this insecurity and all these failed affairs: that I was, in effect, choosing unsuitable partners in order to set myself up for rejection, for reasons that probably lay buried in my past. He also persuaded me, with difficulty, to sign up for some psychoanalysis at the Tavistock Clinic – the pioneering therapeutic unit in Marylebone that had recently begun to specialise in family dynamics. Some people sneer when this kind of thing is mentioned. They are welcome to their cynicism. For me it was a godsend. A few tentative sessions with a Jungian therapist called Dr Ezriel turned into a sustained course of regular analysis lasting six years, in the course of which I became aware of various issues that now seem so obvious to me that I cannot imagine how I ever managed to bury them. For example: I felt rejected by my mother, who had not only sent me away on the Kindertransport but had also chosen to be reunited with Renate in preference to me; I felt rejected by my father, who had not only sent me away but had subsequently abandoned me, along with the rest of his family, a second time; and I felt devalued by the chronic sense, going back to my very earliest memories, that I was displeasing to my mother. The fact that the Nazis had wanted to kill me hadn't done wonders for my self-esteem either.

I had known all this for years, of course. What I had buried was the pain. My conscious mind had focused on the positive side of my story: how lucky I had been to escape the Nazis, and to be shown such kindness by my foster family and my adoptive country (whose NHS, I noted with grateful amazement, was now providing me with this psychoanalysis). Perhaps as a result, I had never thought clearly about how much certain things had hurt me. I had resented my mother's constant criticisms and disapproved of my father's undutiful conduct towards his family. But I had never focused on what these things had done to me and to the unhealed child within me.

Now that I was finally doing so, I was able to consider my feelings rationally. I could see, on the one hand, that there was nothing to be ashamed of in having been hurt, but also, on the other, that most of these rejections were no reflection on me. I had been sent away because of Hitler's cruelty, not because of my own failings; and if I irritated and disappointed my mother, that was largely because of the failure of her marriage rather than my shortcomings as a child. I still felt pain – of course I did. But I also had a choice, now, between letting this pain control my life and leaving it behind.

I resolved, eventually, to leave it behind.

In the same way, psychoanalysis taught me to look differently at another issue that had been eating away at me: survivor guilt. I don't know if I had ever explicitly formulated the thought that I was undeserving of life, when so many millions of others had had life stolen from them, but now that I looked in on myself I realised that this idea underlay much of my long-term unease. Now I turned a more forgiving light on the issue. Yes, I had been lucky: astonishingly so. But my luck was no more undeserved than it was deserved. It was not my fault. Rather than agonising for ever over the unanswerable question "Why me?", I could choose to make more positive use of my luck. In other words, I should make the most of the life that had been vouchsafed to me – and make each day count, so that my life would have been worth saving.

I mention all this partly because it was a significant stage in my personal evolution but also because it explains why these early years of my career were, in general, uneventful. By the time I had fitted in my evening classes – my initial studies in advanced mathematics and physics were followed by a four-year degree course at Sir John Cass College and, after that, a further one-year stint working studying computer logic at Birkbeck College – and my therapy – initially three times a week but later just once a week – there was little time left to do much else except work and sleep.

It also gives a hint, I think, of how the shadow of war still lingered over 1950s Britain. Compared with tens of millions of fellow Europeans, I had been all but unscathed; yet even I was still traumatised by the conflict's destructive effects. If people in general were a little numb and withdrawn in the way they worked and lived, it was hardly surprising.

But things could have been worse, and, in my increasingly frequent moments of maturity, I began to develop a sense of contentment. Yet it was all too easy to slip back into a sense of aggrievement and frustration, especially in the early days of my therapy. This was partly because I was beginning to suspect that my progress at work was being hampered by prejudice. My evening classes had raised me from the bottom of Dollis Hill's intellectual food chain – I was now sufficiently qualified to start studying for a bachelor's degree – and I began to look out for a less menial position. A vacancy for an assistant experimental officer (the next grade up) was advertised internally, and I asked Ettrick Thomson to put me up for it. He looked awkward and, without explanation, refused. I felt, initially, crushed. It took me some time before it occurred to me that the most likely explanation for his refusal was my gender.

Undeterred, I found a public version of the advertisement – published in The New Statesman, I think – and applied anyway. I was interviewed and, in due course, appointed. Ettrick Thomson never forgave me.

I suppose this must have meant that I was growing more confident – or, at least, behaving in a way that suggested greater confidence. I was scarcely out of my teens, but perhaps my fractured upbringing had given me a sense that, if I wanted to make anything of my life, I needed to take control of it myself. It doesn't surprise me at all, in retrospect, that some people saw me as pushy. A kinder analysis would be to say that, like all refugees, I had been forced to develop a strong sense of independence.

I was certainly independent in my lifestyle, by the standards of the day, setting my own agenda rather than being at someone else's beck and call. I kept in touch with my mother, sporadically, by phone – but hardly at all with my father, whose new wife, Maria, wanted as little to do with his previous family as possible. I exchanged regular and warm letters with Renate, who by now was settled in Sydney (where she in due course became an admired social worker, specialising in the care of traumatised children); but the physical distance between us prevented us from playing major day-to-day roles in one another's lives. I also kept in touch with Auntie and Uncle, and I still paid them occasional visits when time permitted. But I had by now begun to look rather disdainfully – with my young woman's arrogance – upon what I saw as their parochial outlook; and, as the years passed, time permitted less often.

Instead, the main focus of my life outside work became Walm Lane, where I gradually settled into more mature habits and began, for example, to give embryonic dinner parties in my little bedsit. I even organised, towards the end of my third year in London, a small 21st birthday party for myself. This was attended by a number of family friends as well as younger colleagues from work and college. There was also an older man present, called Trevor Attewell, who was at that stage my boyfriend.

This was the most important of my various pre-marital relationships, and the longest-lasting. Trevor was much older than me, and married, and in almost every respect unsuitable. Later, when I had untangled some of my subconscious knots, the attraction was obvious. My father had rejected me; my mother had always been criticising me for being immature (an excusable failing, one might think, in a child). What could be a better way of answering them than to be the loved one of a successful older man?

The affair lasted for several years, on and off, and was sufficiently serious for me to be cited as co-respondent in Trevor's divorce. I'm not sure that I was the cause of it: he had been separated from his wife before he met me, and there were faults on the other side as well. But convention dictated that the man should be the guilty party, and so, according to the sordid custom of the day, we spent a weekend at a hotel in Brighton where, by prior arrangement, the hotelier served us breakfast in bed, so that he could later testify in court to Trevor's infidelity.

I relate this not because I am proud of any of it but because it must say something about the kind of person I am, and how I became who I am. I also have a vivid memory of how, many months later, the relationship ended. Trevor was divorced by then, and was hoping that we could start a new life together. I remember feeling a mounting sense of panic as this prospect grew more real and realising with increasing certainty that this wasn't what I wanted at all. I liked Trevor, and enjoyed being with him, but the longer we spent together the more I realised that I was still developing while he was not. He was happy with his place in the world, whereas I wanted more. And while he was certainly not stupid, I knew that I was outstripping him intellectually.

I had, I realised, been hiding this fact from both of us, just as I had with my previous lovers. That was what women did in those days. (For years, I had been in the habit of replying, if a man asked me what I did for a living, that I worked for the Post Office – hoping that he would think I sold stamps or something – rather than admitting to working with my brain at the internationally admired Dollis Hill Research Station.) But now, when it came to a decision that would define who I was for the rest of my life, I realised that I could no longer go along with this kind of self-effacement.

I had to stop playing a part, to stop playing down those very qualities that made me who I was – my intellect and my curiosity and my restless drive to have an impact on the world. It was one thing to pretend to be someone else, in order to fall in with a man's understanding of what a girlfriend's role should be and thus to oil the wheels of a relationship in the short term. It was a very different thing to build my whole life on that pretence.

I realised, with shocking clarity, that if I wanted more from life I would have to go out and insist on it – irrespective of any challenges this posed to received notions of "femininity". That meant moving on from the whole idea of living my life as a supporting role in someone else's drama, whether it was Trevor's or anyone else's.

Perhaps I had finally grown up. From now on, I decided, I would be my own person. I would stop apologising for myself, stop hiding myself and, while I was at it, stop feeling sorry for myself. I wanted whatever talents I had to be fully used, and the only person who was going to make that happen was me.

I also resolved that I would stop congratulating myself on the little I had achieved in my life so far. Resting on one's laurels is the surest route to stagnation. Instead, I would keep aiming higher and higher, giving free rein to my instinct to ask, restlessly, "Is that all there is?" If I failed, so be it; but I would never allow myself to get into a position where I would curse myself for not having tried.

I have not always succeeded in sticking to these resolutions. But, more than half a century later, I am tempted to say that they have defined my life.

6: The Glass Ceiling

By the mid-1950s, I was developing a core of inner confidence that did not meet with universal approval. I had added a bachelor's degree in mathematics to my qualifications. If I hadn't taken my exams in the middle of a pregnancy scare, I might have got a first rather than a 2:1. Even so, I was eligible for further advancement So I signed up for a year's study for a master's degree, at Birkbeck College, and applied for another promotion.

My immediate boss, Ettrick Thomson, supported this, yet my applications for a Scientific Officer's post came to nothing. Word eventually reached me that men were resigning from the interview board that administered such matters rather than recommend me for promotion – they disapproved on principle of women holding managerial posts. I was devastated by this: it felt like a very personal rejection. Even when I tried to rationalise it, it was impossible to know if it was me or my gender that was the problem.

Comparable problems arose when I began to express my growing interest in computers. One of the perks of working for the Post Office was that you got six weeks' holiday a year. The drawback was that I, at least, could not afford to go anywhere. So I had arranged, though a fellow student at college, to spend some of this time working unpaid at the General Electric Company (GEC) Hirst research centre in Wembley. Bill Cameron, the friend in question, had spoken enthusiastically about a new computer he was working on: the HEC4. "You'd love this," he told me. So I went along for a couple of weeks in the summer of 1954 and made myself useful and, in the process, picked up the basics of this pioneering project. The HEC4 was a huge, multi-part machine that to the modern eye would look more like a fitted kitchen than a personal computer (or PC). While primitive, however, it was none the less unquestionably a computer, in a way that the calculator I had been using was not. It received its initial data and instructions on punched cards (80 columns, and six instructions, per card) and processed them using a 64-track magnetic drum. Ultimately, it could theoretically be used for a wide-range of complicated and repetitive data-processing tasks, from payroll processing to production output analysis. But at this stage the challenge was simply to make it work.

*Checking the randomness of the ERNIE premium bond
computer was an important part of my postgraduate work
at the Post Office Research Station in Dollis Hill.*

I spent many weeks watching Bill and his colleagues working on this. (I had to do something with my annual leave entitlement.) My understanding grew. And I became increasingly excited by the thought that this was just the tip of the iceberg. As computers became more reliable electronically, so the possibilities for programming them would be hugely and thrillingly expanded.

Eventually, I went to Ettrick Thomson and said, look, couldn't we use some of these ideas?

The suggestion wasn't well taken.

No doubt such rejections were largely my fault. I wasn't a great communicator and, on the whole, was better at just getting on with my work than at expressing myself. But it was impossible to avoid the suspicion that, had such suggestions come from a man, they might have caused less offence.

Once again, I felt crushed. I was used to sexism (although I didn't yet know that there was a word for it). There were scarcely a dozen female employees in the entire establishment, and walking into the main canteen reminded me of walking into the boys' school in Oswestry: hundreds of heads would turn and gawp at me with expressions that might have indicated a variety of things but almost certainly didn't indicate respect. I had grown used to the need to dress as unprovocatively as possible, in a plain grey suit and white pintucked blouse, like a female version of a man, with a black band round my neck instead of a tie. I had learnt to live with the angry minority of senior scientists who seemed affronted to encounter a girl in the workplace at all and expressed their affront by being as scathing and horrible as possible to their female subordinates. I had even grown used to the fact that women's pay scales were substantially lower than those for men, although I made no secret of my resentment of this injustice. (Sometimes, a man would offer to help me carry my typewriter-like calculating machine – which was exceedingly heavy – only to receive the tetchy reply: "I believe in equal pay, so I'll carry my own machine.")

What shocked me now was the discovery that, the more I became recognised as a serious young woman who was aiming high – whose long-term aspirations went beyond a mere subservient role – the more violently I was resented and the more implacably I was kept in my place.

But although I felt upset by these rebuffs, life went on. The pain passed; before too long, I bounced back. (This has, I think, been another recurring theme in my life.) I applied a few more times for promotion and, eventually, was promoted. I was, however, moved to a different part of the research station in order to sidestep my colleagues' resentment – which meant that I now had the honour of working in Tommy Flowers's division.

Tommy was not just an engineering genius but also, in spite of his diffidence, an inspirational manager, with a gift for getting the best out of everyone who worked for him. One of our main tasks at the time was to develop ERNIE: the Electronic Random Number Indicator Equipment that had been earmarked to select winners for the impending national Premium Bonds scheme (introduced in 1957). The challenge was to ensure that the device – which worked by sampling "white noise" generated by a neon gas discharge tube – was genuinely random. The key (without going into too much detail) was to use two such devices for each number that needed to be generated, subtracting the output from the second from the output from the first, in case one of them went wrong. This meant – we thought – that 32 devices were needed to generate the requisite 16-figure number. Then our youngest lab boy suggested that we could achieve the same result with just 16 devices, pairing the first with the second, the second with the third, the third with the fourth, and so on, instead of having 16 discrete pairs. At a stroke, the cost was halved. The genius of Tommy Flowers – or part of it – was to run his team in a way that allowed such suggestions to be both made and heard. This may have been the most important thing I learnt from him.

There was great public interest in this project, and occasionally groups of visitors would come to watch us at work. The piece of machinery that usually fascinated them most was a futuristic spherical device, on wheels, that we kept in the corner. We could hardly bear to tell them that this was just the vacuum cleaner.

In another version of my life, I might have spent my entire career at Dollis Hill. Whatever its frustrations and limitations, it was a research station – with "Research is the door to tomorrow" carved over its big stone portals – and most of what we were doing was by definition new and challenging. The work that I was able to contribute to was only a few years behind what real mathematical pioneers were exploring, and as we grew interested in computing for its own sake – rather than as a slightly tiresome means to a mathematical end – I began to feel that I had found my metier.

I spent a year studying for my master's degree and began to do some pure research of my own, into the feasibility of speech recognition by computers. I also became a founder member of the British Computer Society, in 1957. (I've always been a great joiner of societies and public bodies, perhaps because of the refugee's desire to belong. Around this time I also joined the Interplanetary Society and, for some reason, the Homosexual Law Reform Society – I suppose because of my innate sympathy with outsiders.) I don't think I made a significant contribution to the development of speech recognition software, or indeed to any other aspect of pure computer science, but it was exciting simply to be involved in the field. I felt that I was finally beginning to fly – and made a point of not taking my lunches with the same old crowd in the canteen any more (even if this meant bringing in my own sandwich), so that no one could be in any doubt that I was no longer at the bottom of the organisational ladder.

It felt good to be making a difference to the world at last, and there were plenty of important projects to be worked on, from helping to design the first electronic telephone exchange (at Highgate Woods) to investigating likely traffic patterns on the first transatlantic telephone cable. And I was above all learning, finally, how to work effectively. I learnt – mainly by trial and error – how to use information, how to prioritise, how to manage money, how to impose structure, how to manage time; and, not least, how to get on with my colleagues.

A lingering sense of prejudice remained: of a glass ceiling that would always prevent me from developing my talents to the full. But in the short term I had plenty on my plate to challenge me, and in the end it was not sexism that persuaded me to leave. It was something more personal than that.

This "something" had its origins back in my scientific assistant days, when I had at some point found myself needing to know more about waveguides – the physical structures (such as cables) through which electromagnetic waves are conducted. I asked around, and one of my female colleagues – Valerie Copper – took me to see a man called Derek Shirley.

He worked in a small office in another part of the research station and initially made next to no impression on me. He was extremely shy, and on our first meeting scarcely made eye contact with me. But he was friendly and helpful and, although I still haven't entirely mastered the intricacies of waveguide theory, his explanations were sufficiently useful for me to return on several occasions for further guidance. In due course we noticed one another.

This is not a book about Derek, and I will not attempt here to express in words everything he has since become to me. Only he and I can ever fully understand what we have meant to one another. For more than 50 years, we have shared joy and sadness, adventure and routine, anxiety and contentment, and, above all, love. He remains the rock on which my life is built. Back then, however, he was just a good-looking colleague who, despite his shyness, seemed curiously undeterred by the fact that, the first few times he asked me out, I turned him down brusquely.

There were other men on the scene back then – including, initially, Trevor. But eventually, many months after our first meeting, I agreed, half-heartedly, to a date with Derek. We had known each other for the best part of a year by then, but, even so, it felt awkward to be alone together. We ate at the old Swiss Cottage in west London, and talked largely of music, about which Derek was both passionate and knowledgeable. My main impression was still of his shyness, and of the way he fluttered his eyelashes, rather as a woman does.

A week or so later we went out again, to explore another of his passions: the Thames. Derek had spent his favourite wartime days on the river, along with a close-knit group of about half-a-dozen friends known, collectively, as the River Boys. They had all been working for the Ministry of Defence – at Dollis Hill – on the production of crystal oscillators, which were needed for all sorts of vital military signals work. But they could do so only when they had the necessary quartz, which was in short supply. When they had some, they would work around the clock, pausing only for occasional snatches of sleep on the on-site camp beds. When the quartz ran out, they would disappear for a week or two to mess about on the river, until the next consignment made it across the Atlantic from, I think, Brazil. Derek had spent some of the happiest times of his life on these excursions, and so it seemed natural to him to introduce me to the joys of the river.

I turned up for our day out in my most glamorous dress and white high heels, under the impression that we were going to be on a grand pleasure boat. It turned out that our vessel was a dilapidated punt, whose sides barely poked out of the water. After an hour of uncomfortable punting, the heavens opened, and by the time we returned to dry land I was bedraggled and shivering – at which point Derek finally succeeded in impressing me by producing an enormous towel from the tennis bag that he invariably carried around with him. Perhaps, I reasoned, such a well-prepared man was worth getting to know better.

Our courtship was long-drawn-out. I remember many happy days on the river – which was, we discovered, a better place than most for a couple to get a bit of privacy. I remember some surprisingly good-natured get-togethers with my mother – who found Derek annoyingly vague but concluded, grudgingly, that on balance he wasn't as bad as some of the other men I had been involved with. And I remember that for a long time our relationship veered between delightful highs and apparently terminal lows. I had, for some reason, decided to take up knitting, and during the good spells I spent many of my leisure hours knitting him a sweater. Then, during the "off" phases, the knitting would stop – while at particularly low points I would even start unpicking the work that I had already done.

At some point, after several years, the subject of marriage came up. I can't remember exactly how it arose; only that I didn't welcome the idea. In retrospect, this seems strange. It seems obvious to me now that marriage to a man like Derek was the best thing that could possibly have happened to me. It didn't then.

There were, I think, two reasons. One was that he had not been what I was expecting. I had imagined that the love of my life would be slicker and more polished – more obviously sophisticated; more like my father. So it took time to accept that, although he was not a good communicator, Derek was none the less a deep thinker, with a profound intellectual curiosity that matched my own. (He was always making journeys to Hammersmith public library, where you could borrow both books and long-playing records.) What I ultimately realised was that he was, simply, a good man: gentle, solid, dependable, honest, unselfish and upright – more like Uncle than my father, though much cleverer and, indeed, probably cleverer than me. As such, he was

*My mother made me a beautiful wedding dress of cream brocade.
The top tier of the cake went to my sister in Australia.*

a thoroughly suitable choice as a lifetime's partner. But it took time for all this to sink in.

The other problem was that – in the early stages of our courtship – I was still in the process of unravelling the mental knots of my childhood through my visits to the Tavistock Clinic. In some hard-to-define way, I felt that I was not fit to marry. Marriage was for normal, happy people – whereas I, I had decided, was too damaged; too much of a victim; too eaten up by resentment; too traumatised by exile.

So the idea of marriage was put to one side, and we carried on, knitting, unpicking and reknitting our relationship without really going anywhere. We saw little of each other at work – we were at opposite ends of the site – and lots of each other outside work. The obstacles preventing us from going further seemed as baffling and elusive as the obstacles that prevented my career from going any further.

Then, in the late summer of 1959, my mother went on a trip to Vienna. At the last minute, I decided to join her. We made the grim train journey across Europe, weighed down with baggage and expectation, before finally emerging in the glorious historic city from which we had escaped 20 years earlier. I looked around at its gracious avenues, ancient walls, grand palaces and elegant squares. And I realised in an instant that, lovely as it all was, it meant absolutely nothing to me. It may look strange in print, but at that moment I felt the weight of my past vanish from my shoulders. It was not that I ceased to be conscious of the traumas of my childhood. It was just that the psychological "ghosts" that had been haunting me suddenly seemed small and manageable – scarcely more than a figment of my imagination. I could not deny my past, or make it go away. But, if I chose to be, I could from now on be as unscarred and "normal" as any other English child of the war years.

I telephoned Derek there and then – no easy matter in those days – and told him that I was ready to marry him. We married six weeks later.

The ceremony took place at Willesden Registry Office, on 14 November 1959. Derek had initially wanted a church wedding, but I felt that, for a non-believer like me, that would be hypocritical. (A few years earlier, my urge to belong had prompted me to enrol for Confirmation classes in the Church of England, but by the end of the course I had realised that I lacked the faith to go through with it.) So instead we booked the last registry office session of a Saturday morning, so that it would feel a bit less like being on a conveyor belt, and then held a small party – for about 40 people – at a hotel in Hampstead. Most of the guests were colleagues, although my mother was there, and Auntie and Uncle, and my aunt Ilse (who had come over from Munich and was shocked by the London smog), but not my father – who had sent a very small cheque which we spent on a very small clock. Derek's parents were there, but many of his family stayed away, disapproving of his marrying a German. Uncle gave me away.

We spent a very short honeymoon in a very grand hotel in Egham, Surrey (chosen because the hotel, Great Fosters, had a four-poster bed). The brevity was linked to the grandness: we ran out of money.

Then we began a new life.

In many respects it was much the same as our old life. For the first eight months, we lived in that same tiny bedsit in Walm Lane – an experience I'd recommend for any newly married couple, because it forces you (eventually) to get on. We wanted to buy a place of our own, but each time we saved up what we thought was enough for a deposit we found that house prices had gone up.

But there was one significant change: I stopped working at the Post Office. It wasn't absolutely obligatory to do so, but the general assumption in those days was that if two people working in the same organisation married, one of them – usually the woman – would leave. (In fact, there was a couple at the Post Office who had broken that convention – and their example alone was enough to turn me against the idea. If they ate lunch together in the canteen, people would gossip about how they were more interested in their marriage than in being good colleagues; if they didn't, people would gossip about how they must have had a row. The thought of my marriage being subjected to such daily public scrutiny horrified me.)

There was no particular reason why it should have been I rather than Derek who left. He was an Experimental Officer, whereas I was by now a Scientific Officer, which made us roughly equal in status. But given the frustrations I had encountered each time I attempted to progress up the Post Office hierarchy, it made sense for me to try somewhere new.

So: I handed in my resignation, cashed in the small pension I had accumulated (which paid for the wedding and the honeymoon) and looked for something else. Before long, I found another job, at a company called Computer Developments Limited (CDL) in Kenton, near Harrow. This was a subsidiary of International Computers and Tabulators (ICT, which was later absorbed by International Computers Limited – ICL – and, later still, by Fujitsu) and of GEC. It was run by John Wensley, who had been Bill Cameron's boss at GEC Hirst. It was, in those days, a small, young, energetic outfit that was really quite exciting to work for. There were about 35 employees, most of them young and bright, and compared with the Post Office their way of working was thrillingly informal. Everyone used to take their breaks together in the canteen, and staff from different departments would exchange ideas freely. People worked with urgency and enthusiasm, and the long days were shaped by objectives rather than routine. This was, I suppose, my first experience of the difference between the staid public sector and the dynamic private sector.

I was part of the company's software group, which provided software for Computer Developments' computers. My particular responsibility – and that of the handful of group members who worked under me – was for software-testing a new computer, called the 1301, that the company was designing and building in Coventry. Essentially, the object of the software was to check that the hardware (which had unbuffered peripherals, for those of you who understand such terminology) was working properly. This didn't involve making radical new conceptual breakthroughs, but for a mathematician with limited technical experience it was quite exciting.

We worked hard – I have many grim memories of snatching a few hours' sleep in cheap Coventry hotel rooms after working half the night on the computer because other people were using it by day – but I felt that I was learning things. I loved those early computers – huge, whirring things that filled an entire room, and I loved the pure, abstract beauty (not unlike musical beauty) of the logic that underlay their design. The process of designing the 1301 had, it was said, included making a huge "logic diagram" of its workings on the floor of CDL's 50ft-by-15ft meeting-room. Volunteers representing electrical pulses were recruited to walk between the various "gates" (jargon for the electronic devices that compute the value of two-valued signals), just as was supposed to happen in the machine itself. If someone tried to go through a gate that wasn't open, or if two people ended up

Newly married and saving for our first home, I could scarce believe that I should be paid so well in industry. It was a happy period – but I still smoked.

trying to stand on the same point at the same time, then there was a problem that needed to be addressed. It was, in short, a triumph of pure reason, and a labour of many people's love. I used to sit down at the controls to begin a session with the same kind of thrill that one might feel on taking the controls of a shiny new racing-car. I also liked my colleagues, several of whom turned into friends. And, as an extra bonus, I was earning much more than I had at Dollis Hill.

We tried to live just on Derek's salary, putting mine towards buying furniture and saving for that elusive first home. But house prices still grew faster than our savings, and bit by bit we moved our sights away from central London. By the time we found somewhere we could afford, we had reached Chesham, a market town in Buckinghamshire, in the heart of the Chiltern Hills. More precisely, we had reached a hamlet called Ley Hill, a few miles outside Chesham, where we bought a dilapidated brick-and-flint cottage – then being rented by a friendly young couple with a baby – on the edge of some woods. It cost us £4,765 and was called Moss Cottage.

Life here required considerable adjustments. Not only were there holes in the floorboards and leaking pipes to be fixed (by Derek, with admirable patience but limited competence), but we soon realised that we were possibly the only urban incomers in a very rural and isolated settlement. The locals weren't unfriendly, but it was clear that they regarded us with a faintly contemptuous bemusement which it took time to wear down. It didn't help when we held a small house-warming party for a few of our London friends, only for our chimney to catch fire. By the time the conflagration had been extinguished, our reputation as inept townies was firmly set. This had its advantages: I remember one neighbour volunteering (in vain) to put down some unwanted kittens with her bare hands, while another, a frail and harmless old lady, helped deal with a rat in our garden by beating it to death with a stick. Conversely, when some gypsies settled on the edge of Ley Hill for a few summer weeks, ours was the only household that would give them drinking-water. This made us unpopular with some villagers, but with my background there was no question of compromise. I said: "I'm not refusing drinking-water to anyone." In an odd sort of way, we seemed to be more respected after this.

Our lifestyle was basic. Our furniture consisted initially of a bed, two deckchairs, a stool and – for Derek – a baby grand piano. But our lives were full enough for any discomforts to seem unimportant. We both commuted to work, although not together. I worked longer hours than Derek, and generally got a lift from a colleague who lived nearby. In the evenings, we were quite content with one another's company. Sometimes, though, I would linger in the garden on my return, to listen to Derek playing the piano. He played beautifully, but was still too shy to play in front of me.

This was a happy time: the kind of innocent, peaceful post-war idyll to which many middle-class couples then aspired. But, inevitably, there came a time – perhaps two years into our marriage – when we (or at least I) began to wonder what happened next.

It wasn't that there was anything wrong with our relationship; it was more a feeling that, somehow, I was once again limiting myself in order to fit in with other people's preconceptions. Working wives were rare and often viewed with suspicion, not least in rural Buckinghamshire, and so I had got into the habit of playing down the career aspect of my life, reducing my employment at Computer Developments to four days a week so that my earnings would not outstrip Derek's and ostentatiously spending the remaining day on chores such as laundry, so that his traditional male role as head of the household should not be threatened. (He had, to be fair, never expressed any insecurities on such matters, but I didn't want to take any chances.)

At work, meanwhile, that same sense of arbitrary limits that had frustrated me at the Post Office was beginning to frustrate me at Computer Developments Limited. I had done well as a programmer: one short piece of code I wrote – a "bootstrap" programme that allowed the computer to pull in more complicated programmes – earned CDL hundreds of thousands of pounds. As my confidence grew, however, I found myself increasingly interested not just in software development but also in the marketing side of our operations. It fascinated me to think: "If a computer can do x, what use could somebody make of that function? And how could our company exploit that?" Strictly speaking, however, this was not what I was employed for, and it soon became clear that there were people in the company who did not welcome intrusions on their territory. Perhaps my gender had something to do with it, but the real problem was a more broadly territorial mind-set. I had my place, and I should stay in it.

The turning-point was a meeting at which I was supposed to be talking about the technical aspects of some project. The discussion came round to something more marketing-related – about pricing, I think – and I began to make a suggestion. One of the senior men cut me short: "That's nothing to do with you. You're technical." And that was the end of my contribution.

It sounds a small thing, but the more I thought about it, the bigger it became. It wasn't just the fact that he had said it. It was the fact that I didn't know how to deal with it, and that no one else had piped up to say "Hang on, let's just hear what she's got to say." Women everywhere, in all walks of business, will have had similar experiences. It wasn't, in this instance, a gender thing; but the sense of dumb frustration was the same. How could they know that what I had to say wasn't worth listening to, if they wouldn't even let me say it?

I brooded on this for the rest of the day, and on my journey home, and for much of the evening. Finally, after talking things through with Derek, I reached a conclusion: it was time to move on.

It wasn't just that I didn't want to work there anymore. There was something else.

I had had an idea.

7: New Beginnings

I resigned the following morning. I gave three months' notice – much more than I had to – partly out of a sense of duty but also from a certain nervousness about the future. The idea that had seemed so irresistible the night before seemed flimsier once my resignation had been accepted.

I had decided to start my own company, selling software. That's an uncontroversial sentence, written nearly 50 years later. At the time, it sounded mad.

Drawbacks included the following. I had no capital to speak of. I had no experience of running a company. I had no employees, no office, no customers, and no reason to believe that there were any companies out there with any interest in buying my product. Nobody sold software in those days. In so far as it existed, it was given away free. Only the most forward-thinking and well-resourced organisations invested at all in what would now be called information technology, and those that did so would generally have been outraged at the suggestion that, having forked out a hefty sum for a new computer, they should also be asked to pay for the code to make it do what it was supposed to do. They expected that to be thrown in for nothing, as the manual is for a new car.

But I knew, as everyone now knows, that the capabilities of a computer are defined not by its solid parts but by the code that runs it – in those days, huge reels of punched tape. If a company wanted to improve its efficiency by using a computer, what mattered wasn't the hardware it bought but the programme – the software – that told it what to do. I cannot honestly pretend that I foresaw how huge the software industry would eventually become. (The combined global market for operating systems and applications is estimated as I write to be worth around $300bn.) My motivation had more to do with the sheer pleasure of working with computers. But I also had a gut feeling that there was a programming industry of some kind waiting to be born, and I liked the idea of being in at its birth. I knew that I was good at programming, and that there was only a relatively small pool of people in the UK who were. At the very least, I thought, I ought to be able get enough freelance assignments of my own to be able to earn a living, from home, without having to be an underling in a male-dominated company. As an added attraction, such a way of working might well be compatible with raising children, which Derek and I hoped to be doing before too long.

The great thing, from my point of view, was that writing a computer programme required neither resources nor infrastructure. It was a very time-intensive business, in which the code had first to be written out as a sequence of logical commands – the difficult bit – before being converted into digital code that could be expressed as punched holes in a strip of tape. But all you needed, for the most part, was pencil, paper and a brain good enough to imagine how complex tasks could be reduced to a series of logical steps. This meant that I could work from home – or, if necessary, on clients' premises – without splashing out on equipment. It also meant that, if all went well, I could hire other programmers, on a freelance basis, for particular projects, and they could do the work from their homes. My new company's name, Freelance Programmers, described exactly what I intended it to do.

Several of my colleagues, told of my plan, laughed openly; I presume that the rest laughed in private. Not only was the plan mad. There was also the awkward fact that I was a woman. Whoever heard of a woman running a company – unless it was a little tea-shop, or a cottage enterprise selling hats? One or two added that, even disregarding my gender, I was surely too brittle in temperament to survive in the unforgiving business jungle.

None the less, I was determined to give it a try. There seemed to be so much potential: not necessarily for making money, but for translating the various challenges that organisations faced into problems that could be solved by a computer. Logistics, planning, management, automation – anything and everything seemed capable of being made to run more smoothly with the help of a well-thought-out programme. Anything seemed possible.

I was 29 years old, and, while I could hardly have been less qualified for the task, I did have the crucial asset of unlimited enthusiasm. Marriage to Derek had given me a sense of stability and security that allowed me to take risks. I loved the field I worked in, and I felt a bright, joyful, optimistic passion for the business that I had imagined.

Making money scarcely featured in my list of motives. If all went well, I would earn a living; if the worst came to the worst, I had Derek's salary to fall back on while I found another job. What I wanted was not wealth but a workplace where I was not hemmed in by prejudice or by other people's preconceived notions of what I could and could not do – a place where, instead, I could exchange ideas freely with likeminded colleagues. And in 1962 that meant an entirely new kind of workplace.

Luckily, I was in a position to create one; in fact, my lack of assets gave me no alternative. I had £6 of capital, a dining-room table, a telephone (with a party line shared with a neighbour who, luckily, rarely used it), and one other mad idea: those who worked for me would all be women, employed on a freelance basis and working from home.

I'm not sure when this women-only principle first occurred to me. It hadn't been part of my initial idea, and, in the early months, it was hardly relevant. I had imagined that the world would beat a path to my door – I was reasonably well-known by then in what was a pretty tiny industry. But it didn't. And when I did eventually get a contract – from the new UK division of the US management consultants, Urwick Diebold – it provided enough work for just one person: me.

But the issue of gender kept recurring. For example: I needed my husband's written permission before I could open a bank account. (Women weren't allowed to work on the stock exchange then, either; or to drive a bus, or fly an aeroplane.) And the letters that I eventually started sending out to other companies touting for business received so little response – not even an acknowledgement, usually – that I began to wonder if the fact that I was a woman had something to do with that, too. Almost immediately, therefore, I felt that I needed to succeed not just for my own benefit but in order to prove a point on behalf of women generally.

Then another, related issue came up. The Urwick Diebold project lasted about eight months. I got it via a former fellow employee of CDL, David Lush, who had joined Urwick Diebold some time earlier. He introduced me to a colleague, Kit Grindley, who was setting up a programming group in the company's new computer consultancy division. The brief was to write software standards – in other words, management control protocols – for this group. This wasn't exactly the kind of work I had had in mind for my enterprise, but it would prove immensely valuable in the long run. Programming was (and is) a maddeningly hard-to-pin-down activity, whose practitioners are notorious for claiming airily that there are "just a couple more bugs to sort out" while uncomprehending clients fret about missed deadlines. The fact that Freelance Programmers could claim to be a source of objective, written standards would ultimately prove to be a major selling-point for us, and would help demonstrate to prospective clients that we were no mere fly-by-night operation.

But the crucial thing about that first project in the short term was that, halfway through it, I realised that I was pregnant. This wasn't exactly a surprise. We had been planning to start a family, and my dreams for our future usually included four or five children in the background. But the actual approach of a real birth date put things in a less forgiving light. Could I really cope? Could the business cope with such disruption so early on? And what would potential clients – who felt dubious enough about my being a woman – feel about doing business with a heavily pregnant woman? ("How many people do you have working for you?" my ex-boss asked me around this time. "One and a bit," I replied; but I didn't tell him what I meant.)

I finished the Urwick Diebold job with just a few weeks to spare. I remember visiting them towards the end of it and having serious difficulty climbing the stairs to their second-floor office opposite Victoria station. I had earned £700 from it: much less than I would have earned in that time had I remained an employee. It occurred to me that I would need to do something about my pricing – just as soon as I had dealt with the more immediate challenge of giving birth.

Giles was born on 9 May 1963, in Amersham cottage hospital. It was a traumatic, 24-hour labour: at one point a nurse complained that my screams were frightening the other patients. But Giles himself was the most beautiful, adorable baby you could imagine. It was daunting being at home alone with him for the first time, and I remember crying a lot on my first days back from hospital. But we bonded quickly – all three of us – and I couldn't possibly have imagined leaving him with someone else in order to go and work in an office. As I didn't have an office, the issue didn't arise. But what about my business? Would I let it fizzle out after just one job? Or would I find a way to keep it going?

For about three months, I hardly cared: I was too busy being a doting mother. Derek would come home in the evening and ask me about my day, and I would struggle to think of anything I had done. The rigmarole of feeding and bathing and cuddling and playing – not

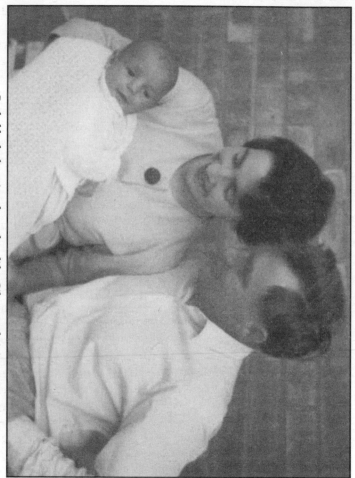

Probably the happiest days of my life. Giles was thriving at 3 months and we had no inkling of the problems ahead.

to mention washing nappies and hanging them out to dry – seemed to fill every waking minute. And if I paused for a moment to gaze into my son's bright eyes, or to contemplate the sheen of impossibly soft and delicate fair hair on his head, I wondered how anyone could ever have suggested that motherhood might be boring. For me, it was utterly absorbing, and I felt a sense of completeness that I had never felt before.

Then, gradually, my enthusiasm for work began to return: not instead of my enthusiasm for Giles but as well. Giles was not just a beautiful baby but an easy one. He ate enthusiastically, warbled quietly in a beautiful treble voice, and spent a lot of time sleeping. I found that it was relatively easy to write letters and work out proposals in between looking after his needs, and before long I felt confident that he and Freelance Programmers could be nurtured simultaneously. A former colleague at CDL asked me to do a fairly straightforward project, which I appreciated (but would have appreciated even more if they could have managed a less miserly fee). Before I knew it, I was working more or less full-time again.

Neither my mother nor my mother-in-law could understand why I wanted to go back to work. Nor could most of our neighbours. "Why? Hasn't Derek got a decent job?" was one comment. Derek took a more practical attitude. "I understand that babies make a lot of washing," he said. "If you're going to be working, we had better buy one of those new automatic washing-machines." It was the only thing we ever bought on hire-purchase – and a much larger investment than anything we had so far put into my new company. It was also one of the best investments I ever made.

Then another project came in, from a City company called Selection Trust, who wanted a Programme Evaluation Review Technique (PERT) carried out on a computer they had purchased. I was too busy with the Computer Developments project, and with Giles, to do this myself, but I hated to turn work down, so I found a freelance programmer, a very nice lady called Ann Leaming, to do most of the work for me, while I just managed the project. I paid her 15 shillings (75p) an hour, and charged Selection Trust a guinea (£1.05) an hour, which sounded suitably grand.

In fact, both projects were laughably under-priced, to the extent that it scarcely made business sense to be doing them at all. But at least we were gaining experience in new kinds of work – PERT projects, in which you analyse the tasks involved in completing various processes, would form a significant part of our future business. And at least I was no longer just a one-woman operation. My company was doing what its name implied.

By the end of 1963 I felt confident that the business could expand. In fact, I felt confident about everything. I remember looking at Giles, and thinking of him and Derek and our home and my exciting new company, and concluding that I must be the luckiest person in the world.

But feeling confident was one thing. The problem remained of how to develop the business. All our contracts to date had come through former colleagues, and these would soon be finished. There would be no more work for us to do, unless I could I somehow sell our services to the wider world. Meanwhile, the financial situation was worrying. I remember bursting into tears on receiving an income tax demand, based on my previous salary, for £600 – that is, for 85 per cent of what I had earned in the 1962-63 tax year. Another year like that and I would be ruined. Somehow, urgently, Freelance Programmers needed to expand.

I had already spent most of our starting capital on some smart headed notepaper, with the words "freelance programmers" all in lower case (partly in deference to the design trends of the day but also as a pun: we were a company with no capital). I had also taken steps to make us sound more like a proper business – and less like a cottage industry – by removing the words "Moss Cottage" from our address. I remember posting empty envelopes to myself from various locations, addressed simply to "Freelance Programmers, Ley Hill, Buckinghamshire", to check that they would reach me.

And I had hired a local lady, Barbara Edwards, to provide half a day week of secretarial assistance, so that I could be certain that my letters would go out looking as though they had come from the chairman of a blue-chip company. She used to come to Moss Cottage on Wednesday afternoons with her own baby, and we would help one another out with childcare as circumstances demanded.

But still my letters failed to produce a response, until Derek suggested that maybe the problem lay not with the letters themselves but with the signature at the bottom of them. Given my experience with previous employers, it was not unreasonable to speculate that many potential customers, seeing the words "Stephanie Shirley" at the bottom of a letter, would refuse to take its proposals seriously, simply because I was a woman.

Derek suggested testing this theory by signing a few letters "Steve Shirley" instead. I did so, and people began to respond. I have been Steve ever since.

Around that time – on 31 January 1964, to be precise – my little enterprise got a mention in a feature in the Guardian about a strange and exotic modern phenomenon: women who worked in the then embryonic computer industry. The article, by Maureen Epstein, was headlined "Computer women" and described how a growing number of women who had decent maths qualifications plus "patience and tenacity, and a common-sense sort of logic" were finding employment opportunities as programmers. "Much of the work is tedious," she wrote, "requiring great attention to detail, and this is where women usually score." I'm not sure what women who read the article would have made of this analysis, but one paragraph that clearly struck many of them mentioned a "Mrs Steve Shirley, of Chesham, Buckinghamshire" who "has found that computer programming... is a job that can be done at home between feeding the baby and washing nappies. She is hoping to interest other retired programmers in joining her in working on a freelance basis."

This unexpected piece of free publicity provoked a flurry of enquiries from would-be programmers, some of whom had worked in the industry at quite a high level before "retiring" to have children. It really marked the beginning of what would become a "panel" of highly qualified freelancers. It also encouraged a certain amount of interest from prospective clients – as did a small advertisement I placed in The Times around this time, seeking two home-based programmers and describing the opening as a "wonderful chance, but hopeless for anti-feminists". It was hard, however, to translate these initial enquiries into firm orders. People got cold feet when they phoned and heard Giles crying in the background. I dealt with this by making a tape-recording of Barbara typing and playing it whenever the phone rang. Then there was the problem of going in to meet someone and – once they had got over the shock of discovering that I wasn't a man – suddenly finding myself the object of unwanted sexual advances. It is hard to sell software when you are having your bottom pinched. And that is what the business world was all too often like in those days.

But bit by bit offers of work began to trickle in. The great thing in our favour was that we had scarcely any competitors. Once we could show that we were a reliable enterprise that had done demonstrably valuable work for serious customers, then even quite large companies were willing to give us a try. Several of our early clients were US businesses, who were more at home with the idea of outsourcing, and I went out of my way to target the Anglo-American market. But gradually we began to build a British customer base as well. Our revenues for the 1963-4 tax year reached £1,700 – still less than I had been earning at CDL but none the less a significant improvement.

But expansion brought headaches of its own. The fact that other people were now writing software on my behalf made me worry about public liability. What if someone's work went wrong? It takes only the tiniest of errors in the coding to cause a software programme to work in a dramatically different way to the way intended. As the projects that came our way grew bigger – we were even in discussions with GEC about a system for a new aircraft – so the potential for making a catastrophically expensive mistake grew bigger too. I made enquiries about professional indemnity insurance, and was quoted premiums that would have wiped the company out. It made more sense, I realised, to incorporate Freelance Programmers as a limited liability company. On 13 May 1964, therefore, I paid £15 for an "off-the-shelf" company registration, and the business became Freelance Programmers Limited.

This was a huge step forward. Not only did it ease my worries about indemnity by limiting our liability, but it also felt, in an odd way, like officially laying a foundation stone. That "Limited" somehow made the whole operation seem more solid, more credible, more real – both to our customers and to me.

Minute Number One in the company's minute book stated that our purpose was "to provide jobs for women with children". Later on, when we began to give more thought to the need for training and development, we changed this to "careers for women with children". Later still, when I realised that many of the women I was employing were caring for elderly relations or disabled partners, it was amended again to "careers for women with dependents". But the main point never changed: this was a company that would offer opportunities to the kind of women whom traditional male-dominated companies considered unemployable.

I don't think I had started out with such a clear-cut social purpose. I had merely imagined a workplace undisfigured by traditional male sexism. Yet a pro-woman policy made obvious sense. Talented female mathematicians had been passing through the universities in increasing numbers ever since the War, and gaining good degrees. Many of them had worked for a while in Britain's nascent IT industry, only to drop out – of the job and the job market – either on marrying or on having children. And, since most companies were far too rigid and male-dominated to adapt their ways of working to suit such employees' convenience, their skills and intellectual energy had been going to waste. By committing my company to making use of this pool of untapped talent, I gained privileged access to some of the best programmers in the country. (Many came from IBM, where part-time systems engineers were simply not allowed.) Not only were these women good: they were delighted to be working for me and determined to make the most of the opportunity.

Perhaps as a result, the company thrived. There were still plenty of potential clients who refused to take us seriously because we were women, but for others it was, if not a positive selling-point, at least a reason for not forgetting us. Our client-base grew slowly but surely. We got a job working for Tate & Lyle, helping to optimise the scheduling of the lorries that carried their sugar around the UK. (Decades later, I still feel a stab of panic if I see a Tate & Lyle lorry on a country road, in case it is lost.)

Our PERT project for Selection Trust led on to a series of other PERT projects, some of which were quite substantial. We were hired by Mars, the confectionery company, to improve the efficiency of their production processes. Their UK base was in Slough, which I used to visit by bus. I remember agonising about the ethics of accepting the goody-bags full of chocolate bars that they always used to press upon me when I left. (This issue arose with Tate & Lyle too. Each of us who worked on the project was given a 6lb tin of their famous black treacle. I have only just finished mine.) And so it went on. Imperceptibly, and unintentionally, we were becoming much more than freelance programmers. We were becoming experts in logistics and operational research.

British Railways was another big early customer. They commissioned a major study of their nationwide freight scheduling, This required me to make several journeys to Doncaster, by train. They always provided me with a first class rail warrant, which eased the strain considerably. It also encouraged me to feel that I was a serious businesswoman.

There was, however, a drawback. I still hadn't the slightest idea how to run a business. I understood software, and I knew how to work – hard, and in an organised manner. But I hadn't a clue about how to run a company. Even the basics of administration – how to register, how to make contracts of employment – involved a steep learning curve, while more subtle skills, such as managing cash-flow, eluded me completely. I didn't even know that the issues existed, let alone that I needed to master them.

As our workload expanded, this became a serious problem. We were being paid to do more and bigger projects, and each project was in itself profitable, yet we never seemed to have enough money in the bank. Sensing that something was wrong, I decided to invest in some expert advice, and asked the consultants of Urwick Diebold (by now a satisfied customer) if they could help. They sent out Kit Grindley, the manager who had liaised with me on the standards-writing project.

He came over for a morning – or more than a morning, as it turned out, although he only charged me for half the day, which was all I could afford. (They charged a terrifying £150 a day.) He looked through what passed for my books and was simultaneously impressed and horrified. I was, he explained, on the point of having to close the business down: there simply wasn't enough cash to pay the freelancers at the end of the month. This seemed mad to me: we had far more money coming in than going out. But the incoming money hadn't come in yet, and wasn't coming in quickly enough.

But Kit – who later became an influential professor and IT consultant – could also see that the business itself was fundamentally sound. The organisations that owed us money, or with whom we had signed contracts for future work, could in no way be described as credit risks. (Other early clients included Rolls-Royce and GEC.) There was clearly a market for what we did, and our long-term future looked astonishingly bright. So he got out his chequebook and, there and then, wrote out a personal cheque for £500 to tide us through. It was an act of generosity that I have never forgotten, and also an example, which continues to inspire me, of the power of intelligent lending. We paid him back rapidly, as I'm sure he never doubted we would; and that cottage industry that he saved went on to become a multinational giant. But without that timely loan, all of our potential and inherent strengths would have come to nothing.

8: Growing Pains

After this, I made a serious effort to educate myself in business matters. But none of the books I found seemed to take much interest in the kind of business I was running. They focused on things like production and logistics and theories of manufacturing efficiency. The idea of a service industry – which is what we were – barely existed in those days. I also considered doing an MBA, and got as far as making inquiries at Harvard before concluding that the disruption to our family life would be too great.

Then I met a local academic, Jack Bungard, who lectured in business studies at Watford College (later the West Herts Management Centre), and an idea occurred to me. Surely, I suggested to him, a theorist of business must need real-life raw material from which to draw his conclusions? So why didn't he come in and treat my business as a case study – free of charge? He did, and the arrangement worked well for both of us. In the course of an attachment lasting many months, he got a front-row view of the birth pangs of a very modern kind of company. I got the benefit of a high-powered consultant with years of top-level experience of how companies usually work. He taught me many things, the most important of which – based on sitting in on various unsuccessful pitches – was how to sell. He taught me to rein back my instinctive desire to show off my insight and technical expertise and, instead, to listen. If clients expressed doubts about my proposals, he explained, it was no good my simply telling them they were wrong. I needed to respond to their worries: to take on board what they were saying and modify my proposal to fit their needs.

I listened. I learnt. I became better at selling and better at running the company – and the work began to pour in. Following Kit Grindley's advice, I began to link payments to programmers to the jobs they had worked on: when the client paid, we paid. (He called this "gearing".) This felt a little mean at first – although we did offer the safety-net that if the client hadn't paid within three months we would pay anyway. But it did do away at a stroke with 90 per cent of our cashflow problems – and, as a result, with the risk that we would suddenly go out of business.

Our lack of financial muscle was, on the whole, an advantage. We had access to a small bank overdraft, thanks to Derek's secure salary and an old-style bank manager called Mr Priddle, but there were next to no fixed assets. So we grew only when our market grew. I hired people only as I needed them, to work from home on specific projects. Many of them became regulars, but only on the basis that the relationship was a mutually satisfactory one. Some didn't want to work all the time – usually because of family commitments – but liked being on our books because of the interesting and rewarding work it provided when they were available. (There wasn't much other interesting part-time work that a woman could do in those days.) Even our project managers – essential for the growing number of larger projects, on which several programmers worked simultaneously – were hired on an ad hoc basis, working from home at whatever times worked best for them. We didn't call it flexi-working, because the term didn't exist, but in due course that concept was to become one of our defining characteristics.

In fact, there were some people who preferred to work away from home, which meant that, after a while, Moss Cottage became very crowded. There were three of us working there on a regular basis, plus Barbara on Wednesday afternoons, plus her baby, plus mine. We usually had two people working in the lounge, with a third in the spare bedroom. There were boxes of files piled high on the piano, and Derek had to make a special collapsible table for the spare bedroom – we had to take it down whenever we wanted to open the cupboard. The photocopier occupied most of the bathroom. In fact, it was a man who had come to service the photocopier who first put the idea into my head that we should get a proper office. He had just been doing a job for a company in Chesham, in Station Road, which was vacating its premises, and he thought they would suit us perfectly. I decided to look into it.

But it was hard to find the time. The need for new clients meant that I had to respond to every enquiry. Most of my meetings took place on Tuesday afternoons, which was the only time I had a babysitter. I funnelled as many appointments as possible into those few hours each week, knowing that – since Derek came home at 6pm – I could remain in London (or wherever the client was based) for as long as it took. But then, since most of these meetings yielded requests for more detailed proposals, there were countless hours to be found, somewhere in the

Moss Cottage, named after the moss rose in the garden, had originally been a pair of agricultural cottages; the large window dated from when it served as the village shop.

week, for preparing reports about what we could and couldn't do for different prospective clients. And, of course, I had to make sure that our existing projects were progressing satisfactorily – which could mean anything from ringing people up for reports to putting more coal on the Moss Cottage fire to keep everyone warm.

It all seemed to work quite well, and new work kept coming in. But it all felt alarmingly happy-go-lucky, even by my naïve standards. I remember us having earnest debates about how to spell "computer" and how many 'm's there should be in "program". Luckily, our clients never got to hear about this.

But one thing that did become screamingly evident as we expanded was the need for quality control. One project, involving Castrol (part of Mobil Oil), nearly ended in disaster. I hired a very high-powered programmer to do it: an Indian lady who came from Dublin University. Everything seemed to be going according to plan, except that the project was taking much longer than anticipated. Then the client began to query the amount of time that the programmer had been spending on their computer. I looked into it, and found that although the programmer in question was, unquestionably, a brilliant woman, her brilliance did not extend to being able to carry out a clearly defined task in a coherent way. Her work was totally undocumented and she didn't seem able to explain where she had got to or why. She may or may not have known what she was doing, but she appeared to have been heading off down a series of blind alleys that made sense only to herself, and I realised that I could not afford to employ her any more.

I had to drop everything, learn a computer language (FORTRAN) that I had never used before, and work round the clock for two weeks trying to unpick the mess she had made. Amazingly, I succeeded – largely because Derek was able to take two weeks' leave from Dollis Hill and look after Giles. But by the end of it, after nearly a fortnight of 18-hour days, I was close to collapse. The project was rescued, however, and we retained our crucial record of having nothing but satisfied customers. Kit Grindley later told me that it was at this point that he knew that Freelance Programmers would succeed. I, meanwhile, was beginning to wonder if starting my own company had been such a good idea after all.

One beneficial effect of the Castrol debacle was that it forced us to become more professional in our approach to quality control. We were already relatively advanced in this respect, thanks to the objective standards that I had created for Urwick Diebold, which we also applied to our own work. But only now did we develop a really rigorous system of process control. Every project was divided into phases, and at the end of each phase we would double and treble check before we moved on to the next phase. No one else in the industry could claim to have anything like such a robust system, and it stood us in good stead: not just because we developed a reputation for reliability, but because the system allowed us to be much more precise in our planning. While others were still saying "There are just a few more bugs to be ironed out", we could say "The job is now 60 per cent done and will be finished in another 10 days". This precision also allowed us to offer fixed prices on our contracts, which was attractive both to clients and to us.

In the short-term, however, I had taken home a more negative lesson from the Castrol episode. Running a company was a headache. Even after two short years, I was beginning to encounter the familiar paradox that at one stage or another demotivates most people who start their own businesses: I had begun to delegate much of what I loved about the business – writing software and designing systems – while filling my time with all sorts of administrative, financial, legal and managerial chores for which I felt next to no enthusiasm. Instead of welcoming each new project as an exciting new challenge, I was starting to see new assignments as potential disasters waiting to happen – and the bigger the contracts grew, the greater the potential for disaster.

I still retained most of my enthusiasm, but I was sufficiently jaded with the management side of things to feel a huge surge of relief when, towards the end of 1964, one of our clients, a company called Business Operations Research (BOR), announced that they wanted to buy us. It seemed too good to be true. They would put up the money, but I would retain day-to-day control. They would pay me a salary – something I hadn't had since the company started. And they would provide investment capital, and pay for offices and other support. All the administrative responsibilities that had been weighing me down would be taken off my hands, and I would be free to return to doing the work I loved.

If it had worked out, I would never have become rich. But becoming rich had never been one of my aims. All I wanted was the freedom to do what I was good at: that is, to explore the potential of information technology for transforming the way people worked. I had never dreamed of fast cars and huge houses. Rather, my ideal was to be part of some kind of high-powered creative commune, full of free, kindred spirits, held together not by rules and conventions but by our shared joy in what we did. It was the business itself, not its potential for generating profits, that I cared about.

The proposed takeover was thus a highly attractive proposition. It took a long time to sort out the details, but, in the meantime, I went out and, on the strength of the provisional agreement, rented the vacant offices that the photocopier repair man had recommended, at 16 Station Road, Chesham. I hired three full-time employees, and, since they all had young children, took steps to ensure that the office incorporated a crèche.

Then something odd happened. I mentioned to our would-be purchasers that I was going to register the crèche through the proper channels. "Oh no," said Don Neville, the man at BOR I was dealing with, "you don't want to do that." But, I insisted, we must do things properly. "No, no," he insisted. "You mustn't. That sort of thing's a waste of time and money." And I realised that, as my owner-to-be, in control of the future purse-strings, he was in effect giving me an order – and was telling me to do something that seemed to me to be wrong.

Suddenly the proposed takeover appeared in a different light. Selling the company, I realised, wouldn't just mean offloading the various administrative and financial chores that I found so tiresome. It would also mean relinquishing the very independence that had prompted me to start the company in the first place.

I told them that the deal was off.

Any satisfaction I felt in having taken a stand on a point of principle evaporated when I considered what a mess I was now in. I had commitments to three employees, a commitment to rent our new office, contracts with numerous clients – and, suddenly, no money to pay for anything. It was a critical point in the company's history. Did we give up? Did we – or I – scale back, or renege on the commitments I had just made? Or did we find the money from somewhere else?

I agonised with Derek for several days. The first two alternatives seemed sensible but unacceptable. I had been trying, in some vague way, to run the business honourably and decently. It would have

'Moss Cottage' · Ley Hill

We lived in this impractical but idyllic home for 8 years.

broken my heart to have let my little workforce down. And it would have broken my heart, too, to have abandoned a business that had so much going for it and that seemed so close to turning my vision into a reality.

At the last possible moment, we made our decision. We would make it work. We re-mortgaged the house – for £1,600 – and, in effect, funded the expansion ourselves.

This was frightening stuff. If things went wrong now, we faced something close to ruin; we would, at best, have been back in a bedsit. But this very scariness was, I think, crucial to our subsequent success. When everything you possess is on the line, you tend to find reserves of drive and commitment that you didn't know you had when you were less exposed.

Steadily, we made things work, although it seemed sometimes to be as much by luck as by judgement. There's a sense of inevitability to the growth in our revenues when you look back at the figures today: £7,000 in 1964-5, £17,000 in 1965-6, £35,000 in 1966-7. But that's not how it felt at the time. We were an almost ludicrously minimalist organisation, with three managers and a secretary operating from our bare offices above the opticians while I flitted about between Moss Cottage, the office and the headquarters of various clients and potential clients. There were also many local freelancers who were so closely involved as to be to all intents and purposes part of the business. An example that springs to mind is Pam Elderkin, a high-powered technical person who lived just down the road in Chalfont. When I had drafted the main outlines of a proposal for a project, I would pass it on to her to assess its technical implications. I rarely got a chance to work on proposals without interruption until the evening, and so I tended to drop my drafts through her letter-box in the small hours of the morning. She could then start on them the moment her husband left for work, and would have finished them, returned them and cleared away all traces of her work before her husband returned in the evening. I presume that he knew that she worked – but I don't think her neighbours did.

I hate to think what some of our blue-chip clients would have thought, if they had fully taken in the fact that the expensive, sophisticated, state-of-the-art computer programmes they were buying from us were being created at home by women surrounded by babies and nappies. Yet there was a steely professionalism underlying everything we did. Just because we weren't versed in the suitbound conventions of the male workplace, that didn't mean that the intellects involved were any less incisive. And although our processes were improvised and homespun, they were remarkably rigorous.

The freelance programmers, briefed by us, would write their programmes on coding sheets, as a series of numbers. (These would usually use the numbers 0 to 9 but would occasionally be in binary.) All they needed for this was a pencil, paper and "access to a telephone" (as we put it in our application questionnaire) so that they could resolve any queries with our managers as they went along. These hand-written numerical programmes would then be sent by post to an independent data centre, whose employees (also female, on the whole, but unconnected with us) would sit and punch the data on to punchcards or paper tape. This would then be verified by a different data centre employee, punching the whole thing again; after which the verified card or tape would be taken to a separate computer centre to be tried out. (Younger readers may find this hard to imagine, but hardly anyone had their own computer in those days.) As often as not a problem would arise at this stage, so where possible we would try to send the original programmer to the centre to fix it on the spot, rather than wait for the results to come back to us by post. An experienced programmer could often tell what was going on inside a mainframe computer just by listening to it.

One crucial regular freelancer was a woman called Ailsa Turner, who wasn't a programmer but, unusually for a woman in those days, had a car. She would act as a courier for important programmes and, when necessary, programmers, even doubling up as a mobile babysitter if the programmer needed to leave a child in the car while she worked briefly in the computer centre.

Our system for managing our growing "panel" of freelance programmers had a similarly improvised, homespun feel. Each programmer would be represented by an index card, with a series of holes punched along its edges. Each hole represented a different kind of skill, either technical (along one side) or more general (along another). So on the technical side there would be holes representing different computer languages – FORTRAN, Cobol, BASIC, and so on – and on the general side holes representing areas of experience such as scheduling, or transport, or payroll. The holes that applied to that programmer (i.e., representing skills or experience she possessed) would be extended, so that they became open indentations. The rest would remain closed. All the cards – and there were getting on for 75 by the end of 1966 – would be kept in a shoebox. Then, when we wanted to find programmers with appropriate experience for a particular job, we would take them all out, put a knitting-needle through the appropriate holes for the entire set, and jiggle the cards vigorously. Those with the right combination of open holes (for example, representing knowledge of Cobol 3 and experience of distribution systems) would fall out .

It sounds ridiculous now, yet I remember our card system fondly: not just as a symbol of my company's modest beginnings but also as a neat demonstration of what I mean by systems. A system can be anything from a computer programme to a physical arrangement of objects but is often somewhere between the two: in effect, an arrangement of ideas or concepts that facilitates efficiency. As Freelance Programmers grew, so, increasingly, the "product" that we sold became systems rather than mere programmes.

And one unexpected benefit of not having a conventional office and a conventional hierarchy – and thus having to create our own systems from scratch – was that, as we learnt to organise ourselves more efficiently, so we became better able to advise others on how to organise things. I don't think the phrase "management consultant" would have meant anything to me in those days, but I do remember thinking, after one visit to the Mars factory, that what they were paying me for was not so much my programming expertise as my insights into how their operations worked. This struck me as a rather exciting development.

As with any business that thrives, success created its own momentum. Word spread through the small world of the computer-literate that there was a company in Buckinghamshire that offered interesting, flexible, rewarding employment to women working from home. Highly qualified people began to seek us out. Some were more suitable than others; and some more available than others. Some wanted work only seasonally. (I had one very good programmer who ran a boating business in the summer but wanted something else for the rest of the year.) Others were available subject to something better not turning up. (One of our best programmers had aspirations to be an opera singer, which meant regular absences for auditions but, luckily for us, few big parts.) On balance, however, the supply of workers seemed to match our demand for work. By 1966, we had relationships with (as I have already mentioned) about 75 regular freelancers, of whom some were working more or less constantly while others were happy to go for long periods between assignments. This meant that we never had to turn business down because of lack of capacity – a huge bonus for a growing enterprise. The only job I can remember turning down was a proposal from a company called EMCON (Economic and Mathematical Consultants) for designing an automated fingerprint recognition system. I simply couldn't see how it could be done (and, indeed, it would be 20 years before anyone else cracked the problem).

It worked in our favour that there was scarcely any other part-time work available in those days that offered the slightest intellectual challenge – and most women, then as now, had at least a stage in their lives when part-time work was the only kind of work they could do. For intelligent, numerate women in mid-1960s Britain, Freelance Programmers was a godsend. (And not just in Britain: I even had an enquiry from a Middle-Eastern potentate wondering if we had any opportunities for women in his harem.)

One key recruit around this time was a case in point. Ann Leach (later Moffatt) had been working as a programmer for about six years, mostly for Kodak, for whom she had programmed a Ferranti Pegasus (the same early computer that I'd used for testing ERNIE) to determine optimum strategies for streamlining production process, locating distribution centres and optimising products to match market demands. She had also worked on loan for Ferranti themselves, for whom she had helped create the pioneering operating system for the Atlas computer (the forerunner of the IBM 158). She was, in short, one of Britain's top programmers. But she had become disillusioned when, as she saw it, the traditional male managers at Kodak realised what an impact computerisation was having on the company's balance sheet and began to muscle in on the territory that she had opened up. Programmers like Ann were in effect pushed down the hierarchy, to be ordered around by self-serving corporate types who knew far less about software than she did. She had left Kodak when her first child was born, in early 1965, but now was looking for interesting work again. Freelance Programmers met her needs perfectly.

But she met our needs perfectly too. We had just been given a large contract by GEC to write programmes that would analyse the "black box" flight recorder for an exciting new aeroplane, then under development, called Concorde. The software – for two purpose-built computers – needed to perform statistical analyses in the outputs of some 40,000 different instruments on the plane. Ann was one of the few people in Britain capable of leading such a project, and she did so very successfully, completing the £40,000 assignment on time and slightly under budget.

Our programmers weren't especially well-paid on an hour-for-hour basis. But the quantity and the quality of the work meant that they generally did well out of the relationship. One very respectable lady was suspected by the Inland Revenue of being involved in some kind of vice: they couldn't imagine how else she could earn what she was earning without leaving her home. In fact, Suzette Harold – who would later play a crucial role in the company's growth – was one of the most upright and respectable people I have ever met. But the Inland Revenue was even more male-dominated than the computer industry. Both groups of men were too blinded by prejudice to notice the obvious: that many of Britain's most brilliant and reliable programmers were female. This general blindness was our opportunity.

In fact, not quite everyone who worked for Freelance Programmers was female. One valued early employee was Jim Hawkins, who had previously been personnel manager at CDL. A former Army officer, he had left that job after suffering a nervous breakdown, and had feared that, despite his subsequent recovery, he would never work again. But I had admired his conscientiousness and honesty, and when I needed someone to oversee staffing matters I offered him a job. He was deeply moved and repaid me with three vital years of dedicated and sometimes inspired service.

Another male employee was John Stevens, whom I hired in 1965 as our first full-time project manager. John was a would-be Liberal politician who had taken up programming because he thought it would provide him with employment in between elections. I had first met him when I needed a crash-course in FORTRAN for the Castrol project. He now became an influential colleague and friend. A passionate believer in the extension of share ownership, he contributed a new strand of idealism to our already rather utopian enterprise, opening my mind to the idea that there were other ways of structuring a company beyond the traditional top-down proprietor-staff relationship. Ultimately, the ideal of staff ownership that he explained to me would become as central to the company's ethos as the empowerment of women, although this was still many years away. But John's radicalism, combined with my innocence, did mean that, even then, our company worked in a very different way from what was then the norm.

Elsewhere in the industry – and indeed in British business generally – people were still clocking in and out, and having their pay docked if they took too long over their lunch break. We paid people for the work they accomplished rather than the hours they put in. Compared with a conventional company, we were treating our freelancers like adults: trusting them, as intelligent, motivated people, to make the best use of the time available to them in order to achieve the goals they had been set. In modern management-speak, they "owned" the projects that had been assigned to them – which was a relatively small step from the idea that they should also participate in the ownership of the company. We introduced our first profit-sharing scheme in 1966.

I think my receptiveness to John Stevens's idealism may partly have been prompted by guilt at the changes that I had been forced to introduce to the way we paid people. My instinct still told me that it was fairer to pay people once they had completed the work they had been hired to do, rather than "gearing" the payment of their fees to the clients' payment of our fees. I knew that there was no realistic alternative to gearing, but I felt better about it when I knew that our freelancers also had a stake in the financial well-being of the company.

I suspect, however, that the most important factor that shaped Freelance Programmers in its early years was, simply, my naivety. Deep down, I still didn't know what I was doing. Not knowing what the rules were, I was free to innovate – as, indeed, was everyone else involved. Our long-term patterns of flexible home-working and remote management came about not just from theoretical idealism but also from practical necessity. They evolved because they were what worked. Paying for work done rather than hours worked made it easier to cost projects in advance; trusting people to manage their own time was not just effective but considerably easier than trying to keep control of every detail of every project remotely. It helped that there were so many high-powered programmers out there, who were available simply because more conventional companies disliked employing women with dependants. It also helped, I think, that they were women

– who traditionally take responsibility for running family and home and, as a result, tend to develop finely honed self-management skills.

We had a collective naivety, too, which on balance worked in our favour. Pointed musings by potential clients about cars and holidays fell on deaf ears because none of us realised that they were intended to elicit bribes. We didn't get the business in question, and we were better off without it. Another time, we blew the whistle on a senior civil servant who explicitly asked for a bribe while we were negotiating for a contract with the Department of Health; it was a long time before we got any more work from that quarter. It never occurred to us to behave otherwise. We were normal, decent people, and no one had told us that, in business, many people feel that the normal rules of decent behaviour don't apply. The consequent short-term loss for our balance sheet was more than off-set by the long-term gain for our reputation. Another time, we were bidding with IBM to a major government department that then asked us to team up with ICL instead. We refused – and IBM were so impressed by our loyalty that they went out of their way to partner us on a number of other projects.

It is startling, looking back, to think how many of the characteristics that came to define us as a company evolved by accident. For example, we were one of the very first companies to allow job-sharing – something for which we were later much admired. We did so for the simple reason that a husband-and-wife team suggested it. "Why not?" we thought; and another innovation was added to the Freelance Programmers repertoire of employment practices.

But that was what made it such a rewarding company to work for: a lot of the things we were doing were things that had scarcely been imagined before, let alone done. None of us knew where the business – or the industry, for that matter – was going. We never looked further than the next project, asking ourselves: "How could we do this?" or "How could we do that?" And that was one of the main reasons for our success.

Of course, the more projects and programmers we took on, the more scope there was for things to go wrong. Inevitably, the bigger the projects that we took on, the more I worried that a small slip might lead to disaster. (The Concorde black box project was one that concerned me particularly in this respect.) But one of our accidental strengths was the fact that our lack of resources forced us to be relatively conservative in our use of software. We tried to keep abreast of new programming developments, but we couldn't keep training people in every latest cutting-edge innovation. So our software tended to be tried-and-tested rather than experimental; and, as a result, we acquired an enviable reputation for reliability. We might not have been pushing back the frontiers of computer science, but we knew how to design systems, we knew how to control the quality of our work, and we knew how to run projects efficiently.

But the possibility of programming errors wasn't the only thing we had to worry about. There was also the fear that a small mistake in costing might plunge us into the red. One such mistake involved a project for Sheffield Regional Hospital Board, who paid us £16,000 for a project and were very satisfied with the result. Unfortunately (because we had agreed a fixed price, while they had kept changing their mind about what they wanted), our direct costs for the work came to more than £24,000. A few more satisfied customers like that could have killed the company off.

There was also the question of getting our customers to pay up in a reasonable time. The Concorde job for GEC was a particularly bad example of the problems we faced. They took so long over part of their payment – £20,000 of it – that eventually I was reduced to visiting their headquarters in Mayfair and demanding to see Arnold (late Lord) Weinstock, their managing director, who was notorious for being a slow payer. I made a considerable nuisance of myself but didn't quite succeed in getting into his office. But I did persuade a senior executive to take a message into him and, later that day, received his reply: "Tell Mrs Shirley that £20,000 is a significant sum for any business and that if she cares to come round tomorrow there will be a cheque waiting for her."

There was. So that was that problem sorted out. But GEC's contract was just one among many, and I really could have done without devoting whole days of my time to debt-collecting.

There were times when I simply lay awake at night worrying, but at least I was able to alleviate such worries by putting in place more rigid and robust systems – for monitoring progress, for checking quality and for controlling costs. Luckily, we were still at a stage in our development when it was relatively straightforward to do this. And, in the meantime, most of the debts came in more or less on time, income just about exceeded outgoings, and the feared disasters never materialised. Imperceptibly, Freelance Programmers Limited was beginning to acquire the solidity of an established, reliable company.

But that was by no means the end of my sleepless nights. Unfortunately, it was not just the company that I was worrying about.

9: The Lost Boy

The catastrophe had crept up on us. It must have been in early 1964 – when he was about eight months old – that we first began to worry, on and off, that perhaps Giles was a bit slow in his development: not physically, but in his behaviour. He was slow to crawl, slow to walk, slow to talk; he seemed almost reluctant to engage with the world around him. These concerns took time to crystallise – as such concerns generally do – and the first time I went to a doctor about them I couldn't even admit to myself what was worrying me. Instead, I asked about the "funny shape" of his head – which at the time was rather flat at the back – and I remember the slightly odd answer: "It will get worse before it gets better." This turned out to be correct. It was, however, a red herring. What I was really concerned about was not the shape of Giles's head but what was going on inside it.

This deeper worry remained unarticulated for a month or two longer. The fluctuating fortunes of Freelance Programmers gave us plenty of other things to fill our minds, and for as long as we could we tried to persuade ourselves that everything would be all right. By the end of that year, however, there was no avoiding the observation that Giles was losing skills that he had already learnt. He had talked for a while, for example. I remember that his first word was not "Mummy" or "Daddy" but "car" (which may, in retrospect, have told us something). But he had never become chatty. And now he fell silent.

Months of desperate anxiety followed, in which there seemed to be little that we could do except fret. Visits to our local GP alternated with consultations with a succession of experts and specialists. We became regular visitors to The Park, the children's diagnostic psychiatric hospital in Oxford; and, later, to Great Ormond Street Children's Hospital in London. Meanwhile, inexorably, Giles's apparent disabilities became more pronounced.

My lovely placid baby became a wild and unmanageable toddler who screamed all the time and appeared not to understand (or even to wish to understand) anything that was said to him. He no longer showed any interest in either me or Derek, and never once raised his arms to be picked up by either of us. His only interests seemed to be bouncing up and down – he destroyed two cots in quick succession –

and tearing paper (books, newspapers, money, vital correspondence) into tiny strips.

By mid-1965 Giles had taken up weekly residence at The Park, while the doctors there tried to work out what was wrong. Nothing I can write can capture the enormity of the sorrow that that short sentence now brings flooding back to me. This was my son, my adored boy, my beautiful Gilesy – and he had been taken from me by some sinister, invisible force that I could not understand. Every day for months – even as my dreams for Freelance Programmers appeared to be coming true – I would feel as though I had been wrung out by some emotional mangle; and it was no better for Derek. Our domestic idyll was in ruins. In fact, for the first month or so that Giles spent in The Park, I spent my nights in the hospital's mothers' unit and, by day, ran my company from there – a striking if unhappy example of the flexibility that our new kind of working conferred. Eventually, the staff persuaded me to go home, saying that I should be looking after "all the family", not just Giles. But wherever we were in physical terms, the pain, for me and Derek, felt much the same. Irrespective of any successes at work, our days were just a question of hanging on until nightfall; of feeling the waves of pain and anxiety breaking over us, but grimly refusing to be broken by them.

And there was worse to come.

After Giles had been in hospital for about eight months, the consultant at The Park, Professor Ounsted, pronounced that in his opinion Giles was suffering from a degenerative brain disorder and would eventually lose not just his speech but his sight, hearing and balance. This seemed such a horrifying prognosis that we insisted on a second opinion. So Giles found himself spending two weeks at Great Ormond Street Hospital for Children: a wonderful institution that in those days was clearly more geared to the treatment of the ill in body than the ill in mind. I stayed at a very cheap hotel nearby and spent a lot of time physically restraining Giles from tearing down the hospital's extruding electrical cables or throwing himself from its unenclosed staircases.

Finally, in mid-1966, the excellent specialists overseeing Giles's case – Professor Wolff and Dr Bentovim – delivered the devastating but unarguable verdict: our son was profoundly autistic, and would never be able to lead a normal life.

In the 45 years since then, I have learnt more than I would ever have believed possible about this perplexing disorder. I have read hundreds of books and thousands of articles about autism, and have consulted experts in the subject from all over the world. It has become, in a sense, the dominant theme of my life. (I have even funded research into autism spectrum disorders at The Park.) Back then, however, "autism" was just a word, conveying little meaning to us, apart from some vague, horrible idea of "mental handicap".

We soon learnt more, and everything we learnt was like a skewer in our hearts. People with autism have an impaired capacity for social interaction and communication. They are prone to restrictive, repetitive and destructive behaviour. Unable to make real sense of the world, they cannot form viable human relationships. They are at increased risk of other brain disorders, such as epilepsy. Many have lost the power (or habit) of speech. Scarcely four per cent go on to achieve a degree of independence in adult life.

It was as if all our hopes and dreams for Giles's happiness had been snatched from us and trampled on.

Shock was compounded by guilt. Every parent of a sick or disabled child is tortured by the thought that the problem might somehow be their fault. With autism, the medical orthodoxy of the day stated clearly that it was the parents' fault. Leo Kanner, director of child psychiatry at Johns Hopkins Hospital from 1930 to 1959, had famously proclaimed that the condition was caused by cold, unloving "refrigerator mothers"; a theory subsequently popularised by his disciple Bruno Bettelheim, professor of psychology at the University of Chicago, whose 1967 bestseller, The Empty Fortress, would suggest that such mothers had traumatised their children by behaving like "concentration camp guards" towards them.

That theory of autism's causes has since been discredited, while Bettelheim was later exposed as a plagiarist and fraud. But we had no way of knowing that – beyond a gut feeling that the theory must be false. We had loved Giles with all our hearts – and, indeed, still did. To say that we had crippled him with our coldness simply didn't make sense. Not that that prevented us from torturing ourselves with self-reproach.

None the less, we had to come to terms with the situation. We had, somehow, to move on from agonising questions about the past to no less agonising questions about the present and the future. We had to mourn the child that we had hoped for; to learn to love, in a different way, the child that we had; and to work out how best to look after him; and, somehow, to carry on living.

There were few helpful pointers in those days for parents in our position. One medical professional advised us bluntly that we should put Giles in an institution, forget about him and start again. The advice horrified us. Neither of us was in any doubt that we wanted to do anything that was in our power to give Giles as fulfilling a life as possible, and to communicate to him – in so far as he was able to understand – how deeply we loved him.

So back he came to Ley Hill – now aged three and a bit – to be welcomed into the chaotic, overcrowded, cheerful, low-ceilinged cottage that served as both our home and my workplace. Derek continued to work at Dollis Hill, although how he managed to do any creative scientific work there, with all this on his mind, is beyond me. I divided my time between our home, our Chesham office and the various locations to which I was taken by my role as Freelance Programmers' chief ambassador. I had back-up from a baby-sitter (one afternoon a week) and, increasingly, from Derek, outside his regular working hours. But it still felt like an enormous burden to be shouldering more-or-less alone.

Renate was sympathetic, but was increasingly preoccupied at the time with her own affairs – specifically, a lengthy on-off romance that she finally brought to an end by leaving for Australia, where, on the rebound, she married a man called Peter Tankard and (as previously mentioned) settled permanently. My mother, on the other hand, was surprisingly supportive. She was living quite near us by then, in a quiet Amersham cul-de-sac, having retired from teaching. She had quickly become besotted with Giles and remained so even when his problems became apparent. Drawing on her classroom experience, she would take him for a couple of hours a week, supervising him in pre-prepared activities such as biscuit-making that he seemed to enjoy. Her confident manner, developed through two decades of exerting authority over unruly pupils, seemed to calm him, and his wildness never exasperated her. I was grateful for this, but also, sometimes, felt slightly undermined by it: Giles, in her eyes, could do no wrong, whereas she still couldn't bring herself to give me the approval or reassurance that I yearned for.

But it was my mother-in-law's reaction that upset me most. She and Derek's father lived in Queensbury, in what had until recently been Middlesex (now the London Borough of Brent), and we used to make regular visits. Once Giles's problems became evident, she let it be known that she would prefer it if they could come to us instead, so that their neighbours would not see Giles visiting them. Needless to say, we found this deeply hurtful and insulting. She remained far from supportive for a long time, constantly suggesting that I was bringing Giles up badly. Her husband, a relatively conventional military man, was, in his straitlaced way, more empathetic, and at some point I told him how upset we felt at my mother-in-law's attitude. He must have had a word with her, because soon afterwards she became much more understanding, and remained so from that point onwards.

My own father played no more role in this stage of my life than he had in most of the previous ones. Early in 1966 I had learnt, by chance, that he was dead: he had died some months earlier, in 1965. Maria, his second wife, had not thought to inform his first family, and it was only a passing reference in a letter from his sister Alice that alerted Renate to his passing. The news must have given me pause for reflection, but I can't honestly claim that it bothered me greatly. Our relationship had rarely been anything but distant, and I still find it hard to think of him with love. Yet I do remember him, increasingly, with admiration, and the older I get the more I feel that I have much in common with him. He cared too deeply about his work, as I do; he too was an idealist. The defining tragedy of his life – as of so many millions of other lives – was Nazism. In a happier age, he might have done great things, as a judge and perhaps as a father too. As it was, he went to his grave frustrated – even though he eventually rose to be head of both the judiciary and the police in the state of Hesse. Some time after his death, I was moved to discover that, all through his war-time exile and beyond, he had kept with him the brusque letter of dismissal that he had received from the Reich justice ministry in July 1933.

But any warmth I feel towards his memory is abstract rather than personal. The love that fuels family life is ultimately dependant on people being there for one another, and as a father he had emphatically not been there for me. I resolved that, whatever else happened, I would be there for Giles. I had no idea then how much easier it is to make such resolutions than to keep them.

In a sense, compared with what was to come, Giles's autism was relatively manageable in those early days, when he was three or four. He was wild, and often unresponsive in what could be a desperately upsetting way. He had already taken to headbanging: bashing his head repeatedly against walls, furniture or people, which was both dangerous and agonising to watch. But he was at least small enough to be kept or snatched away from the worst troubles, and quiet enough to be able to pursue some of his less harmful interests, such as paper-tearing, without causing intolerable disruption to others. What broke our hearts was the thought of what the condition meant for his future, rather than what it meant for his present.

In due course we learnt to stop comparing what was with what might have been (including the other children we might have had), and to think instead about the difference between what was good for Giles now and what was bad for him now.

Derek was convinced that the key was getting him to speak again, but we were unable to find a speech therapist who was prepared to take him on. Eventually we settled for learning by experience how to interpret some of the noises Giles made, from the quiet hum that meant that he was happily engrossed in what he was doing to the frightening roars that indicated distress or frustration.

Meanwhile, we attempted various forms of education, with limited success. I began by taking Giles to a local nursery, St George's Hall, for two mornings a week. It soon became clear that they were not equipped to deal with such a challenging pupil. (One member of staff was sacked for losing her temper with him.) Then we took him for a term or so to a training centre in Chesham. Training centres were places where children and adults with various kinds of learning disability went for a primitive form of occupational therapy. The adults would perform simple and repetitive tasks such as envelope-stuffing in the hope that this might ultimately equip them to do some kind of productive work, while the children would be given the same kind of play-based teaching that they might have received in a nursery.

This was a heart-breaking time. The staff at the training centre appeared competent, but there was something unbearably bleak about the whole business, and I never felt that Giles was contented there. One of my most vivid memories of this period is of going to watch the little nativity play that they put on at Christmas, after Giles had been there for about four months. I went with a friend, Jane, the wife of a former colleague, whose daughter, Suzannah, was at the same centre. We smiled politely at the clumsy efforts of the older children. Then, near the end, half-a-dozen smaller children, including Giles and Suzannah, were brought on stage on a trolley. They were all non-speakers, and none of them seemed to understand what was going on. None the less, they were dressed as angels. I wept as I had never wept before. The contrast between the sentimental "English dream" of Christmas and this cruel, botched reality was too painful to bear. Jane wept too; and, since we had both dressed up as smartly as possible for the occasion, we soon made a grotesque spectacle, with floods of mascara streaming down on to our previously immaculate blouses.

But that, I reminded myself, was my disappointment, not Giles's. All that really mattered, ultimately, was that he should be happy – or, at least, have some kind of quality of life. The difficulty was working out whether he had this or not. One of the cruel things about autism is that it is so hard to tell what the autistic child is feeling. You have to work at it, and learn to interpret often subtle signs.

One less-than-subtle sign gave me a horrible shock a month or two later. I waved goodbye to him as he was being collected to go to the training centre, and, as I raised my hand, he flinched. I realised with chilling certainty what this meant: somebody had been hitting him. He never went to that training centre again.

But the heart of the problem was not so easily solved. Giles's condition remained intractable, and, the bigger he grew, the harder he became to deal with. I didn't sympathise with our babysitter when she called him a "stupid boy". On the contrary, I resented it bitterly. But I also understood that, for any adult charged with looking after him, Giles was almost impossibly difficult. He was disruptive, destructive, unresponsive – it was hard not to become exasperated from time to time. Even I, once, in the heat of the moment, slapped him on the leg. It was meant as a warning rather than in anger: a fierce "Don't do that!" None the less, I was horrified at myself. I had never have imagined that I could ever strike a child: only a monster would do that. And now, suddenly, that was exactly what I had become.

This incident seemed to sum up the grotesque things that were happening to me and my emotions. I loved my son, and yet was tormented by the occasional thought that I would better off without him. I longed for him to be protected from pain, and yet could not help feeling resentful, sometimes, at the utter absence of any sign that he appreciated anything that I or Derek did for him. Sometimes I wasn't even sure that he knew who I was. I hated to be parted from him, and worried desperately when he was not there; yet I could not stop myself from wondering what life would be like without this all-consuming responsibility for this inscrutable tyrant.

We had long since given up any pretence of a normal, happy family life. We snatched food when we could rather than sitting down together for meals. Derek and I resorted to sleeping in shifts. (You can imagine what this did for our relationship.) But what really frightened me was how the strain was changing me as a person. Emotions and ideas that I neither recognised nor approved of seemed to pop up in my head without prompting. I even wondered, in my wilder moments, if Giles was possessed, and if I ought to get some cleric in to come and exorcise him. Another time, I wondered if I should get a sheepdog to help me manage him – at which point both Derek and I agreed that I was totally losing the plot. (Interestingly, though, specially trained "assistance dogs" are now sometimes used for precisely this purpose.)

It is painful to recall this period of my life, even half a century later. But perhaps the saddest thought of all is that there are probably tens of thousands of parents of autistic children who will recognise immediately the kind of emotional agonies I am talking about. The harsh fact is that it is almost impossible to provide a satisfactory life for a child with severe autism without expert help – and that parents who try to do so risk destroying themselves in the attempt.

Eventually, shortly before Giles's sixth birthday, we were lucky enough to find a wonderful little weekly boarding school which specialised in non-communicating children, including many with autism spectrum disorders. Called The Walnuts, it was (and is) in the north Buckinghamshire village of Simpson, near Milton Keynes. It hurt terribly to leave him there: he was so young. But the head, Janet Pratt, was an inspirational figure, and it was clear that the children there were (relatively speaking) thriving. After much agonising, we decided that it would be unfair to Giles not to enrol him there. An ambulance used to collect him on Monday mornings and bring him home on Friday afternoons, leaving us the whole of each weekend to spend together as a family. Within a term or so he had become visibly calmer and happier.

Weekends, and school holidays, were exhausting but manageable. Sometimes it felt as though our parenting was largely a matter of containment and damage limitation; but there were also periods of relative calm, when we felt love and togetherness and even a degree of optimism. There was, for all his problems, something very lovable about Giles. He was extraordinarily handsome, with an ethereal quality that made me sometimes wonder if he was a creature from another world. At other times, I thought of him as an "innocent" – as people with disabilities like his were once called.

Janet Pratt and her colleague Judith Waterman taught him to ride a bicycle – but not, unfortunately, to brake. Derek tried to play rudimentary tennis with him. Occasionally, the chaotic results of these experiments would be heart-warming rather than heart-breaking.

But I could never really tell what Giles was feeling, or whether or not we were doing the right thing for him – especially in those early years, when the challenges of autism were new to us. So it was a relief to know that for at least some of the time he was in more expert hands than ours. And it was also fairly crucial to our survival that there were extended periods in most weeks in which, while never forgetting Giles, we could give at least a reasonable part of our brains to our work.

Quite how we did so, or how I combined all this heartache with running Freelance Programmers, is no longer clear to me. The records show that the company continued to expand, steadily and rapidly, both financially and in terms of our workforce. I invited Ann Leach to take on a more managerial role, effectively overseeing our panel of freelancers. She had a knack both for accurately estimating the work that any given project would require and for understanding the different strengths, weaknesses and working styles of our programmers. This allowed us to make the very most of our flexible workforce, and gave us a huge advantage over potential rivals. We reckoned that our programmers were forty per cent more productive than programmers in traditional companies, which made it easy for us to offer competitive prices. Meanwhile, my policy of targeting big, blue-chip clients had begun to pay off, as we were able to point to a growing number of high-profile satisfied customers. Contracts began to pour in: from Bird's Eye, from Esso, from Littlewoods, from Stewart & Lloyds (later absorbed into British Steel), from Wallasey Buses, from Hille (the furniture people, in Watford), from Griffin & George (the scientific educationalists), from British Insulated Callender's Cables (BICC – later part of Balfour Beatty). The names may mean little today, but at the time they were instantly recognisable as some of the biggest beasts of British business. Their presence among our clients proved that we must have something serious to offer; we had, in effect, been accepted by the establishment. We had even been hired by the Government, whose Admiralty Underwater Weapons Establishment (AUWE) commissioned us to do some work on a command-and-control system.

But I remember such landmarks only dimly, through a grey fog of misery. My memories of that period are dominated by Giles. I suppose, to an extent, some of these projects would sometimes run themselves – for limited periods, at least. At other times, I would immerse myself in work to forget my pain. But I don't remember neglecting either my company or my son. I suppose that, like Derek, I just muddled on, driving myself to physical and emotional exhaustion every day with the combined challenges of work and family and then, somehow, dragging myself up to do it all over again the following morning.

I cannot deny that, at times, our marriage seemed near to collapsing under the strain. We were both so miserable that neither of us was able to give the other the emotional support he or she craved. But nor did either of us relish the prospect of dealing with this ordeal alone. So we stuck grimly together, argued a lot about what was best for Giles, and, a long time later, realised that the roots of our relationship had been stronger than we had feared. We were lucky. All too many marriages never recover from the blow of discovering that a child has special needs.

Nor can I deny that, at times, work was a relief from the trials of parenting. It wasn't that I didn't want to be with Giles, or to think about him. It was just that it was refreshing to immerse myself in problems to which I could usually find a satisfactory solution – in contrast to the terrifying and heartbreakingly intractable problem of how to give my son a tolerable life.

I also found a level of emotional support in Freelance Programmers that might have been harder to find in a traditional workplace. The more established we became, the more we developed a trusted elite of top programmers and managers. Some of these – names like Jean Fox, Suzette Harold, Alison Newell, Mary Smith, Rosie Symons and Penny Tutt spring to mind – would become influential senior figures in the company over a period of many years. Some of them, as we got to know one another better, became friends.

There was one colleague in particular who became very close. Pamela Woodman was a bright, attractive woman who had been working for the Commercial Union insurance company but had had to leave because she was expecting her first child. She was unmarried – which was considered scandalous at the time – and anxious to carry on working. She was also highly qualified and motivated, and seemed to offer to the company skills that complemented mine. I hired her on the spot, and before long had been so impressed by her that I suggested that she might want to become a partner in the company. She declined, preferring the security of a salary. But she had the same ferocious commitment to her work that I had. She bought a house nearby, in Great Missenden, so that she could be on the spot, and she insisted on working right up until the final week of her pregnancy. I could hardly have asked for anyone more amenable with whom to share my workload, and from early on she was not just a colleague but a friend. Derek in due course became godfather to her daughter, Fiona Jane, and we soon got into the habit of having our most productive business discussions on long walks around Ley Hill common, with our children in pushchairs or, later, toddling along beside us. I got used to sharing my worries with her, both about work and about Giles, while she in turn used to pick my brains about computers in general and Freelance Programmers in particular.

We even took a brief holiday together, to Bournemouth: me, Derek, Pamela and our children. The first thing we did when we arrived was go and look at the sea. Giles walked straight into the waves, and Derek was only just quick enough to rescue him. The two of them were thus both soaked to the skin when we checked in to our hotel – and Pamela and I roared with laughter at what might, without her, have been rather a dispiriting incident.

It was lovely to be working with someone with whom I felt so at home, and I remember wondering if the men who ran conventional companies were able to enjoy proper, warm human relationships with their colleagues in the same way. Not only was I able to share some of my workload with Pamela, who was a properly trained manager with great organisational skills, but I could also share some of the emotional burden that came with the work. I have always been a worrier, and the bigger the company grew the more things I found to worry about. And always, of course, beyond those worries, there was that terrible unceasing background anxiety about Giles: about what was happening to him at that moment, about what was about to happen to him, and about what would happen to him in the long run. Pamela had a practical, solution-finding approach to life that I found hugely reassuring on the various occasions when I shared this load of anxiety with her.

We made such a good team that, over the next few years, Pamela's role in the company grew and grew. By early 1969 we had established what we called a "dual management system", whereby she was more or less entirely responsible for the day-to-day running of the established part of the business, while I focused on expansion, evolution and new business.

But although I was happy to share the responsibilities of internal management, and happy to accept that Pamela knew more than I did about commercial systems, the core responsibility of the enterprise – devising, proposing and refining computerisation strategies that we could perform for our clients – remained mine. In a sense, this was creative work: not programming, not sales, not even – quite – marketing, but, rather, a kind of visualisation: looking at what companies did and what they wanted and imagining software solutions that had never been dreamed of before.

In terms of sales, I used to set myself very simple, quantifiable targets, such as making two new contacts every week and maintaining my existing contacts. That meant following up every lead, asking for introductions, writing to people, networking tirelessly, keeping half an eye always open for new opportunities. I made myself go to lots of conferences and receptions – whenever Derek was free to keep an eye on Giles. We had experienced another flurry of new business after featuring on the BBC television programme Tomorrow's World in March 1966, on the eve of the general election (Pat Lovelace, my then secretary, had previously worked for the show's producer), and it was clear to me that we would continue to grow only if we continued to make ourselves visible. I remember a small item in a newspaper around that time that referred to me as "the ubiquitous Steve Shirley" – a dig that I decided to take as a compliment.

But most of my time, for several years, went on proposals. We developed a system of pink folders. Each folder represented a project and would pass between various members of our network. I would explain the basic background of the initial discussion and what the client wanted, then someone else (usually Pam Elderkin) would assess the technical implications, and someone else (often Penny Tutt) would go through our database of programmers and find out who was suitable and who was available. And then it would all come back to me and I would spend ages writing it all up into a very detailed proposal (which would then have to be neatly typed up, since there was no word-processing then). It was exhausting but enjoyable. A typical proposal would take me five hours to write, so I used to do them in the evening, when I could work without interruption.

I remember spending a holiday in Norfolk around this time. We had rented a bungalow in the countryside, with rolling fields just outside, where Giles could watch the combine harvesters at work through the windows. Every day, packages would arrive in the post from the office, containing pink folders which needed to be converted into proper proposals. Every evening, I would work far into the night, working out and writing out detailed explanations of the systems that we would create. When I eventually dragged myself out of bed the following lunchtime, I would post my finished work back to the office on my way to the beach, where Derek and Giles would already have been for several hours.

Perhaps that sounds rather a grim, obsessive way to have lived, but I have no doubt that Freelance Programmers could not have succeeded without that kind of commitment. For all the advantages of our new kind of workforce – more flexible than a traditional firm yet with a depth and breadth of expertise and support unavailable to solo freelancers – the company remained a fragile organism, with little to hold it together beyond the personality at its centre: me.

Indeed, if I had to offer a single, simple explanation for my company's survival and ultimate success, it would be just this: my hard work. For reasons that I don't entirely understand, but which I imagine are rooted in my childhood, I never slackened off for a single day during that first decade of Freelance Programmers' existence. Yes, the core idea of the business was a good one; yes, I had a talent for programming; and, yes, I was lucky in my timing. But there were, increasingly, other software-producing companies appearing, including a few that mimicked our approach of using freelance home-based programmers. Any one of these could have taken our business; and there were, in any case, lots of other things that our clients could have spent their money on. (According to one study, in 1974 there were 80 software companies in the UK – and a mere 4,500 computers.)

What saw us through was the fact that I stuck with the idea and made it work. All those days when I worked for 12 hours rather than eight, all those weeks when I worked seven days rather than five-and-a-half, all those years when I worked through my holidays – if you add them all up over a decade, the compounded advantage is considerable. There were, as I say, others who could have succeeded instead of us. If we came out on top, it was because we gave time and energy to the challenge that our rivals were simply not prepared to give.

I don't doubt that Giles's condition had something to do with this. A whole houseful of happy children – which was what we had originally planned to have – might have been a hard distraction to ignore had they and their friends all been clamouring for my attention. Instead, the pain at home may have sharpened my hunger to ensure that one aspect of my life, at least, worked out well. Perhaps more significantly, that irreducible core of pain at the centre of my life may have given me a toughness – a relative indifference to such minor inconveniences as exhaustion or workplace stress – that I would not otherwise have had. I was used to shutting off my feelings – a skill I had first developed in my own childhood. And I knew that, whatever else happened to me, I somehow needed to make sure that Giles would always be provided for. That meant that, at all costs, Freelance Programmers had to succeed.

10: Survival Of The Fittest

By 1970, things were looking up. That, at least, is what I told myself as the old decade ended. Giles seemed contented at The Walnuts and was reasonably settled in his routines at home. Derek, while continuing his weekday commute to Dollis Hill, was gaining confidence as a hands-on father. And I was learning to switch roles, from mother to businesswoman and back, abruptly and completely; by which I mean that, whichever role I was currently in, I would banish the other from my mind. Between us, we had reached a degree of acceptance of Giles's condition, and we felt that we were now achieving a balance between giving him the care that we wanted to give him and allowing him to receive the expert care that his condition demanded.

We had also moved house. This had been prompted by the break-up of Renate's marriage and her subsequent return – along with her adopted daughter Clare – to England. We all felt that we might benefit from joining forces for a while, but there was no room in Moss Cottage for two extra people. So we put it up for sale, found a buyer quickly and moved for a year into a large rented house in Amersham, in Longfield Drive. This proved a big improvement: not just because it was more convenient but because extended family life seemed to suit Giles. He must have been six by then, and he and Clare, who was about 18 months old, developed a special rapport. He appeared to like the routines of a toddler's life, while she had a way of demanding a relationship with him – hugging him relentlessly with no thought for his indifference, or bouncing up and down in the bath as if she was taunting him with love – that occasionally provoked a hint of a response. Both of them were fascinated by the railway line beyond the garden fence, and would rush down to the end of a garden whenever a train went by. Many a tantrum was interrupted in this way, usually never to be resumed.

It was a big house, with one rather smart sitting-room that we rarely used. At Renate's suggestion, we designated this "The Good Room", kept it locked and only went in there as a special reward, when everyone was behaving in a gentle, civilized way. Sometimes it went for weeks without being entered. Eventually, however, we found that we were able to spend a surprising number of relatively extended periods in there, just sitting quietly and reading or listening to music.

Then, after about a year, we moved into a house of our own – the Old Schoolhouse – also in Amersham. Renate and Clare came with us, and Clare in due course began to go to school, and to bring back friends to play. Giles was sometimes able to sit with them at mealtimes. Life was chaotic, but it felt like the benign chaos of a big family rather than the cold, negative chaos of a life ruled by one relentlessly destructive child. Renate, who had a lifelong rapport with troubled children, was very good with Giles. Most evenings, she would more or less sit on him and read him a story, undeterred by his obvious lack of interest; and eventually this became one more piece of positive routine.

I wouldn't go so far as to say that these were happy times – it was hard to observe Clare's "ordinary" childhood without feeling occasional heart-piercing stabs of jealousy. But they were times that had happiness in them, and I was grateful for that.

My company, meanwhile, was thriving, with annual revenues of around £50,000. We were getting interesting assignments – everything from big pay and personnel systems to stock control for ice-cream vans – and with each successfully completed project it became easier to persuade the next client that we were a serious, grown-up business with a worthwhile product to sell.

I had a delightful new PA, Penny Tutt, whom I had first met years earlier when we were buying Moss Cottage: hers had been the young family renting it; and, since they had not moved far, we had stayed in touch over the years and become friends. She was not a programmer, or indeed a computer expert of any kind; but she had a common sense, feet-on-the-ground understanding of life's basics that would become crucial to the company's long-term stability, and she would soon move into a more senior administrative role.

There could be no doubt by this stage that we were a proper company rather than a cottage industry. We had hardly any employees in the conventional, full-time, office-based sense. But we had all sorts of people working for us: freelance, part-time, full-time, home-based, office-based . . . Altogether, we used around 100 freelance programmers and analysts on a regular basis, all working from home, with a growing number of managers and administrators either working from home or, in a few cases, based in our headquarters in Chesham. We had even had to rent new premises to accommodate this last group, across the road at No 7 Station Road. (We gave our address as 7-16 Station Road, which sounded more impressive than it was.)

For simplicity's sake, we referred to all these people as "staff" or "the workforce" – terms that I shall use in this book. They were not, however, employees in the conventional sense.

All of us were women, apart from John Stevens. (Jim Hawkins had moved on by then.) And the media had cottoned on to the idea that we could be written about as an amazing feminist success story. Women's liberation was becoming fashionable – Germaine Greer's The Female Eunuch was published in 1970 – and the notion of an all-woman company had begun to seem less like an abomination than a rather jolly encapsulation of the spirit of the Swinging Sixties (which, as anyone who was there will tell you, took place largely in the early Seventies).

Opinion-formers began to warm to us. (One journalist told me later than the media treated us kindly because they considered us a good source of upbeat stories.) The fashionable broadcaster Anona Winn, who since 1965 had chaired an all-female radio chat-show called Petticoat Lane, gave some of us lessons in telephone diction. The Times took to referring to us as by what it obviously thought was the rather witty nickname "computerbirds". Academics began to write about us too. I remember seeing myself described as an entrepreneur – and thinking, once I had looked the word up, "They're right. That is what I am."

The learned article that sticks in my mind today was by someone from the London Business School, who managed to include in his essay the outrageously shallow and sexist jibe: "Like many women of her ilk, she is indifferent to the appearance of her home." But most of the coverage was flattering, and, predictably, I found myself starting to believe in it. Perhaps I really was a business genius. Perhaps I really had caught the spirit of the age. Perhaps I really was set irreversibly on the path to riches.

On Christmas Day in 1970 – which we celebrated in our usual way with our old friends Frank and Doris Hewlett – I gave an enthusiastic toast to the success of Freelance Programmers. "We're flying now," I said. "Nothing can stop us now."

A few weeks later, things began to fall apart.

The first crisis was one that it had never even occurred to me to look out for: a recession. The economic downturn of the early 1970s struck early for the computer industry: two or three years before the 1973 oil shock with which it is generally associated. The computerisation of British business had got ahead of itself, and firms that had been investing heavily in IT realised – more or less simultaneously – that they needed to wait for some return on this outlay before investing further. It took a while for the orders to dry up completely, but more and more companies started to hold back, and our flow of new work slowed alarmingly. Pamela and I began to worry and resorted to our first ever mass direct mailing to drum up business. It had little effect.

Things still looked healthy from the outside. We had an impressive range of current and recent clients, including – in addition to those already mentioned – ICI Paints, Penguin Books, Glacier Metal, Watney Mann, the Atomic Weapons Research Establishment at Harwell, the Family Planning Association and the Council of the Stock Exchange (despite the fact that women still weren't allowed to work on the Exchange itself). Our work ranged from straightforward programming to more complex consultancy projects such as feasibility studies, benchmark tests, equipment selection and systems analysis. We had also been working on a big cost-sharing contract from the Ministry of Technology, creating package programmes based on British Standards for fluid-flow and design.

As the year unfolded, however, and the contracts were completed one by one, it became harder to ignore the frightening truth: new contracts were not appearing to take their place. By the end of the year, the wider economy was showing signs of faltering, and we realised that clients and prospective clients weren't just cutting back – some were actually going under. In February 1971, I managed to extract a large, late payment from Rolls-Royce two days before it went into receivership.

The suspicion dawned on me that, in developing Freelance Programmers, I might not have been nearly as clever as I had imagined. Perhaps our success had been attributable to lucky timing and had been driven simply by wider economic growth. Perhaps I should have given more thought to the fact that economic cycles can go down as well as up. Now that our luck had run out, the company's hard-earned assets were – even with our minimal overheads – haemorrhaging away.

It is easy to feel helpless in such circumstances, but Pamela and I both realised that our best hope lay in vigorous activity. We threw ourselves into finding new business – or, failing that, at least making new contacts. When work is scarce, you must network or die. I had, as it happened, been elected a Fellow of the British Computer Society and, a bit later, a Vice President (with a mission to get the society chartered status). This might sound like a tiresome distraction. It was actually an invaluable opportunity for keeping in touch with people and new developments in the industry – while my position in the Society added greatly to our credibility within the industry. Many members would at some point or another be awarding contracts of the kind we were looking for; and, when they were doing so, it was a huge advantage if I was aware of it and they, in turn, knew who we were. We wouldn't necessarily win the contract, but at least we would be in with a chance.

In a similar spirit, we formed a loose consortium, in early 1971, with three other software companies: Business Software, Applied Computer Sciences, and Programming Sciences International. We called ourselves Allied Software Houses. The idea was that, while continuing to pursue our individual businesses, we would widen the options available to us with a collaboration that would let us bid for contracts that would otherwise be too big for any of us to handle. It didn't make much difference: it was 18 months before we won our first contract. But doing almost anything – even just seeking safety in numbers – was better than doing nothing.

Around the same time – February 1971 – I launched a new company: F2. This was largely a formalisation of the "dual management system" that Pamela and I had already established, and was partly prompted by a sense that Pamela was growing frustrated with her subordinate status. She became managing director of Freelance Programmers, which continued to concentrate on the home-based programming services on which the business had been founded, while I became managing director of F2, which focused on more ambitious services such as systems analysis and consultancy. This kind of work had grown to represent around 40 per cent of Freelance Programmers' business, and there was a certain logic in dividing the operations: not least because consultancy arguably required a more full-time, less home-based workforce. There was also – again – the attraction of being seen to do something. The last thing we needed was for potential clients to believe that we were struggling. F2 at least got us noticed for a while. We gave the company its own address in Amersham. Ann Leach became group technical director.

To the casual observer, we appeared to be expanding. But the bottom line was that both parts of the business were struggling. The work was running out, and our hard-earned wealth was evaporating. In the 1971-72 tax year we posted a £3,815 loss. As I agonised over how much money we could afford to spend on a morale-boosting celebration of Freelance Programmers' impending 10th anniversary, it occurred to me that this could be the last anniversary we would celebrate. If things didn't start getting better very soon, we were done for.

Instead, they got worse. I arrived in the office in Chesham one summer morning to find a letter from Pamela. She was handing in her notice. A series of fraught conversations, with her and with others, revealed that that was not all. She was setting up a rival company, Pamela Woodman Associates, to carry out exactly the same kind of business as Freelance Programmers, in exactly the same market. She was also approaching most of our best programmers to invite them to work for her and (it emerged later) offering their services to the same prospective clients that I was targeting.

People with long experience of the tooth-and-claw struggles of the business jungle tell me that such breakaways are simply a painful fact of life; some experts say that it is surprising that they do not happen more often. Young companies in hi-tech sectors are particularly vulnerable to them, because the talent they employ forms such a large part of their assets. I am sure that this is true. But for me Pamela's breakaway wasn't just a set-back: it was a brutal, horrifying shock, like a kick in the stomach. I felt – perhaps unfairly – that it was a monstrous betrayal.

Part of the joy of the first decade of Freelance Programmers had been its loose, informal structure. We were all highly skilled, in a sphere that required the most precise, disciplined and logical thinking. Yet our way of organising ourselves had been largely improvised and intuitive – one might almost say "feminine", in contrast to the rigid structures and conventions of the traditional masculine business model. Paradoxically, this looseness had also made the company quite centralised, because the invisible ties that held it together came mostly from me and my personality. Perhaps it was this that Pamela and her fellow-defectors wanted to escape. The fact that they did so made me feel that I was under personal attack, and that my world was collapsing around me.

I can see, nearly 40 years on, that Pamela was perfectly entitled to have her own ambitions and to do anything legal to further them. But I have never recovered from the disillusionment – and especially not from the realisation that, even as we had been sharing our dreams for the company's future, she had been plotting a move that she knew might destroy it. This did something to me as a person. I still find it hard to take friendship at face value, and I have allowed very few other work relationships, no matter how satisfactory, to become proper friendships.

In the short term, however, it was not just an emotional blow. It was a catastrophe for the business. Overnight, we had lost many of our most skilled and experienced programmers and a large slice of our future business, at a time when we could least afford to do so. I had also lost some of our best project managers – including the highly valued Suzette Harold (mentioned before as the early programmer suspected by the Inland Revenue of running a house of ill-repute). And of course Pamela had almost as good an idea as I did about which parts of our business were most profitable, which clients we were planning to approach, what sort of ideas we were intending to discuss with them, and what kind of prices we were likely to quote. From her point of view, we were sitting ducks.

I say "we". To all intents and purposes, the burden of this crisis fell on me. Most of our programmers kept themselves aloof from the schism, making themselves available to whoever booked their services first. Some made a point of rejecting Pamela's advances, out of loyalty, and several offered emotional support and encouragement. But as far as I was concerned there was no one else who was "under attack" and no one else who was actively involved in the question of the business's survival. All sorts of people offered helpful advice, but I don't think I really listened to any of it. I was the one who decided what costs could be cut, I was the one who had to cut them and deal with the consequences of doing so, I was the one who had to ensure that the positive morale that had helped drive our expansion did not now turn into a hopeless fatalism – and I was the one who somehow had to find the time and strength, amidst all this, to carry on going out in search of new business.

Every day, throughout every waking hour, I was working at frenetic, breathless speed. I felt constantly as if my heart was in my mouth, as if my very life depended on my making the best possible use of every minute. And in a strange kind of way, I relished it – as if the adrenalin were addictive. This, I said to myself, was my big moment, my Battle of Britain. Anyone who thought I would give up without a fight was very much mistaken.

In the outside world, conditions worsened – and carried on worsening. January 1973 saw a huge stock market crash. In October 1973, the OPEC nations' anger at US support for Israel in the Yom Kippur war led to a devastating rise in oil prices. In 1974, a crash in UK commercial property prices provoked a medium-sized banking crisis. By 1975, UK inflation was touching 25 per cent. If we had relied on economic recovery to save us, we would have gone out of business.

Instead, we fought. I drastically reduced our staff of full-time managers. I quietly reabsorbed F2 (after a decent interval) into the main company. I resumed the overall managing directorship, while Frank Knight – whom Pamela had brought on to the board from Commercial Union in 1971 – remained chairman. I also did most of the clerical and administrative work, and all the sales, and, it seemed, more or less everything else. Treating every day as a battle for survival, I explained to each remaining member of our panel that work was in short supply and that they were likely to earn little or nothing from Freelance Programmers for the foreseeable future – but that I still earnestly hoped that our long-term relationship with them would continue. I started looking for ways to replace our disparate bases (at my home in Amersham and on both sides of the high street in Chesham) with a single, cheaper premises in Chesham. In short, I developed a liquidator's mentality, getting rid of almost anything that could be got rid of, until there was scarcely anything left of the company but its name and its core ideas.

The personal cost was huge, but perhaps there was no other way to survive such a storm than by taking the battle personally. To me, this was no longer just a financial matter. It was about me and my dream. I had come up with a kind of business that no one had imagined before, and had run it in a way that the small-minded traditionalists who blocked women's career paths in the conventional workplace considered mad. If the company failed, the whole idea would be discredited: the idea that companies could be run on trust, the idea that women had as much to contribute as men – and the idea that I was a proper businesswoman rather than just a dreamer who had got lucky.

I realised by now that, in a sense, I had got lucky. But I also realised, as never before, just how much I cared about the business. Drawing conscious inspiration from the way Britain had stood alone in the Second World War, I resolved that, no matter how bad things got, I was not going accept defeat.

One incident that illustrates my embattled mentality at the time had nothing to do with the business. I was driving one morning along a familiar country lane near Amersham and noticed that a huge swastika had been painted on the outside wall of a remote farmyard. (The National Front was enjoying a brief spell of headline-making popularity.) My first reaction was horrified panic, as old wartime fears were re-awakened. My next was to take control of the situation. I found the farmer and told him how offensive the symbol was to me. He shrugged and said that it was nothing to do with him. So I visited the local police station, who, in turn, shrugged and said that it was nothing to do with them either. Finally, having toyed with the alternatives of (a) embarking on a lengthy correspondence with the relevant department in the local council or (b) letting the whole thing lie, I realised that there was only one thing for it. I bought a large tin of paint, got up at 4am the next morning and, shortly before dawn, painted over the offending symbol myself.

I mention this episode of arguably delinquent behaviour because it shows just how fired up I was. (It also reminds me how much energy I then had.) In my mind, my fight for business survival had become part of a much wider fight to defend everything that I held dear: my business dream, my family, my gender, my values. "Never give in," Winston Churchill had said, in a much-quoted speech in 1941 – "never, never, never, never, in nothing great or small, large or petty; never give in except to convictions of honour and good sense..." It had worked for him. It might just work for me.

It was a crucial advantage, in the struggle to keep Freelance Programmers alive, that we had few fixed costs, and that many of our regular freelancers were used to surviving on an irregular income. Most of them seemed to understand that this was the flipside of flexible employment: there was little or nothing to shield our workforce from the economy's icier winds. The fact that many of them had not been employed before we came along made it easier for all concerned to accept that the company's pain had to be shared. This didn't make it less painful, but it gave us a fighting chance of survival.

Derek was unfailingly supportive too, as he always has been. But I don't think he really realised quite how bad things were. That £3,815 loss in 1971-72 sounds petty by modern standards, but in our terms it was huge. The company had next to no assets, and there was nothing with which to cover further losses apart from our personal wealth – which, given that we were already double-mortgaged, was negligible. If we did not get back into profit the following year, that would be the end of our story.

At one point the F2 side of the business was down to a single contract – with Unilever. Yet still, somehow, we refused to give up, keeping our spirits up by putting an extravagantly positive spin on things. For example: back in 1969, when business was booming, Derek had persuaded me to mark our tenth wedding anniversary by splashing out on an extravagant fur coat. It was second-hand but gorgeous, in dark leopardskin with a beautiful black mink collar; I had imagined that I would wear it on special occasions but in practice had never had an opportunity. Now, having briefly considered selling it (it might have raised anything up to about £1,000), I took to wearing it every day – so that anyone who saw me would assume that the company was still prospering.

Morale seemed to me to be a crucial issue. In business, as in life, good things rarely come to those who appear desperate. I was determined to put everything in a positive light – even our 10th anniversary party, which took place just days after the launch of Pamela Woodman Associates. I smiled bravely through the champagne reception, which we held at the Institute of Directors in Pall Mall, and was rewarded with some positive press coverage the following day.

Everyone – well, all three of us who remained in the office – entered into the spirit of things. My part-time secretary, Muriel Messider, epitomised our collective attitude when one of our few, precious customers rang up with a query about an invoice. "Would you mind telling me the invoice number?" she asked, before making a huge song and dance about tracking it down among an imaginary department full of other invoices.

Those were difficult days. Yet, as sometimes happens when you have your back to the wall, there was a grim pleasure to be taken from the daily battle. And, the harder the fight, the greater the pleasure to be taken from occasional victories – such as the day in 1973 when a very sheepish Suzette Harold rang up, asking if she could re-join us. Several colleagues were aghast when I said yes. But my view was, and is, that people should be allowed to make big mistakes – or one big mistake at least. Few of us are infallible, and the brightest people learn their most important lessons from the things they get wrong. I certainly never regretted giving Suzette another chance. By May 1974 we had appointed her to the board.

Bit by bit, we began to believe that we would pull through. We ended the 1972-73 tax year back in the black, with profits of just under £2,000, on hugely reduced turnover, and the sense that my hard work was making a difference proved highly motivating. I spent a lot of my time on the then unheard-of practice of telephone marketing: not cold-calling, but ringing round existing contacts just in case any opportunities were in the air. I had a crude but effective system of little cards, each summarising what I needed to know about each target (e.g., name of company, name of the person I was dealing with, what sort of equipment they had, what we had last talked about, and so on), and I felt proud of my ability to make a large number of effective calls in quick succession. Only a tiny percentage yielded so much as an appointment to meet – but without that handful of positive results we would have had no new business at all.

We also looked further afield for openings, in the US and in continental Europe. When I formally reabsorbed F2 into Freelance Programmers, I had given their controlling company the grand-sounding new name of F International. The "F" was an echo of the original "Freelancers", although I liked to say that it also stood for "female", "flexible" and, indeed, more or less anything else that people wanted it to stand for. The "International" was more problematic. We had, at that stage, had only one truly foreign client: an Antwerp-based company called Agencie Maritime Internationale (who became so exasperated by our well-meaning attempts to translate all our documents into French that they pleaded with us to leave them in English). But "International" sounded good, and we decided to start looking for opportunities overseas. I remember gate-crashing a big insurance industry function in Paris with Frank Knight around this time: I felt terribly embarrassed doing it, but Frank was well-connected in the insurance industry, and we felt that we couldn't afford to neglect even the remotest chance of making a useful contact. The short-term benefits to the company were minimal, but such thinking would ultimately yield considerable dividends, and, in the meantime, it did wonders for morale to be thinking in terms of expansion rather than contraction.

Eventually, after extensive market research across Europe, we set up a small subsidiary in Denmark, whose manager, Charlott Skogøy, ran a team of seven (six of them mothers with young children) from her stylish home in Fredensborg, near Copenhagen. The adventure contributed little to our finances but did teach us valuable lessons – not least about the perils of market research if you don't interpret it correctly. We had chosen Denmark on the basis that it had one of Europe's most educated and numerate female populations, which meant that we ought to be able to recruit plenty of top-quality programmers. What I hadn't taken into account was that Denmark was so far in advance of the UK in terms of equal opportunities, with an excellent state-funded childcare system, that there was nothing like the untapped reservoir of frustrated female talent that we had found at home. Talented Danish women who wanted to work tended to be in jobs already.

The whole venture was fraught with problems – including the breakdown of our relationship with Charlott, who eventually formed a breakaway operation. But at the time that scarcely mattered. The important thing was that we believed in ourselves again. We were growing. We were no longer clinging on by our fingernails. Instead, we had (as Franklin D Roosevelt had urged Americans to do during the Great Depression) converted retreat into advance.

The creation of a further subsidiary in 1976, in the Netherlands, brought with it a different set of unanticipated local difficulties, chiefly relating to employment protection legislation – which played havoc with our traditionally relaxed approach to freelance hiring. But, again, there was symbolic value in the fact that we were still growing. Back in the UK, potential clients that had hesitated to do business with a struggling little company from Chesham felt quite differently about hiring a fast-growing concern that appeared to be a major international player.

There was never a recognisable moment when our troubles ended. We just carried on struggling, week after week, and the weeks turned into months and the months into years, and somehow we always managed to return some sort of profit at the end of each year, however pitiful. Eventually I began to feel that, since the crisis hadn't killed us off, it must have made us stronger. I don't think I ever again felt entirely relaxed about the future. But I did begin to contemplate our prospects with more equanimity.

Unfortunately, my troubles were by no means over.

11: The Great Crash

By 1975, the worst of the economic storm was over. A blizzard of red tape came fluttering in behind it. More or less simultaneously, the Department of Health and Social Security and the Inland Revenue began to take what seemed to us to be an oppressive interest in our affairs. Both were exercised by the unorthodox nature of our employment arrangements – and had decided that now was a good time to call us to account. We wondered if the large job we had just completed for the DHSS – compiling an early database called CUBITH – might have drawn us to their attention.

I have no intention of revisiting the detail of these tiresome episodes, or of the endless correspondence and interrogations they involved. I would merely say that I resented them. Both inquiries concluded that we had done nothing wrong. But both seemed to be predicated on the idea that our flexible approach to employment in some way constituted "cheating". This seemed to me an outrageous view to take of an approach that had brought rewarding work to a whole class of people who had hitherto been entirely excluded from the workplace. And what seemed scarcely less outrageous was the thought that my taxes (and those of my flexible workforce) were funding a series of bureaucratic intrusions that were scarcely less debilitating for the business than the recession. Had the various inspectors involved made such exorbitant demands on our time and woman-power a year or two earlier, it might well have finished us off. I shudder to think how a smaller or weaker company would have coped.

But one of that year's run-ins with the state provoked a more ambiguous response. In November, the Sex Discrimination Act was passed. You might have expected me to applaud such a landmark in the struggle for gender equality at work; and with part of my soul I did. But in our case, as several commentators enjoyed pointing out, the legislation had an effect almost diametrically opposite to the one intended. We were one of the few companies in the UK that already provided real opportunities for women who wanted to work. Now our policy of "providing careers for women with dependants" was illegal.

It caused us no difficulties to make the necessary amendment to our methods of working. I had never objected to hiring men, and, indeed, there had rarely been a moment in our history when we hadn't had a few men working for us. In 1975, all but three of our 300-odd freelance programmers were women, and all 25 of our project managers were women, but nearly a third of our 40 or so systems analysts – on the F2 side of the business – were male. (Our Netherlands subsidiary even had a staff member who had started off as a woman and then had a sex change.) Conversely, I don't suppose we would have ended up with a radically different gender profile had we never explicitly espoused a pro-women policy. The preponderance of women working for the company was partly a reflection – the mirror-image – of the gender bias in the wider workforce. Most male programmers of sufficient calibre were already in conventional employment and had no interest in the kinds of opportunity we offered.

None the less, it was a striking irony – and one that rather irritated me – that, because we mentioned gender in our mission statement, we became one of the first companies to be brought into line by this landmark piece of pro-women legislation. I don't think Freelance Programmers had been a consciously feminist organisation when I founded it. I hadn't even heard of "feminism" in 1962. But by 1975 F International was seen by many as part of the women's liberation movement. One of the things that had helped us through the dark days of the recession was the conviction that we were working not just for money, but because we believed in a particular way of doing business. And I, at least, was convinced that, in fighting to save the company, I had also been leading a crusade for women. Without that idealism I might have found it easier to throw in the towel.

Now, as the realisation dawned on us that the company had survived the storm, I think we became collectively even more aware of our feminine identity as an organisation. We had, we realised, come through a test that countless "male" organisations had failed. Surely the fact that we were women – and ran our organisation in a distinctively different way – had something to do with this?

I felt strongly that my "female" approach, which had attracted such scorn in the business's early years, had been vindicated, and it irked me that the state, in addition to its other meddlings, had now declared that approach illegal. Still, there was no point in quarrelling with the law, especially such a well-intentioned one. At a board meeting that December we amended our personnel policy again. Our purpose was now to provide employment for "people with dependants unable to work in a conventional environment".

It felt like an important landmark in our history, marking the end of our 13-year adventure as an "all-women company" but also seeming to draw a line under the trials of the previous five years. Times were still hard, but businesses were starting to invest in the future again, and our survival no longer seemed in doubt. We had got back into the habit of ringing up freelancers to offer them work, while our core of permanent staff seemed stronger than at any point since Pamela's defection – a fact that I recognised at around this time by making Suzette Harold group managing director in my stead. In so far as all can ever be well with a business, all seemed well with F International.

As any woman with a demanding career will tell you, however, what happens in the workplace is only half the story. And in my case, the other half of the story had taken a turn for the worse.

In the summer of 1974, Giles had finished his time as a weekly boarder at his special primary school. It was a sad moment for all concerned. They had understood his needs at The Walnuts, and had had the time, the patience and above all the staff to manage his idiosyncrasies. We had been dreading the moment when his time there came to an end, as had the school, who kept him on until the latest possible moment. He was loved there – they used to call him their "ewe lamb" – and it was hard to believe that we would ever find another institution that would care for him so well.

In fact, it turned out to be hard to find another institution that would care for him at all. We tried him at a succession of day placements, from the general to the specialist, but none could cope with his increasingly difficult behaviour. He had, after all, been legally classed as "ineducable". Others gave blithe reassurances that all would be well, only to find that it wasn't. I grew to dread the almost inevitable phone call that would come a few hours after I had dropped him off somewhere, saying that they couldn't manage him and (through gritted teeth) please would I come and collect him, now.

Unfortunately, puberty had hit Giles like an out-of-control lorry. It does so with many autistic boys – and, to a lesser extent, with boys generally. In Giles's case, the hormonal turmoil turned what had been an almost benign eccentricity into a raging nightmare of unpredictable violence against inanimate and animate objects, including his parents and himself. He had periods of calm; then, without warning, he would lash out with fists or feet, punch himself, hurl furniture over, bang his head against the wall – and all with the force of a strapping young man rather than a tantrum-throwing toddler. He once tried to throw our piano across the room, and nearly succeeded.

At around the same time, Renate and Clare moved back to Australia. We had all been suffering from the lack of privacy that results from two families living right on top of one another, and, now that Clare was old enough to start proper schooling, it made sense for them to pick up their lives in the country where they meant to live. I imagine, too, that they must have been relatively pleased to see the back of Giles. They had both been very good with him, but it was hardly fair to expect their lives, as well as ours, to be dominated by his tragic agenda. (A few years later, I wrote to Renate to ask if she would be prepared to become Giles's guardian if anything were to happen to Derek and me. After a delay, she wrote back with a thoughtful letter in which, in the kindest possible way, she declined. She wished Giles well, she said, but simply did not think that she could cope.) But while I entirely understood Renate's migration, I did not relish trying to manage Giles's frightening new problems without an older sister to fall back on for advice or moral support.

My mother was still nearby, just around the corner from our new house, but age was catching up with her, and the bigger, stronger and more violent Giles became, the harder it was for her to deal with him. Nor was there much comfort to be gained from the fact that we had acquired another new neighbour: my beloved Uncle. Auntie, who had been poorly for some time, had died in 1974, and after a few months of adjustment he had been persuaded to come and live round the corner from us. It was lovely to be able to see more of him, and to be able to repay some of the kindness he had shown me. But he too was frail – more so than my mother – and in my mental categorisation of the extended family came under the heading People to be Looked After rather than People to Help with the Looking After.

There was, unfortunately, a lot of looking after to be done. Giles, on top of all his other problems, had developed epilepsy. This is not uncommon with autistic children, but no easier to deal with for that. In the midst of, as often as not, a violent rage, his body would abruptly go into spasm, his limbs would twist inwards, his face would contort and he would fall to the ground. Sometimes, this would be preceded by a terrifying, primordial scream – a ghastly sound, in a voice that it was impossible to recognise as his.

Derek, in particular, found Giles's fits desperately upsetting. He felt that the screams were screams of physical and spiritual agony. I took a more matter-of-fact approach: to me, these were physical symptoms of a physical problem and, in that sense, less distressing than Giles's underlying autism. But the fact remained that the condition had to be dealt with, and that this new propensity to seizures made Giles even more of a hazard to himself and to others than he had been before. With medication, the seizures became relatively infrequent – perhaps half a dozen a year. But the threat of them was constant, and it was not a threat to be taken lightly. I still feel numb at the thought of some of his more disastrous seizures, such as the one that he had in a swimming-pool, or the one where he fell and smashed his head on the radiator.

It is hard to convey to anyone who has not experienced it how harrowing it is to deal with such problems. Your emotional involvement with your child remains as intense as ever – yet you also begin to see him as, in some sense, the enemy. What horror will he come up with next? What disaster will he inflict on you, or himself, next?

In some ways, Giles's seizures could feel like a relief. They would generally follow a period of several days in which he had been growing steadily more troubled and, as a result, more violent. When the convulsions came – assuming that you could see him through them without injury – they would usually be followed by a day or more of very subdued behaviour. I don't think he was happy during these quiet spells, but at least he wasn't dangerous.

Of course, you don't really wish the misery of a seizure on your child. But there were certainly times when, cowering in a corner with my elbows over my head as he rained blows down on me, I would think: if he's going to have a seizure, I hope it comes soon.

It was easier for Derek than for me to deal with the violent side of Giles's autism; but it was easier for me than for him to work from home. So, even when my company's future was hanging in the balance, I spent most of my working days from May 1974 onwards at home with Giles. I tried repeatedly to get help, and every now and then I would find a day care centre that would share the burden for a while. But no one seemed to have a long-term answer to the question of how

Giles steadied up at The Walnuts weekly boarding school and we went through a couple of very good years.

to look after a big, strong, violent boy who had no notion that there were agendas in the world other than his own.

I suppose those brief episodes of succour explain why I was able to keep steering F International through its troubles while all this was going on. There were a few particularly stable months, when I used to drive Giles to The Manor hospital in Aylesbury, where a lovely Jamaican-born nurse called Blossom would care for him for a large chunk of the day and even, occasionally, overnight. But then that, like everything else, came to an end, for bureaucratic reasons which I now forget, and the whole desperate search for help began again.

As anyone with a vulnerable child will know, there is a great deal of theoretical support available from state agencies, but getting practical access to it usually means negotiating an administrative maze that can reduce even the most switched-on citizen to despair. (I suspect my mother experienced something comparable trying to organise our escape from Nazi Vienna.) The greater the child's needs – and children don't come much more expensive to look after than a profoundly learning-disabled autistic boy – the greater the number of bureaucratic hoops that have to be jumped through. For parents who are often already close to breaking-point, the difficulties can sometimes seem insuperable.

Eventually, after a morning at Amersham social services when I simply couldn't stop weeping, I was allocated a social worker, which probably didn't make that much practical difference but did at least give me someone else with whom to share the mental burden. I also managed to get an hour or so of daily help from some teenage sisters who lived nearby. They were called Eke, and used to take it in turns. They had no special expertise, but simply having an extra pair of eyes and an extra pair of hands – and an extra heart – can, in such circumstances, make the difference between survival and despair.

But the involvement of the social services brought with it a fresh problem. The approved policy in state agencies for dealing with adolescents as violent as Giles was to sedate them. This was understandable: the only alternatives were physical restraint – itself fraught with problems – or letting him run amok. But there is something distasteful, to the parent, about letting your child be drugged into submission, and Derek, in particular, was horrified by the whole idea.

We never did resolve the issue. Sometimes Giles would be sedated; often he wasn't. Sometimes, when he was, life became briefly more tolerable, although it always left me with a slightly sick feeling to see him drugged. But the subject provoked some terrible rows between Derek and me, in which he would argue that Giles's needs had to come before ours, and imply (very hurtfully) that I was putting my business before my son, while I would argue that it simply wasn't possible for me to manage Giles without some kind of medical intervention. I would have given up work altogether, for ever, on the spot, if it would have done Giles any good; but it wouldn't. The sedation issue and the working mother issue were unconnected.

There was no middle ground: Derek's aversion to "drugs" was more instinctive than theoretical. So we argued until we could argue no more, or until some crisis involving Giles distracted us, and then we fell into miserable exhaustion. This went on for months. I don't think our marriage ever fully recovered.

Once, we watched a snatch of a nature documentary together on television. (We never watched an entire programme together: there would always be some kind of interruption.) The programme showed a cuckoo laying an egg in the nest of, I think, a sparrow, and the resulting fledgling gradually taking over the nest. The mother and father sparrows were working themselves to exhaustion trying to feed the young cuckoo, which simply grew bigger and bigger and more and more demanding, dominant and aggressive. In a rare moment of marital harmony, Derek and I looked at each other and shared the unspoken thought: this is what our lives have become.

The depressing thing was that, no matter how hard we worked, things never got better. We never had proper meals – just grabbed mouthfuls of food as the opportunity arose. Every waking moment when we weren't at work was devoted to clearing up after Giles or trying to forestall the disasters he seemed intent on causing. We had bolts on all the windows and locks on all the cupboards (although most things we possessed were broken anyway). We lived in a perpetual state of high alert. And Giles just grew bigger, his rages stronger, his seizures more alarming.

I simply cannot understand, now, how we got through this period, which coincided with some of the most stressful business episodes of my career. When I try to describe what it was like, I inevitably focus on particular examples and incidents; but my overwhelming memory is of a misery far more pervasive than that. It was like living half my life in a different world, permanently soured with pain; or perhaps like living in a horror film. Sometimes I thought I was going mad. In retrospect, I probably was. There was certainly a phase when we talked again, but seriously this time, about the possibility of calling in an exorcist. And there were many black months when I contemplated a more extreme solution.

One image still makes my body tense up with remembered horror. In the Old Schoolhouse there was a big, double-height room, with high windows, which had once been the school room itself. The ceiling sloped steeply upwards from two sides, parallel to the roof, and a huge oak beam crossed the room at the base of these slopes. There was also a kind of gallery at one end of the room, with steps leading up to it, where pupils' younger siblings had once been left to amuse themselves during lessons.

One day, at the end of some long, exhausting tantrum, we found ourselves up in the gallery, all in a heap on the floor. I looked through the railings at the beam, and the thought came into my head that it was at an ideal height for all three of us to hang ourselves from it. We could put the nooses round our necks while in the gallery and then simply jump over the railings. Perhaps that was the only answer, so that all three of us could finally be at peace.

I said as much to Derek. Did I mean it? Yes. At least, it was, unquestionably, a serious thought. It had been a long time since I had had any long-term thoughts about our futures beyond "When will this all be over?", and I had been sufficiently tempted by such ideas already to have bought a guide to voluntary euthanasia a few months earlier. (The book in question was banned in the UK, but I had picked it up on a business trip to the US.) Perhaps I was exploring such issues with the unconscious intention of using them as a way of crying for help from Derek. But now, as we lay in our unhappy heap on the gallery floor, I simply proposed to Derek, quite calmly, that we should make a family suicide pact and bring this miserable parody of a life to an end.

It was typical of Derek, with his visceral traditional values, that he refused; but indicative of our misery that he did not dismiss the proposal out of hand. He could follow my reasoning but couldn't overcome the objection that, ultimately, it felt wrong. He also pointed out that, for Giles, it wouldn't be suicide – which I think was the point at which I more or less dropped the idea.

But the trouble with intractable situations like ours is that the alternative to despair is not acceptance or hope. It is simply a different form of despair. We struggled on, at home and at work. But we remained at breaking-point.

In November 1975, the Post Office moved its Research Station from Dollis Hill to Martlesham in Suffolk. Rather than move with it, Derek opted to switch to a fairly lowly administrative job, for the same employer, based in Old Street, in central London. This was a considerable sacrifice for a man of his intellect and creativity, but relocating to Suffolk would have meant leaving me to manage Giles – and the company – single-handed all week. For all the strains that our marriage was now under, he would never have contemplated doing a thing like that.

So he knuckled down to his unstimulating new role (never once complaining), while I got used to the fact that – even with this compromise on his part – he would now be leaving home earlier each morning and getting back later each night. I could hardly complain: it was Derek, not I, who was making the sacrifice, and part of his thinking was that he could put his under-utilised brain-power and energy towards finding ways of bettering the family's lot. In the short-term, however, it felt – as most things did by then – like one more burden to be endured; one more thing to add to the great mass of things that threatened to break me.

Finally, towards the end of the long, hot summer of 1976, I broke.

The strain had been showing for a while, even outside the home, in undramatic ways. I was tense, irritable, joyless; I doubt if I had laughed all year. Work had begun to seem like a series of burdens rather than a series of challenges to be relished. I was smoking 60 cigarettes a day, which can't have helped, and I had forgotten what it was like to have a proper night's sleep – which can't have helped either. I don't think my decision-making had become erratic, but it was certainly becoming uninspired. I was tired all the time, prone to headaches and inclined to snap at people for no good reason.

Then something more frightening happened. I was driving along a dual carriageway one afternoon and, going over a fly-over, felt suddenly agitated. The road seemed terribly frail and narrow; the drop below a huge, gaping abyss. I clung tightly to the steering-wheel, heart pounding, as the car seemed to teeter on the edges above the windy void. By the time I had reached ground level again, I was shaking with terror.

A week or so later, it happened again – and then again and again, on bridges, fly-overs, anywhere where it was possible to imagine a car slipping off the edge of a road and plunging downwards. I had never suffered from vertigo before, but now it began to loom in the background of every working day.

By the autumn, it was in the foreground. I had stopped driving by then, but I would suffer vertigo if I saw a bridge on television. Big staircases made me giddy. Sometimes, too, the walls of rooms would seem to be closing in on me, angrily, threatening to crush me.

I gritted my teeth and carried on, treating these occasional panic attacks as just one more trouble that had to be endured. But I did recognise that the pressure must have been getting to me, and, as a result, I looked into the possibility of giving myself a break from work, now that the company's fortunes had stabilised. Derek and I got as far as agreeing that I should try to take a trip to Australia to see Renate. But it was too late. I was growing more hysterical by the day, and, as the year's end approached, my panic attacks became more frequent and more intense.

I was on my way to Manchester for a business meeting when I realised, abruptly, that I could not continue. The train I was travelling in seemed to be lurching forward at a suicidal speed; the walls of the carriage were alternately closing in on me and threatening to fall apart; the blur of ground outside the windows seemed miles below; my heart was racing and everything was spinning around me. Nauseous and terrified, I scrambled off the train when it paused at Altrincham. For a while, I just stood on the platform, sobbing, as the train pulled away, seeming to take with it all my hopes and ambitions; all my inner belief that, somehow, I would always stay on top of things.

Then I found a pay-phone and called for help.

We had been making corporate use of a medical service provided by the Institute of Directors (because with a company as large as F International now was there were always health issues of one kind or another to be dealt with). I spoke to the doctor who handled our corporate check-ups – Dr Harvey-Smith – and was summoned to see him immediately. I am not sure how I got to London. I suppose I must eventually have got on a train, but I have no recollection of doing so. None the less, by the end of that afternoon I was in Dr Harvey-Smith's surgery, weeping and trembling on his couch.

By the end of the evening, I was in hospital. Dr Harvey-Smith wouldn't even let me go home. That is more or less all I remember. I was, it seemed, having a full-scale nervous breakdown.

All those years of fighting, all those years of accumulated emotional scar tissue, seemed to fragment and fall away from me, leaving me as vulnerable and helpless as the five-year-old child I had been the last time my life had changed irrevocably at a railway station, 37 years earlier.

12: Time Out

People with no experience of such traumas sometimes imagine that a nervous breakdown must be rather pleasant. If your life is normally an unrelenting ordeal of stress and exhaustion, what could be sweeter than an interval of complete peace, in which all responsibility is taken from your hands and all the worries that you have been grappling with are simply released, like captive birds?

I had probably indulged in such speculation myself. I will never do so again.

The reality of losing control of your mind is so awful, so destructive of your sense of self, that the trauma overshadows all other considerations. Thirty-five years later, I can still hardly bear to contemplate this episode – perhaps for fear that, if I try to re-live those experiences, I may actually bring them back to life.

All I can say with confidence is that I was in St Anthony's Hospital – in North Cheam, Surrey – for a month or so. I slept a lot; I wept a lot. I felt overwhelmingly weak. The image that always comes into my mind when I think of that time is of trying to get out of a bath one morning and being unable to complete even that simple task without crying for help.

I suppose that there must have been a momentary relief in this unconditional surrender, after all those years of believing that no challenge in the world was too great for me to overcome. But behind the relief was a raging frustration. I had vowed never to give up, and here I was, unable even to get out of the bath. I had vowed never to abandon Giles and was now doing nothing for him at all. I had vowed to conquer the world with my company and instead couldn't even make the simplest telephone call. I had let down my colleagues, let down my son, let down my husband, let down my elderly dependants. Lots of women drop the occasional ball when trying to juggle competing responsibilities. I had dropped the lot.

Somewhere in the back of my mind was the additional tormenting thought that all those doubters in the past – all those people who had said "She'll never cope" – would now be saying "I told you so." Each time this thought came into my head, I would be filled with a furious urge to pull myself together. Each time I tried to do so, I found myself falling apart again.

Derek visited as often as he could, and tried to reassure me, but he was in a scarcely better state himself. Giles had been temporarily hospitalised, as a necessary response to the emergency, in Borocourt subnormality hospital (formerly Borocourt Certified Institution for Mental Defectives), in Rotherfield Peppard, near Henley-on-Thames. I think this may have been part of Dr Harvey-Smith's intention in sending me to hospital. He had realised that, whatever else happened, Derek, Giles and I could not carry on as we had been. Neither Derek nor I would voluntarily accept that necessary conclusion, so he had to make us do so.

Derek now had to divide his time between visiting Giles (on the Oxfordshire-Buckinghamshire-Berkshire border), visiting me (in Surrey) and going to work (in London), while continuing to live in Amersham. He had no one to confide in or to turn to for advice, no one with whom to share the burden. Like me, he had been sustaining himself with the simple mantra: "I will not give in." Yet now circumstances were forcing him to do so. For 13 years, he had spared himself nothing, making every possible sacrifice rather than take the "easy" option – which we had been advised to take when Giles was first diagnosed – of putting him in an institution. And now he was being given no choice. Dr Harvey-Smith had repeated conversations with him, as he did with me at St Anthony's, and each time the gist was the same: I would not be allowed to leave hospital until Giles was receiving proper medical care in a proper medical institution.

What he hadn't said (but could have done) was that I would never become well enough to leave hospital until I gave up my cherished sense of indestructability. The belief that I could control my destiny by will-power alone had been central to my world-view – and had been exposed as an illusion. And the idea that "recovery" meant picking up my life at the point where I had lost my grip of it was equally fallacious. "Business as usual" would have meant going back to living on the edge of a breakdown, pretending that nothing could damage me. But none of us is truly invulnerable, and those of us who deny our vulnerability are merely storing up trouble. For real recovery, I needed a new world-view.

Slowly, we accepted the inevitable. Our lives needed to change, radically. The only question was how.

Giles remained in Borocourt while options were explored for a more long-term solution. I was allowed to leave St Anthony's and went to convalesce in a hostel attached to the old Quaker meeting-house at Jordans, near Beaconsfield. Here I began to feel that I was healing. It was hard not to. The accommodation was plain, with a communal dining-room and a simple garden, but the atmosphere was extraordinary: there was no hint of the noise and haste of the wider world, and the air seemed to glow with stillness and peace. Nobody asked questions; nobody sought anything from me; nobody expected me to be anything more than a simple human being, with basic needs for food, sleep and spiritual contemplation. When, years later, I came across Max Ehrmann's poem, "Desiderata", its opening lines immediately put me in mind of Jordans: "Go placidly amid the noise and haste, and remember what peace there may be in silence..." The poem and the place have been associated in my mind ever since.

Derek visited regularly, crisscrossing England in the stifling heat in an old car with no air-conditioning. My mother was in Australia, visiting Renate, so through no fault of hers this episode in my life largely passed her by. But I did receive one rather moving visit from Uncle. I don't think he really understood what had happened to me: people of his generation didn't have nervous breakdowns. He certainly didn't know what to say to me. Yet he somehow managed to convey (though he would never have used the phrase) the fact that he was "there for me", and it was reassuring to reflect that, in that case, perhaps my world hadn't entirely collapsed.

Within a couple of weeks, I was well enough to go home. It would be another six months before I felt well enough to go back to work, but at least I had begun to pick up the pieces.

It felt strange being with Derek again. After all the traumas of the past 18 months – including the great battles about sedation – it was hard to recover a sense of intimacy or trust. We wished one another well, but I think we had got into the habit of each thinking of the other as part of the troublesome world that needed to be dealt with – part of the problem rather than the solution. There was still love between us, but I no longer thought of him as the other half of my soul. He was a separate human being, with many virtues and some faults. Any closeness with him would need to be worked at.

Derek, for his part, felt betrayed. His battle to protect Giles from (as he saw them) the twin evils of institutionalisation and sedation had ended in defeat, and I must have seemed less like an ally than one of the enemy who had defeated him. He still did his best to care for me. But there wasn't, at that point, much trust.

I tried to persuade him – and part of him accepted – that, when someone is as big, strong, violent and irrational as Giles was, love alone simply isn't enough: that person needs to be contained in some way. Borocourt was highly spoken of, and there was no reason to believe that Giles would not be well cared for there. Perhaps the most loving thing we could do for him was to let him go.

Derek had little to offer in the way of counter-arguments, beyond a gut feeling that he didn't like the look of Borocourt. When I was eventually well enough to visit it, I could see why. It was an old-fashioned "subnormality" hospital: a big, gothic Victorian building of the kind that most people probably imagine when they encounter the phrase "lunatic asylum". Formerly a manor house, it had been bought by Berkshire, Buckinghamshire and Oxfordshire County Councils in 1930 to be an institute for "mental defectives". But by the mid-1970s it had acquired a more modern focus, with an emphasis on training and rehabilitation and an aspiration to "enable patients to move on to sheltered accommodation or independent living". Its various wards and buildings included occupational therapy centres for day patients, accommodation for more than 300 long-term patients, and educational facilities for younger patients.

With heavy hearts (but reminding ourselves that "asylum" originally meant a place of sanctuary or safety), we agreed that Giles should be transferred from his temporary ward in Borocourt to a permanent, secure ward there called Laburnums Ward. This was in a two-storey modern block adjoining the main house and seemed at least to have been built with patients like Giles in mind. It was bleak and bare inside – but then how could it be otherwise, when the dozen or so young men it housed were all, like Giles, prone to acts of irrational destruction?

It was agreed that we would take him out every weekend, picking him up every Saturday morning and returning him on Sunday afternoon. The first time we took him back, it felt as if we were going to die of sadness on the lonely homeward journey. We had done all we could for him, and all we could do had turned out to be. . . nothing.

And yet, as I tried to explain to Derek, there had been no alternative. We had tried doing it all within the family, and had more or less destroyed the family in the process. We had to accept expert help, in whatever form it came.

Looking back now, I still shudder at the recollection of having let Giles go into Borocourt (although good would come of it in the end). But I recognise that it was, literally, a question of survival. If Giles had not been institutionalised then, I would have been. It was him or me. And although I will never feel entirely comfortable at having chosen my own survival, I also know that it was never really an option to choose for him to survive while I went under. (This principle also explains why airlines advise parents, in emergencies, to put their own oxygen mask on first before trying to do the same for their children.)

The fact was that Giles could not survive unaided. To have any hope for a tolerable existence, he needed me to survive and thrive. If I broke down again, I could do nothing for him. If I became strong again – and ideally if I could derive some financial security from my business talents – then the possibility remained that I might yet be able to give him a better life than any of us imagined possible.

13: Common Ground

Returning to work must rank among the two or three hardest things I have ever done. On my first morning back, I had to decline a much-needed cup of tea, rather than risk drawing attention to the wild shaking of my hands.

It wasn't the prospect of the work itself that worried me: it was the fear of what people would be thinking. I had been used to being seen as Superwoman. Now, surely, people would see me as weak, damaged – a victim instead of a champion. The very fact of having been proved to be vulnerable increased my vulnerability.

In fact, my colleagues couldn't have been kinder. They were supportive and tactful and gave me space to rebuild my confidence. But those first few weeks still felt alarmingly similar to the last few weeks before my breakdown. My world seemed brittle, as though it might shatter at any moment.

There was, however, a difference. Each day, instead of feeling like a little bit more of a struggle than the one before, felt a little bit easier. I gritted my teeth and told myself that, if I could just keep going, all this would become second nature to me again. So it proved.

Before I knew it, I was forgetting to think about the nightmare behind me and was thinking instead about the day-to-day challenges in front of me: decisions, proposals, meetings, plans, ideas. Within a week or two I was looking back in the evening with satisfaction on what I had accomplished that day. It seemed that, contrary to my worst fears, I still had my intellect, my focus, my vision, my technical skills. Perhaps, in short, I was still the person I had been before.

When self-doubt troubled me, I boosted my determination by focusing on a private sense of anger – at those in the outside world who had been watching my company's progress sceptically for years and who would, I knew, have treated my breakdown as a gender issue. Of course, they'd have said, she's a woman; of course she can't cope. The thought of them saying this maddened me. Yes, it was true: for a while I hadn't coped – but not because I was a woman. Rather, it had been because of an intolerable personal situation, of a kind which few men ever even attempt to cope with. How dare anyone patronise me in such an unfair, ignorant, sexist way? I fanned my resentment into a flame of motivation. The best way to refute this slur on my gender was to get back in the saddle and make the company even more successful than it had been before.

Then I thought about how to do so, and my spirits rose. There was still much in my business to get excited about.

F International had flourished in my absence. Annual turnover for 1976-77 had grown to £738,671 (from £403,969 the previous year), with pre-tax profits more than doubled to £45,244. We had a regular workforce of around 340 and an expanding client list – including such prestigious names as ICI, Kleinwort Benson and the Department of the Environment. Our reputation for efficiency and reliability was as strong as ever. Nothing significant had changed, but nothing significant had gone wrong either. Instead, the company was continuing to re-establish itself, slowly but surely, as a long-term success story.

At one level, this was a disappointment. If you're used to thinking of yourself as indispensable, it's humbling to find that everything hasn't gone to ruin in your absence. But I wasn't foolish enough to take this response too seriously. Instead, I focused on what this development could mean for the future, and on the lessons I could learn from all that had happened.

Suzette Harold, who had replaced me as group managing director about a year before my breakdown, had been acting as what would now be called chief executive. Her approach to the job was quite different from mine. She had little interest in – or flair for – creativity or innovation, but she thrived on the less strategic aspects of running a business: that is, on making the right things happen day-to-day. She was organised, strong-minded, calm, principled, a good communicator and good at dealing with pressure. Unlike me, she enjoyed public speaking. If running the company made her stressed, she never showed it. As long as no big strategic innovation was required, she was the perfect chief executive.

With me, it had been the other way round. My talent is for being an entrepreneur, in the widest sense. I love thinking of new ideas, questioning first principles, sensing new opportunities, starting things, changing things, recruiting new teams, attacking new challenges. That kind of work, for me, is indistinguishable from pleasure.

But I had always resented the way that my company also flooded my time with business chores: administration, budget-balancing, tax and legal issues, personnel problems, trouble-shooting, making things happen. They all had to be done, and I was quite capable of doing them satisfactorily – now as before. But they were things that I made myself do. Only when I was exploring ways of doing things better did I fling myself into the work with joy.

This being the case, what was the point of taking back from Suzette those parts of the job that I disliked and that she did better than me? Why not leave things as they were? True, everyone expected me to take back control from her, and, true, that would have been the comfortable option, in the sense that it would have allowed us to go back to doing things as we had done them before.

But when did anyone, company or individual, achieve anything worthwhile by pursuing the comfortable option? And, in any case, look where doing things as we had done them before had got me last time...

I brushed aside my insecurities and announced that Suzette would remain in day-to-day charge, while I took a less hands-on role. Within days I was having second thoughts: had I just conceded publicly that Suzette was more able than I was? But it was too late for agonising. I stood by my decision and soon realised that this letting-go was one of the smartest things I could have done.

Every company needs the kind of firm, confident, hands-on management that ensures that it carries on performing its core functions well. Equally, no company can thrive for long without innovation, inspiration and strategic vision. My ceding of day-to-day control to Suzette gave F International the best of both worlds. And what was good for the company must ultimately be good for me.

I remained the public face of the company. I carried on using my strengths as a people person – inspiring excellence and identifying and developing the stars of the future. I trained myself to become a more confident public speaker. I carried on networking, stepping up my activities in professional bodies such as the British Computer Society and accepting invitations to serve on government committees such as the Computer Systems and Electronics Requirements Board (which advised the government on its future IT needs, and on which I served from 1979 to 1981).

Some people seem to feel that someone who didn't need to "get a life" would have better things to do than to sit on such worthy bodies. All I can say is that, for me, this kind of networking was crucial to my professional development. It was, for a start, stimulating: the company of clever, high-achieving people generally is. It was sometimes reassuring, too. (I am thinking here of Forum, a personal and professional support network for successful women that I joined around this time, with members as various as Prue Leith, Katharine Whitehorn and Elizabeth Butler-Sloss. Each of us had made our way more or less alone as a woman in a man's world, and we found that we had a lot to learn from one another.)

Above all, though, it was by mixing with business heavyweights outside the narrow context of my day-job that I learnt about such unfamiliar subjects as corporate governance, patents, company law, lobbying, demography, long-term strategic thinking, and so on; or simply what the next big thing in computing or regulation was likely to be, a few years down the line. Nobody teaches you these things, when you start your own business from scratch; nobody else is responsible for making sure that you are kept in the loop. But if you do not learn these things at some point it is hard to make the leap from cottage industry to substantial, established business; or, indeed, to keep your enterprise going at all. So I am glad to have spent so much time mixing with what might be semi-derisively called the great and the good. The more time I spent in such circles, the more I learnt to raise my eyes from the desk in front of me and to think again about long-term, global perspectives. You could almost say that I learnt to get out more.

It was also around this time that I took the significant step of persuading the board of F International to agree that from now on one per cent of all pre-tax profits would be given (with the encouragement of a now defunct organisation called the PerCent Club) to charity. This decision was little noticed at the time, but over subsequent decades it would do an enormous amount of good, both to the beneficiaries and, I think, to the culture of the company.

At the same time, I carried on selling, enthusiastically – because coming up with the right vision for potential clients was arguably the most creative thing we did, and was one of the things that I did best. But I had less input than before into the technical detail of our proposals – which increasingly tended to be beyond my competence anyway – and focused instead on the broader brushstrokes of our visions. (This self-limitation had three advantages. It meant that I understood what I was talking about. It prevented me from expressing our proposals in technical gobbledegook, which meant that clients, too, could understand what I was talking about. And, because I was talking clients' language rather than ours, it forced me to see things from their point of view – something that the IT industry is notoriously bad at doing.)

That apart, I put my energy and enthusiasm into exploring strategic opportunities, in the UK and beyond. It was around this period, for example, that I wrote my first paper on the potential benefits to Western companies of outsourcing IT functions to India – an idea that would bear enormous fruit a couple of decades later but that seemed outlandish at the time.

I also looked at ways of expanding and invigorating our overseas operations, not just in Denmark and the Netherlands but also, following a chance encounter with an American consultant at a conference in Barcelona, in the USA. Heights Information Technology Systems Inc., a computer consultancy managed by and for Americans in New York and California, opened under licence from F International in 1978, using our work methods, working proformas, control techniques and recruitment expertise; five years later it would become a wholly owned subsidiary.

Such explorations had little immediate impact on our balance sheet (and little positive impact even in the medium term), yet I quickly became certain that this was the right kind of thing for me to be doing. The business as a whole was continuing to grow rapidly, with turnover for 1977-78 passing the magic £1m mark (to £1,330,819, to be precise). This meant that my old trick of saying airily that our revenues were "in six figures" – which people for some reason always took to mean over £1m rather than over £100,000 – would no longer be needed. It also meant healthy pre-tax profits of £83,246. It was almost as if, the less I concerned myself with the day-to-day running of the company, the more we achieved.

This was partly thanks to Suzette's commercial good sense and calm, decisive management. I hope, too, that my own more symbolic leadership may have played a part. But it was also obvious – to me at least – that there was another crucial factor in play: the company itself was sound.

F International was thriving because of strengths that over a decade and a half had become embedded in its corporate DNA. Unlike its competitors, it was an enterprise founded on trust. Its workforce were not sullen, submissive employees. They were self-motivated self-starters who loved and understood what they did and took pride in and responsibility for their work.

In the late 1970s, much of British industry was held back by a debilitating "us and them" mentality that by the end of the decade would bring the economy to the brink of collapse. At F International, everyone was "us". Our workforce had never had much in the way of job security: few of them even had jobs in the conventional sense. What they did have was a sense of ownership of their work and careers that encouraged each one of them to make the most of their professional potential.

This was of huge value, to both company and staff. Our people tended to be working not just to earn a living but to escape from the domestic obscurity and impotence that society had ordained for them. They knew that the company trusted them to make sensible use of their time: they were paid according to the work they accomplished, not the hours they clocked up. But many were also driven by the thought that, having been considered unemployable once, they might one day be considered unemployable again. This made them keen to develop their careers, to acquire new skills and to develop a reputation for excellence – just like the company as a whole. They generally cared as much as I did that a project should be completed on time and on budget, and that it should produce a satisfied customer. We were, by this stage, a large organisation, dispersed nationally, whose UK operations involved not just programmers and project managers but senior project managers, project directors and even regional directors. Roughly 500 people would probably have said, if asked, that they worked for F International. But I don't think any of them felt that the company owed them a living. They thought of themselves as responsible, independent adults, and so did we.

The average employee in a traditional male-dominated company was (in those days) suspicious of change; for our staff, keeping abreast of new technological developments was part of the point of working. Many of our panellists had carried on going to conferences and courses even in the depths of the recession, describing themselves as representatives of the company despite the fact that we were not paying them at the time. No one had asked them to do so. It was their insurance against being relegated to the kitchen again.

In the same way, whereas employees in traditional companies tended to resent being monitored or criticised – and could barely comprehend the American notion that "the customer is always right" – collective self-criticism was part of our way of life. We were a learning organisation.

Right from the beginning, when we had written those software standards for Urwick Diebold, Freelance Programmers had made a selling-point of its ability to monitor objectively the quality of its work. Our early crisis with Castrol had taught us how important it was to incorporate rigorous quality control into our working practices. And my chronic naivety had made us simply oblivious to the common industry practice of producing two sets of reports when reviewing projects: one for internal consumption and one, toned down, for the client. We were brutally frank to everyone about our failings – and, as a result, had never settled into bad habits.

For much of the previous decade meanwhile, our contracts had insisted on a formal post-project review to get feedback from the client after our system had been up-and-running for a while. (This had been Derek's idea, and was intended partly as a means of getting us back inside the door to tout for new work.) So the idea that there is always scope for learning to do things better was central to our culture, as was the idea of listening to the customer.

Individually and collectively, everyone was always looking for ways of adding value to their work. We encouraged staff to keep their skills up-to-date – but usually they came to us first, pressing us to give them more training and often paying for courses themselves.

As a respondent in a workforce survey around that time put it: "We want to be the best. Not necessarily the biggest, but the best."

How could such a company fail to thrive?

Thrive it certainly did. Between 1977 and 1979, our revenues would more than double, to £2.5m. But what struck me now, freed from the daily administrative burden and thinking strategically about where the company could go from here, was not the question of sales and profits but, rather, the question of ownership. Here, surely, there was scope for another transformative innovation?

F International's overwhelming strength was the fact that, in contrast to most companies of the time, its employees felt that they "owned" the projects they worked on. Yet in legal and financial terms they didn't. The only person who owned the company was me.

This seemed neither fair nor desirable – even from my point of view. The fact that it was "my" company had had little effect on my personal wealth: I paid myself a modest salary, with any profits going back into the company. I had, in any case, little desire to be rich and little prospect, as I saw it, of becoming so. What ownership meant to me was motivation – and responsibility.

Now, looking back at my collapse and the events surrounding it and asking myself what lessons I could learn, I realised that the issue of ownership had been part of the problem. When the company's survival had been hanging by a thread, I had had good people all around me, but I had insisted on taking all the burden on myself.

This was partly because I am a bit of a control freak; and also because, when you build a business up from nothing, it is difficult not to think of the whole enterprise as an extension of yourself. But there had also been a deeper reason: I had been the only person whose whole life – wealth, reputation, home, company, self-image and more – was on the line. I had been the only person who really owned the problem.

Perhaps that was inevitable. I was, after all, the proprietor. But now that I had seen the benefits of sharing the burden of leadership with Suzette, I was reminded of an idea that John Stevens (the Liberal idealist and programmer mentioned in Chapter Eight) had planted in my head a decade earlier. Maybe ownership was a more flexible concept than was generally assumed.

I had realised in Freelance Programmers' earliest days that – in the now-familiar cliché – the people who worked for us were our greatest asset. It could hardly have been otherwise: we had no other assets. But the fact that hardly any of our workers were employees in the formal sense had made me think more actively than I might otherwise have done about how to ensure that they were fairly rewarded for any success that the company might enjoy.

I had started a profit-sharing scheme in 1966 – which was pretty much the first year that we had any profits. It was a basic scheme. I would decide how much we could afford and then write to all our workers telling them how much their share came to. The letters went out twice a year, in summer and at Christmas, and, for the first few years, it worked pretty well. The payments were seen as a bonus and, since not many other companies operated such schemes, the recipients felt appreciated and appreciative. Then came the recession and the collapse in our profits in the early 1970s. I was forced to write to all our workers explaining that, since we had no profits, we were not in a position to hand out a share of them. Everyone seemed to understand; but then it happened again the next time, and the time after that. By the time I had sent out six such letters – summer, Christmas, summer, Christmas, summer, Christmas – I began to wonder what the point was. Their main effect seemed to be to dampen people's spirits by drawing their attention to the fact that times were hard and that we – and they – were not doing well. For a programme whose main intended effect was to raise morale, this was unfortunate, and after the sixth apologetic letter I quietly put the scheme out of its misery.

Perhaps, though, there was another way of doing things. What if our workers had a share not just of the profits – when they returned – but of the company itself? This idea had first entered my head at around the time that the profit-sharing scheme started, when John Stevens was part of the closely packed group that ran the company from Moss Cottage.

John believed passionately that shared ownership could alleviate many of the day's social and economic ills, and had drawn my attention to such successful examples as John Lewis (turned into a partnership between 1929 and 1950); Scott Bader (the Northamptonshire chemical company given to its workers by its founder, Ernest Bader, in 1951); Kalamazoo (the Midlands stationery company whose employees had owned a majority stake in it, via a trust, since 1947); the various Spanish co-operatives, set up by José María Arizmendiarrieta, that would eventually form the Mondragon Co-operative Group; Tullis Russell (a paper-making company in Fife, Scotland, which was in the process of being bought out by its employees); and the Geographers' A-to-Z Map Company (which had been transferred to its employees by its founder's daughter, Phyllis Pearsall, in the 1960s).

John Stevens admired such companies for their principles as much as their practical achievements. Shared ownership, he argued, was, simply, fair. But there was also a practical advantage to it. If employees are treated with respect, and are given a stake in their employer's success, they will usually work better. And if the rewards of ownership are shared, then the responsibilities of ownership will tend to be shared as well. That might have made all the difference when Freelance Programmers – and I – had been struggling to survive.

I had been attracted by the idea of running my company along some such lines from the moment that John first raised the idea, but with all the other challenges the company had faced it had been rather forgotten. Now, with the day-to-day headaches of running the company no longer demanding my urgent attention, I was free to revisit it. And since it was clear that the crises of the previous few years might have been considerably alleviated if I had been able to share the burden of ownership, it seemed worth pursuing energetically.

Guided by an organisation called the Industrial Participation Association, and advised also by Professor Keith Bradley at the London School of Economics, I visited a number of employee-run companies in the UK and abroad, as well as exploring other examples of proprietorial idealism, such as Bourneville and Port Sunlight. Stanislas Yassukovich (future chairman of Merrill Lynch) initiated me into the financial mysteries of Esops (Employee Share Ownership Plans) in the US. I also spoke to several proprietors who had given away their companies, always concluding my enquiries with the same question: "Would you do it again?" Most said yes, although I was struck by the long, doubtful pause that generally preceded the answer.

I soon learnt that transferring ownership of a company is more complicated than it sounds. Apart from anything else, there is a major tax problem. From the Inland Revenue's point of view, if you give away a business, it's a gift, and that gift has a financial value, of which they want a slice. The difficulty of determining objectively what that value is (especially with a privately owned service company such as F International) does not concern them. Nor does the fact that all the value is tied up in the business – and that to release it to pay tax would wipe the company out. For the would-be donor, however, these are huge obstacles. Unless either donor or recipient has enough ready cash to pay the tax from a separate source, it becomes almost impossible to transfer ownership without destroying the gift in the process.

There are various elaborate ways of getting round this problem, but money and time are required: money to pay for lawyers and accountants and time to listen to their arcane explanations. I fitted such encounters in when work and cashflow permitted. Inevitably, however, the process became protracted, spreading out over months and, in due course, years.

The most practical solution seemed to be (to simplify) to transfer shares a little at a time into a trust, which would own them on the staff's behalf. There would be no direct financial benefit to staff, but they would get a genuine say in how the company was run. But even this was more complicated than it sounds, because most of the relevant legislation applied to employees, and most of F International's staff were not employees in the legal sense. This was not something that I could sort out single-handedly, and my enthusiasm was not shared by the board of directors – especially Suzette, a very conventional thinker who had twice stood for Parliament (in the two general elections of 1974) as a Conservative. In one early presentation, I made the mistake of using the word "co-operative". "If that's what you want," she responded tartly, "I'm off."

I think Suzette was wrong about this, and she did in time become less suspicious of my proposals. I have never considered myself left-wing – I'm more of a floating voter – and I certainly don't see shared ownership as some form of disguised communism. If it has an ideological component, it is simply the idea of fairness – within the existing economic system. "To build co-operativism is not to do the opposite of capitalism, as if this system did not have any useful features," wrote José María Arizmendiarrieta, justifying the Mondragon venture. "Co-operativism must surpass it, and for this purpose must assimilate its methods and dynamism." John Spedham Lewis said much the same: "The present state of affairs is a perversion of the proper working of capitalism. It is all wrong to have millionaires before you have ceased to have slums. Differences of reward must be large enough to induce people to do their best, but the present differences are far too great."

But Suzette's objections were not just political. She also resented the amount of my time – and the company's money – that was being spent on this project. At one point, 10 of our most highly paid personnel – including me and Suzette – were summoned to spend the best part of a week being cross-examined by the Special Commissioners of the Inland Revenue. This was a remarkable experience, in a special courtroom in Holborn, full of gravitas and elaborate formality, and I was grateful to have had the opportunity of observing for myself this obscure piece of British tradition. But I also resented being made to spend all day being quizzed as if I was a criminal, and several of my colleagues felt strongly that the company simply could not afford to devote so much of its resources to what most of them saw as my own personal crusade.

It was hard to answer such criticisms, but, at the same time, I couldn't bear to let the idea drop. Everyone who starts a successful business comes up sooner or later against the question of what happens to it next. Many seek to sell, translating what they have created into hard cash. The trouble with this, from my point of view, was that new ownership was bound to mean an end to the company's unique way of doing things: its social purpose would be submerged by financial imperatives. Others seek to give their company an assured future by keeping it in the family, grooming a son or daughter to take the helm after them. There are pros and cons to this approach. In my case, it wasn't an option.

But, not being immortal, I still needed to do something with the company, and there was little to be gained from hanging on to control for too long, when it was clear to me that my talents were as an innovator and entrepreneur rather than as a manager. I wanted the company to continue, and to thrive, and to carry on providing a uniquely collaborative and creative working environment in which people, regardless of gender, could realise their full potential. Shared ownership offered by far the best hope of achieving this.

So I kept plugging away at the idea, patiently and intermittently, and eventually the wheels began to move. No one really seemed to notice – least of all our staff – but in 1981, after three years of haggling over the small print, the F International Shareholders' Trust was established, to hold shares on behalf of the staff and represent their interests. Its first chairman was Wallace Bell, whose 1973 book, Financial Participation, Wages, Profit-sharing and Employee Shareholding, had made a big impression on me. (Wallace's successors in the role would include David Erdal, who had managed the employee buy-out at the aforementioned Tullis Russell.)

I gave the Trust four per cent of my shareholding to get it going – the maximum tax-efficient amount – and, over the following years, the slow transfer of ownership continued, with the company making annual grants to the Trust which it would use to purchase shares from a separate mentally handicapped discretionary trust to which I had already been giving shares. (This trust's beneficiaries included Giles, Suzannah – the colleague's daughter mentioned on page 100 – and some charities.)

It was a small and obscure step. But it marked the beginning of a process that I would come to see as one of the greatest achievements of my life.

14: Slings And Arrows

By the early 1980s, it seemed as though Freelance Programmers could do no wrong. Whatever we did, we made money. As we did so, the world showered us with praise.

Our overseas ventures thrived (briefly), at one point accounting for eight per cent of our revenues, which by 1981 had reached £3.4m. We also began to make serious profits – £561,000 in 1981 – as Suzette continued her common-sense work of correcting the historic imbalances in our business model. We had devoted much of the 1960s and 1970s to achieving a "profitless prosperity", whereby demand for our services kept growing and the scale of our operations grew to match but – because we didn't charge enough – our profits remained minimal. This turned out to have been an excellent way of building market share, but the company's story would have been a lot less fraught if we had got our pricing right in the first place.

We barely noticed the recession of 1980-1982. If it had an effect, it was that demand grew for the efficiency-boosting systems that we sold. By 1983 our revenues had reached £5.5m; by 1984, £7m.

Meanwhile, it had become clear that the world once again saw us – and me – as a success story. Having been runner-up for the Times/ Veuve Clicquot Business Woman of the Year award at the end of 1979, I was appointed OBE at the beginning of 1980. I could not and cannot disguise my delight in this award. It represented the ultimate proof that I was no longer an outsider, no longer here on sufferance, but, on the contrary, a valued member of the British establishment. I was particularly gratified to have received it for "services to industry" rather than "services to IT". It was not my technical vision or expertise that was being honoured: it was F International's way of working – the flexible, home-based, female-friendly, job-sharing, trust-the-staff approach that had attracted such scorn from establishment types when we first began.

I consolidated my newfound respectability with other public duties. In addition to the Computer Systems and Electronics Requirements Board, which I have already mentioned, I stepped up my activities as vice-president of the British Computer Society, helping to restructure it to reflect more accurately the new shape of the industry while continuing to guide it towards chartered status. I also served, from 1981 to 1983, on the Electronics and Avionics Requirements Board; worked on a number of government projects relating to the use of IT to help disabled people (1981 was the International Year of Disability); served on the Advisory Council for Applied Research and Development's – or ACARD's – Working Party on Information Technology (1982 was the International Year of IT); worked on the Manpower Services Commission's Open Tech programme (from 1983 to 1986); served (from 1984) on the Council of the Industrial Society; became the first woman ever to receive an Information Technology Achievement Award (in 1985); advised the Department of Industry on the challenges posed by the rise of Japanese technology (in 1982); became a regular if informal adviser to various ministers and civil servants; and made any number of speeches and media appearances, with which I gradually learnt to feel more comfortable.

Some of this work was stimulating; much was tiresome. Occasionally it was embarrassing. My work for ACARD took me on one occasion to a function at 10 Downing Street, where, feeling a bit out of my depth, I introduced myself to an unremarkable-looking man and asked him who he was. "The name's Thatcher," he replied.

But I enjoyed the recognition and the sense of belonging that came with all these activities. And I also felt – correctly, I am sure – that F International's image as a top-of-the-range consultancy was significantly enhanced by its chairman's presence in prestigious public positions.

Despite such recognition, however, these were not easy times. There was still too much to worry about.

Our overseas ventures, for example, refused to take off. They functioned, more or less, but they never flew. Where F International seemed to have success programmed into it, and shone with collective confidence, our Danish, Dutch and American offshoots always felt like disasters waiting to happen. No sooner had we resolved one problem than another would appear on the horizon. Eventually, we asked ourselves why we bothered – and decided to stop doing so.

Specifically: we didn't renew our contract with our US partner, Heights, in 1982; then, in 1983, acquired it as a wholly owned subsidiary; and finally sold it in 1985, having realised that the US market was already too mature, and too flexible, to permit the kind of spectacular growth that F International had experienced in the UK. (There was also the little matter of having assumed, when we bought it, that its self-description as a Computing Services Consulting Company meant that it was a consultancy in computing services. In fact, it was a consultancy to computer services companies, and – for example – the "Boeing" on its client list was actually the Boeing Computing Services subsidiary. So it had never been as good a fit for F International as we'd hoped.) We sold off our Danish subsidiary to local management in 1986; and we offloaded our Dutch company in 1987 by allowing one of its clients to merge with it.

If that sounds like a catalogue of failure, perhaps it is. Yet none of these ventures was entirely unsuccessful (although the American one ultimately left us nearly £300,000 out of pocket). It was just that the balance between risk and potential benefit was wrong: too much work was required just to stave off catastrophe, with too little scope for reward if everything went right. In each case (though in different ways), the market was inappropriate: too saturated in Denmark, too inflexible in the Netherlands, too mature in the US. Perhaps we should have worked that out in advance. Yet without those early experiments in overseas expansion we would never have been as well prepared to grow rapidly and effectively when the opportunity to become truly international arose in the 1990s.

Meanwhile, I had, as ever, other things on my mind. Giles was settled in to his subnormality hospital at Borocourt. To say that he was happily settled in would have been stretching even my wishful credulity. Laburnums Ward was a bleak, joyless place. His fellow patients – around a dozen of them – were all teenage boys, with handicaps comparable to Giles's. I couldn't confidently say that any of them was less afflicted than he was; and, as tragically happens in such environments, the problems of each added to the pains of all. There was one boy who was always breaking windows; one who ate paint; one who chewed up his and others' clothes; another who was always trying to play with the fire-extinguisher. Giles himself liked tearing up paper. Another boy was constantly urinating in the wrong places. Several liked to expose themselves, and several were inclined (under certain hard-to-identify provocations) to lash out at their fellow-patients. Put all these challenging behaviour traits in one place, along with a dozen others, and you get something pretty hellish.

It was a locked, prison-like ward, upstairs in a modern building just outside the main Gothic house. You had to ring the bell to get in. Once you were in, you were generally escorted, for your own safety. Everything in the ward was bare. There were no toys, no pictures, just plastic covers over the windows, a few plastic chairs, with bare walls of whitened concrete and a basic dormitory and communal eating area. The kitchen door was locked; the wardrobe door was locked; the toilet doors had no locks; the toilet seats had been removed; one toilet didn't even have a door. Common prudence demanded such precautions. Yet the combined effect was an environment devoid of stimulation. And mentally handicapped teenagers, like any teenagers, do not respond well to boredom.

There was no way of determining with confidence what Giles felt about being at Borocourt. He had reacted badly to the initial move, but that was to be expected. Subsequently he had quietened down, as he grew used to the new routine. But what was his quality of life? We could only guess. It was hard to imagine, though, from the inarticulate cries that echoed periodically from the ward's hard walls, that our son was in a very happy place.

He would spend some time most days at an educational facility in the hospital grounds, where they did things like pottery and drawing; this appeared to function reasonably well. The rest of his time was spent in the ward, where the quality of life was determined by whoever was that day's lowest common denominator among the patients. As the months passed, Giles seemed to grow moodier and more troubled. Perhaps that would have happened anyway, as he passed deeper into adolescence and epilepsy. Or perhaps – as we feared – it was his environment.

To begin with, we would take Giles home with us at weekends. But this proved increasingly difficult as his behaviour grew wilder. Car journeys, in particular, became impossibly dangerous – always assuming that we could coax him into the car in the first place. At one point, when we were about to take him back on a Sunday afternoon, he simply refused, with all the strength and violence at his disposal, to get in the car at all, and I had to get the hospital to send an ambulance to collect him. Eventually it grew clear that we had to find another way of doing things.

This horrified Derek. If we can't do anything else for him, he argued, at least we can still give him his days out. But the truth was that we couldn't. If a raging, violent, strapping, 6ft teenager doesn't want to be in a car, you cannot safely drive him. It's also fair to assume that the teenager himself isn't particularly enjoying the journey. Eventually I was reduced to contacting the hospital and imploring them to accept that, irrespective of anything that Derek might tell them to the contrary, we simply weren't able to look after Giles at weekends any more.

Thereafter, we took to making weekend visits to Giles at Borocourt. He seemed to welcome this, and Derek rapidly agreed that it was an improvement on our kidnap-like weekend car journeys. We would take Giles out for a walk in the hospital grounds, usually stopping for a picnic; sometimes, as he grew comfortable with the routine, we would take him a little further. It seems such a small thing now, in print; yet at the time it felt like a huge achievement, to have found a way of sharing a little happiness between the three of us. Even in winter, when our picnics were as often as not eaten hurriedly while huddled under a heat-reflecting blanket to keep out the rain and the cold, they still felt like a cheering approximation to family life. They were the only scraps of such life that remained to us.

Only one other boy in the ward received family visits. His parents, whom we got to know slightly, wore crash-helmets when they went in to see him. Experience had taught them that it was unsafe not to. The other patients fended for themselves as best they could, buffeted by their various disorders (not all of them related to autism) and befuddled by their various medications. The staff seemed to be doing their best, but there was no sense of visionary zeal – just rather desperate damage limitation.

We agonised constantly about entrusting Giles to Borocourt. We knew that we had no choice but to do so – yet there was something about the place that encouraged dark imaginings. The architectural historian Nikolaus Pevsner had described the building (which has since reverted to its original name, Wyfold Court) as "a nightmare abbey in spirit", and it was hard to watch its ornate towers receding into the twilight after a weekend visit without entertaining dark fantasies about misery and despair.

It emerged much later that some things about Borocourt had indeed been as bad as fantasy painted them. There were, for example, perfectly sane patients who had been shut up in the main hospital for 40 years or more for no better reason than that they had had an illegitimate child, causing relatives to declare that they were "morally defective". There were people whose families had abandoned them so totally that there was no record of their next of kin. There was even a woman whose family had put her there on the basis of a close teenage friendship she had formed with a man with the wrong-coloured skin. She remained there for 33 years.

But we had no way of knowing that then, any more than we could have known the very worst of what went on in Laburnums ward. We could only fall back on the few certainties that we had: the fact that we could not keep Giles at home; the fact that we were dependent for his care on the assistance of the state; and the fact that our local health authority had identified Borocourt as the most appropriate – and indeed only – place for Giles to be looked after.

So we struggled on, hoping for the best, wishing that the voices of doubt at the back of our minds would quieten down, and trying to make the most of those short, precious weekend excursions in the hospital grounds.

Meanwhile, there were other troubles to contend with – notably a devastating deterioration in Suzette Harold's health. This began indistinctly, around 1979, manifesting itself initially as a slight propensity to tiredness and clumsiness. But the symptoms worsened, and, after about a year of mounting physical weakness, she was diagnosed with multiple sclerosis.

She bore it bravely, carrying on for the most part as though nothing was wrong. But there was no getting away from it, and it was heart-breaking to see this strong, brilliant, beautiful woman gradually withering under the disease's relentless attack. One of the cruellest moments came when, after some public function, complaints filtered back to me that Suzette had been drunk. She hadn't been – she never drank alcohol – but her illness had made her stagger and slur her words. Thereafter, on my advice, she never went anywhere without a silver-topped stick: not because she usually needed its support but as a kind of public statement that she was, among other things, an invalid.

She carried on working for several years – and the company continued to prosper under her management. But eventually the handicap became insuperable, and she retired on a total disability pension in 1981. It was a tragic end to a brilliant career, and she never quite came to terms with it. I missed her greatly, both as a colleague and, later, as a human being. (She died a dozen years later, her full potential tragically unrealised.)

There then followed an extended period of management turmoil. I briefly resumed day-to-day control of the company myself, appointing another chairman who, for reasons too tiresome to go into here, did not work out and did not last long. I then switched back to being chairman and appointed our most high-powered regional director, Alison Newell, to be managing director in Suzette's place.

Alison had a huge amount going for her. She had been with F International for more than a decade, including a substantial and successful spell managing our southern division. (We had at that stage in our growth divided our activities regionally. Later, as the UK economy became less localised, we found it less cumbersome to partition our organisation by function rather than geography.) She had recently spent several months in Scotland in preparation for her new role, and had successfully developed a new division for us up there. She was clever and beautiful – clients often seemed to fall in love with her – as well as being energetic and entrepreneurial, with a strong sense of ethics and professionalism and a gift for cost-management that predisposed the organisations she managed towards profitability.

Yet in some hard-to-define sense she was not (in contrast to her predecessor or, for that matter, her successor) the right woman at the right time.

This was probably my fault as well as hers. I was committed in principle to staying in the background and letting the managing director manage, but I'm not sure that I had entirely absorbed the idea at an emotional level. Suzette's illness had sharpened my sense of life's transience, and I was full of impatience for many things to be achieved. I wanted the company to become more profitable. I wanted our management structures to grow more solid and mature, so that I could be sure that the business could thrive without me. I also wanted, increasingly, to earn money for myself and my family. And I wanted to push on towards my goal of a staff-owned company.

I tried scrupulously to stay out of Alison's hair, and indeed eventually relinquished the chairmanship, recruiting Leighton Davies, formerly of

Racal Electronics, to take my place in February 1984. (Thereafter I was merely group chief executive.) But she must have sensed my shadow behind her even when I wasn't there. When I was there, she made it pretty clear – though not out loud – that she didn't want me around. I found this hurtful but told myself that it was the price that had to be paid for letting go. So I focused on my strategic and international work and left Alison to get on with it. I felt less comfortable about doing so than I had done with Suzette, but I made myself do it – and, as a result, stored up trouble for the future.

There was plenty for me to keep myself busy with, and, in the meantime, sales and profits continued to grow respectably. I was also distracted by my own health. Increasingly, over a period of many months or perhaps even years, I had been weighed down by a sense of exhaustion. My energy and drive had evaporated; even my intellect seemed to be fading. I would be taking part in a technical discussion or committee meeting, and the ideas would start to seem slippery, so that I couldn't quite get a grip on them. I was overwhelmingly tired all the time and had only to sit down in a quiet place for a minute to feel my eyes closing with sleep.

I put it down to sheer physical tiredness – I was driving about 30,000 miles a year at the time and probably travelling as many again by air – but, given my previous breakdown, I felt more concerned about this than I might otherwise have done. And when I realised that, for the second or third time in a week, I had been too tired in the evening to go upstairs except by crawling on hands and knees, I began to suspect that something more significant was happening.

Then, on a business trip in the US, I mentioned my worries to a trusted colleague, Elizabeth Virgo. She looked at me closely for a minute or two and said: "That's not exhaustion. That's what my sister has. You've got diabetes."

Not long afterwards, my doctor confirmed the diagnosis. I began to take the appropriate medication and, bit by bit, my symptoms eased. I was lucky. Had I soldiered on regardless, as instinct told me to, I could have suffered a fatal collapse.

By the time my medication kicked in, my head had cleared sufficiently for me to focus on the problem of Alison. There was no longer any denying that it was a problem – nearly three years into her tenure. The company's results were healthy, but it was becoming harder to know if the company itself was healthy. We had recently moved into new offices in Berkhamsted, just across the county border in Hertfordshire. (We paid £300,000 for the freehold in 1981 – a spectacularly good investment.) For perhaps the first time, the company had a headquarters worthy of its public image and its human assets. Yet Alison was rarely to be seen there: she had taken to doing more and more of her work from our Horsham office, near her home in West Sussex. My fellow directors and I had no objection in principle to such an arrangement – this was, after all, a company built on flexible working. But the physical detachment, in this case, mirrored an operational detachment. It was not just I who was being frozen out: it was the whole of senior management. Alison was running everything herself, from Horsham, rather as I had once run things: as a one-woman band. Unlike me, however, she didn't seem to be developing new senior management talent who might lead the company into new territory in future. She was making a good fist of the short-term management of the company, but it simply wasn't what F International needed at this stage in its development. It needed robust management structures, structures that would facilitate expansion and guarantee its long-term future; not one woman sitting in a private office, spider-like, running everything herself.

When I took Alison to task about this, she brushed my concerns aside. "What are you worried about?" she said. "I'm doing it, aren't I?" I urged her to appoint a deputy. She refused. "But what if you fell under the proverbial bus?" I asked, more than once. "It would be fine," she insisted. But it wouldn't have been.

From Alison's perspective, I was the one at fault. I was being the over-controlling founder, refusing to accept that the company had moved on. I can see why she felt this, but I think that, if anything, the opposite was true. If I hadn't been so anxious not to be controlling, I might not have allowed communication between us to deteriorate so badly. As it was, what with my imperfect communication skills and her rather reserved persona, it was becoming almost impossible for us to have a constructive conversation.

But it wasn't just a question of personality. Other directors made similar representations to Alison: she needed to delegate, she was told; she needed a deputy, she needed to push down responsibility to the regional directors. She stood her ground. Eventually, towards the end of 1984, I took matters into my own hands and, at my instigation, the board told her to add another layer of management (reporting to her) – creating the kind of formal structure that one would find in a public company. This weakened the role of regional managers – which caused some ill-feeling – and brought control of a single, enlarged, nationwide sales force back to head office. Shortly afterwards, Alison handed in her notice, and in due course left.

I have tried to be fair in telling this part of my story. I am sure that Alison would tell it differently. But neither of us would dispute that it was an unhappy time for both of us. There was no question about Alison's talent: two years later (with another former F International employee, Ann Budge), she set up her own software consultancy, Newell & Budge, and made a spectacular success of it. But she hadn't been a perfect match for F International's needs at the time, and I think we were both relieved – once the bruises had healed – to move on.

From my point of view, there were lessons to be learnt. Most importantly, I had to think more specifically about what kind of leadership and management F International now needed. A decade earlier, Alison might have been an ideal managing director. But the company was now too big for that kind of management. Like a child turning imperceptibly into an adult, F International had become a proper grown-up company, with blue-chip clients and a multi-million-pound turnover. It needed to be run as such.

I also needed to come to terms with the changing relationship between me and my company. The harsh truth was that, if I wanted it to stand on its own two feet, without my constant intervention, I needed to stop thinking of it as my company. Part of my difficulty with Alison had been personal: I hadn't felt comfortable with someone else – someone I trusted less than Suzette – treating the company as if it were hers. Yet that, in practice, was what letting go was going to feel like. I could make sure the right management structures were in place, try even harder to get the right people in place; but ultimately I had to leave them to make their own decisions and, if necessary, their own mistakes. Inevitably, this would hurt.

I also realised that my vision of a self-sustaining company was closely tied to my vision of a staff-owned company. Having achieved my initial goal of building a successful, sustainable business, I wanted to be sure that, whatever else happened to it in future, it retained its special character as a flexible, ethical, female-friendly organisation whose staff were listened to and trusted. Transferring ownership to the staff seemed the surest way of achieving this.

Since 1981, I had continued to transfer shares to the FI Shareholders' Trust at a rate of about 4 per cent a year. I feared, however, that this might be too little, too slowly. After briefing headhunters to leave no stone unturned in finding the best possible successor to Alison, I moved the issue of staff ownership back to the top of my agenda.

Meanwhile, I was pleased to see another project reach fruition. Some 18 months earlier, I had initiated the creation of a mission statement. This must have seemed an eccentric step at the time, and it took endless discussion, and input from most of the staff, before it was finalised. Finally, however, the F International Charter was agreed, printed, distributed to all our staff and displayed in all our offices. Every company has a mission statement these days, and most are full of weasel words and platitudes. Ours was among the first, and I doubt if there have been many since that have described so accurately the invisible forces that drive a particular enterprise forward.

The F International Charter of 1984 reads as follows:

F INTERNATIONAL CHARTER

F International is a group of companies which have sprung from seeing an opportunity in a problem: one woman's inability to work in an office has turned into hundreds of people's opportunity to work in a non-office environment. Because of its unusual origin, F International has a clear sense of its mission, its strategy and its values.

MISSION:

F International's mission is to stay a leader in the rapidly growing and highly profitable, knowledge-intensive software industry. It aims to achieve this by developing, through modern communications, the unutilised intellectual energy of individuals and groups unable to work in a conventional environment.

STRATEGY:

F International's strategy is to maximise the value of its unusual asset base by establishing a competitive advantage over conventionally organised firms, and imitators of its approach, through cost and quality competitiveness. This occurs by the development of a methodology which ensures quality and by establishing a company ethos which binds people who work largely independently and often alone.

VALUES:

People are vital to any knowledge-intensive industry. The skills and loyalty of our workforce are our main asset. Equally important is the knowledge which comes from the exchange of ideas with our clients and their personnel. It follows that human and ethical values play a pivotal role in the way in which an organisation like F International conducts itself. This is even more true in a structure as open and free as F International. To maintain a high level of creativity, productivity and coherence in such an environment requires a set of high ethical values and professional standards that any member of the organization can identify with and see realised, and reinforced, in the organisation's behaviour. F International has defined for itself such a charter of values:

1. Professional excellence
Our long-term aim is to improve our professional abilities so as to maintain a quality product for our clients. It is also our aim to develop fully our professional potential as people and to develop our organisation in a way which reflects our own individuality and special approach.

2. Growth
We aim to grow our organisation to its full potential, nationally and internationally. We aim to grow at least as rapidly as the software industry as a whole in order to maintain our own position as an attractive employer and a competitive supplier.

3. Economic and psychological reward
We also aim to realise and enjoy fully the economic and psychological rewards of our efforts resulting from the development of the unique competitive advantage of our structure and capabilities. We aim to achieve profits, reward our workforce, maintain the Employee Trust and provide an attractive return to our shareholders.

4. Integrated diversity
We have a commitment to consistent procedures worldwide as a means of lowering cost, but aim to conduct ourselves as a national of each country in which we operate.

5. Universal ethics
We respect local customs and laws, but see ourselves as members of a world society with respect for human dignity and ethical conduct beyond the profit motive and local circumstances.

6. Goodwill
An extension of our ethical view is a belief in the goodwill of others: colleagues, clients and vendors. We also believe that goodwill results in positive, long-term relationships.

7. Enthusiasm
Finally, we believe that enthusiasm for our people and our product, and the ability to engender that enthusiasm in others, is the most essential quality of leadership within the organisation. Enthusiasm promotes creativity, cooperation and profit.

I quote this charter in full partly because I am proud of it, but also because it illustrates how intangible – and yet how vital – a service company's assets can be. Without that defining set of ideas, F International would have been – well, not quite nothing, but nothing out of the ordinary: just one software company among many, loosely linked to a number of talented personnel but otherwise with no unique selling-point.

Instead, with that set of ethical and practical ideas running through it like the words in a stick of rock, the company was able to sell a special something that no one else could offer.

Given what the company would achieve over the next couple of decades, it is amusing to think that any of our competitors could at any time have discovered all the main points of our corporate strategy simply by looking at this publicly available document of – including my signature at the bottom – just 580 words. In most companies, the master plan is a closely guarded secret. Ours was there to be seen and copied by all who had eyes to see. Luckily, few of our rivals seemed interested. Instead, we used the charter to keep reminding ourselves and our clients what it was that we stood for; what we were aiming for; what it was that we were selling. It would have been hard to think of a better foundation for future prosperity.

But that, in turn, was what made me worry and fuss about the long-term ownership of F International. I was reconciled to letting go of the company both managerially and financially. But – like a parent when a child leaves home – I could not bear to think of it letting go of its values.

15: The Great Escape

While the company I had given birth to was growing and changing and learning to make its own way in the world, with all the excitement and occasional pain that such developments generally involve, my son remained as dependent as ever, locked – metaphorically and literally – in a closed, unchanging world where there seemed to be neither progress nor hope of progress.

The bitter irony was not lost on us; but what could we do about it? Derek and I spent much of the early 1980s fretting about what we should do for Giles, without finding a satisfactory answer. Derek had even taken early retirement, in order to devote more time to the issue. It was a big sacrifice for such a brilliant man, at the age of just 57, but he was determined that Giles should come first. Unfortunately, his extra input didn't initially do much good. Derek's first innovation was to start visiting Giles on Wednesdays, in addition to our regular weekend visits. Giles reacted with fury at the disruption to his routine, lashing out, roaring and throwing things across the room. I remember Derek returning home ashen-faced after each of his first few midweek visits.

He kept at it grimly, however, and, after a few months, Giles began to show signs that he had learnt to expect and accept these visits. Yet the effect on our peace of mind was minimal. Most of Giles's life continued to be lived behind locked doors, far from his parents' oversight or love. These short snatches of extra contact did little to alter this sad fact; they merely encouraged us to worry about what Giles was going through the rest of the time.

It was hard to point to any specific failing in his care at Borocourt, beyond what the head of West Berkshire's mental handicap service would later call the results of "years of neglect". There were so few staff – typically just two nurses for a ward of around a dozen unruly youths – that nearly all their energy necessarily went into preventing major incidents of violence, self-harm or escape.

Derek and I each independently concluded that the staff had more or less abandoned hope of bettering their patients' lives and had become almost entirely reactive to whatever problems their charges might throw at them, rather than aspiring proactively to help them

Giles remained a handsome man despite various cuts and bruises over the years and the medication which seemed to coarsen his face.

deal better with the world. I used to telephone the hospital most days, just to check with the staff how Giles had been getting on. More often than not, the question "What have you been doing today?" elicited the answer, "We have been hoping to go out" – the subtext being that at no point had they been able to get the patients sufficiently controlled and motivated actually to leave the ward. Sometimes I thought that they seemed more like prison warders than nurses; indeed, one nurse later admitted to a journalist that it was "like a concentration camp". The residents were kept alive and physically safe, but they had been deprived of most of their human rights.

Even West Berkshire health authority, which owned Borocourt, was losing faith in it. In 1983 it drew up plans to close the hospital and move its residents into "care in the community". Such transitions were widely mooted at the time, and widely criticised as mere money-saving exercises, but I have no doubt that, for children like Giles, such care is (where practical) infinitely preferable to segregation and incarceration among fellow-sufferers. It allows stimulation and thus the hope of development. (It does not, however, save money.)

But in the short-term this weakening of official support for Borocourt added to the sense of it being an institution that had lost its way. Staffing levels were in long-term decline: the number of nurses would fall by nearly 25 per cent between 1983 and 1990. As for management objectives, Borocourt's main ambition, it seemed to us, was to serve as a repository for troubled souls whose families and communities wanted to wash their hands of them. This "out of sight, out of mind" approach had become central to its approach to its patients. Such staff as there were on the ward welcomed the active interest that Derek and I took in Giles's wellbeing, but I wasn't convinced that the management felt the same.

One Saturday, we turned up to find that a big programme of redecoration had been embarked upon, initiated by a new member of the management team. Our spirits rose: perhaps this signified a new, more positive approach. Then, some weeks later, we realised that it was only the staff areas that were being spruced up. Decorating the areas the patients lived in was considered a waste of money; indeed, their area was actually being made smaller to allow more room for the staff.

Another time, we turned up to find that Giles had been moved. He had had a particularly violent tantrum a few days earlier, and had been transferred temporarily to an extra-secure ward, where 17 of the hospital's most intractable cases were kept in conditions even starker than those of Laburnums ward. The staff's initial reaction to our arrival was to refuse to let us see Giles. They said it was for our own safety, but we soon realised that their real concern was to protect us from what we might see there.

In fact, the special ward was scarcely bleaker than Laburnums ward. It was, like Laburnums, devoid of anything that could possibly be considered warm or stimulating. Many of the patients (several of whom carried signs of recent violence) were obviously sedated; Giles seemed much lower than usual. And that was it: no horrors per se; just a bare room full of bruised, bewildered youths, each groping blindly through his own emotional fog, guarded by nurses who maintained a semblance of order without seeming remotely interested in what their charges were feeling.

It wasn't that the nurses lacked human sympathy. On the contrary, they seemed very sensitive to what Derek and I might be feeling. It was just that the question of the patients' feelings didn't seem to be on the agenda. There were probably zoos in Britain where the quality of the inmates' lives was a higher policy priority. And, in the meantime, what else might the staff be keeping from us?

By 1984, we were both resolute: things could not go on like this. Yet the old impasse remained: what could we do instead?

Then fate intervened.

My mother was in her eighties, and had been growing frailer. With Renate still in Australia, Derek and I had been devoting an increasing amount of time to looking after her. Now, without warning but not unexpectedly, she died, from a heart attack in her sleep.

I don't remember shedding a tear. We had been reconciled in later years, but had never become close. I had never lost the feeling that she disapproved of me, and, although I had looked after her attentively, I was always a dutiful daughter to her rather than a loving one. I respected her, but I was not distraught to lose her. (By contrast, when Uncle died, a few years later, I was inconsolable.)

But I did weep, a few months after my mother's death, when I learnt that she had cut me out of her will, dividing her estate instead between Renate and Giles. These were tears of pure self-pity, but they were no less bitter for that. It was not the money that mattered – it was not a huge estate – but the injustice, the rejection, the cold, deliberate snub. The will had been written some years ago, but she had updated it quite recently, and I had been excluded from both versions. My mother must have been conscious of this, even as I was shouldering the burden of her support, and must have known the effect that the rejection would be likely to have on me when I discovered it. And yet still... The thought of what must have been going on in her heart makes me flush with defensive indignation even now. I am sure that I was at fault in our relationship in many ways, and I daresay I had no right to expect anything from her. Yet that final message from mother to daughter still feels like a cruel, spiteful rebuke from an angry adult to a little girl who doesn't know what she has done wrong. And that still hurts.

Yet much good would ultimately come of this episode. Some months later, wondering how we could spend the money that had been left to Giles for his benefit, we had the idea of buying a cottage near Borocourt. We had seen one for sale – a plain but cosy two-up-two-down called Redcot, within walking distance of the hospital – and Giles's legacy (around £40,000) was just about enough to cover it.

All sorts of legal niceties had to be observed: we had to be scrupulous in spending the money for Giles's benefit and not ours. But, in brief, we bought the cottage, on Giles's behalf, and weekends were immediately transformed for all three of us. We could take Giles there as part of our Saturday excursions – a welcome alternative to shivering picnics in the rain – and could even stay there the night before to maximise the time we could spend with him. He needed close supervision: the cottage could hardly have been less fit for purpose in terms of being bare and indestructible. But despite its awkward beams and rickety stairs, it did allow us a few more precious hours as a family each week. And if things did get too wild or difficult, it was only a short walk back to the hospital.

It is hard to over-state the difference that this made. The fact of having a base exclusively for Giles, combined with the security of having the hospital so close by, allowed us to approach our time with him in a completely different way. Instead of having half an eye always on travel logistics, we were able to focus entirely on him. The big question of the weekend ceased to be "Will we get him safely out and back again?" and became instead "What can we do with him this time to help him to respond more positively to the world?" It also allowed me to grab some sleep after returning from the US on the "red-eye" shuttle, leaving Derek in charge until (inevitably) things got dicey.

It was a lovely place, serenely quiet. There were plenty of disasters, from banged heads to smashed furniture, but it always felt – as it hadn't felt for years – as though we were doing the best for Giles that could be done.

Yet however much things improved at weekends, the fact remained that the rest of the time he was locked in Borocourt. And if his quality of life seemed better when he was with us, it was hard not to suppose that he must notice the difference when he was locked back into Laburnums.

Then things took a turn for the worse. We had been concerned for many months – perhaps even years – with Giles's propensity to mouth ulcers. Derek took a close interest in Giles's dental health (nightly teeth-cleaning was one of the few little rituals of normal family life that had always run smoothly in Giles's life, and helping him with it whenever possible had been one of Derek's few opportunities for normal father-son bonding); and he had come to see the state of Giles's mouth as a kind of barometer for his wider well-being. So Derek would check Giles's mouth on every visit and regularly quizzed staff about medication, oral hygiene and so forth. Then, in one such conversation, at some point in 1985, one of the nurses said something rather startling: "Of course," he said, in a half-whisper, "it would be better if he didn't drink from the toilet."

It took a few supplementary questions, and a few minutes' thought, before we understood what this implied. Once we did so – and understood that the staff had known that he was drinking from the toilet bowl for years, and had not thought to mention it – we agreed, instantly and irrevocably, that we could no longer meekly accept the situation.

We fired off a formal complaint to West Berkshire health authority, agonising far into the night about the precise wording. The final draft (the seventeenth) itemised nine different shortcomings in Borocourt's practices, from the general to the particular. We wrote it with a heavy heart, because there were one or two individual members of staff of whom we thought highly – and it was not their fault that recent changes on the ward had denied patients access to the kitchen, reducing their access to water. But we could hardly let the matter lie, and the health authority, having received our complaint, had no alternative but to investigate. Before long we were summoned to a meeting, where our complaint was discussed by representatives of the health authority and members of the hospital management and staff, including the very people we were complaining about. It would be hard to imagine a more stressful situation, and I suspect that we did not press our case as convincingly as we might have done. At any rate, the outcome was inconclusive, and the investigation dragged on for months.

Meanwhile, what little warmth there had been in our relationship with the Borocourt management vanished abruptly, and a new fear gripped us: what if this hostility also expressed itself in the way Giles was looked after? There was, I hasten to add, absolutely no reason to suspect that any of the staff on the ward would maltreat him, yet it was impossible to eradicate that fear entirely from our minds. If nothing else, he was desperately vulnerable.

I'm not sure which of us first had the idea that we could take what we had done with Redcot a stage further. I think we had both voiced the vague wish "If only he could stay here all the time"; but neither of us had really thought it through. Then, gradually, we began to discuss it as a serious proposition.

We realised within minutes that it was an impractical idea. Looking after Giles in Redcot would be no easier than looking after him in our own home; harder, in fact, because Redcot was smaller and more hazardous. Why would it work now when it hadn't worked before?

Derek pointed out that at least he was now retired; I pointed out that he was 62 and no match physically for Giles, who was 22 and strong as a bullock. The only way Giles could live full-time outside Borocourt was with full-time professional help. And how could we possibly afford that? We got as far as investigating some of the figures (official estimates at the time put the cost of the most basic "care in the community" at £30,000 per patient per year) before giving up in despair.

The only step forward was that Derek began to take Giles to Redcot during his Wednesday visits and – since Giles could be extraordinarily violent and destructive when the mood took him – began to pay an unemployed local nurse called Phil Bunce to come and help him. This caused further tensions in our relationship with the hospital, where Phil had once been an employee. He had left under a cloud after allegedly disregarding rules about taking patients into the local pub. But he was obviously competent, and experienced, and what he lacked in professional discipline he made up for in human warmth – which was what had been so painfully absent from Giles's life over the past decade. We knew him from Borocourt, where we had been impressed by him and had been sorry to see him leave, and Derek, who is a good judge of character, felt comfortable working with him.

So Wednesdays, like weekends, began to see a distinct improvement in Giles's situation. Unfortunately, the opposite was true of the rest of the week. Even before our complaint, not everyone in Borocourt seemed very enthusiastic about the active interest that Derek and I took in the details of our son's care. I am certain (now) that they would never have harmed a patient in order to get back at his parents; but, equally, it was impossible (then) not to imagine that they might. Every time we gave Giles back into their care, we felt as though we were betraying him. And yet – to repeat yet again a question that we repeated to ourselves many times each day – what else could we do?

Some time later, a colleague, George Zahler, found me sitting alone, weeping, in the conservatory at The Bury, the office that FI still retained in Chesham. (Our headquarters were in Berkhamsted by then.) George asked what the matter was, and I explained that I was at my wits' end, trying to work out how I could save Giles from spending the rest of his life in his prison-like subnormality hospital whose staff hated the Shirley family. We talked it through for a bit, and then he said: "But what about the company?"

I didn't understand at first, but gradually he pressed the point home. Over the past few years F International had grown from a liability into a valuable asset. The value was still all locked up in the company; but what was to stop me selling some shares in it?

I don't think the idea had even occurred to me. I was dimly aware that, as profits had grown in recent years, so the value of the company had increased; I had even vaguely contemplated the implications of that rising value for my personal paper fortune – laughingly wondering if an extra nought or two had been accidentally added to the figures. But until this moment I had never considered that I might turn some of this notional value into hard cash, here and now.

The obvious reason for not doing so was that, once some of the company was owned by outside investors, there would no longer be any possibility of transferring ownership of the company in its entirety to the workforce. My colleague countered this by asking which dream was most important to me. My dream of a staff-owned company? Or my dream of finding Giles a future outside Borocourt?

It was a painful question, and it took me some time to come to terms with the obvious answer. But subsequent discussions with Derek left me in no doubt that Giles's needs had to come first, and in due course I set in motion the process of selling part of my stake in F International to institutional investors. It was a long-drawn-out business, but by the end of that year – 1985 – some 13 per cent of the company was in outside hands, and Derek and I had enough ready cash to change Giles's life.

It was, even then, a slow process. It would be more than two years before we were able to remove Giles from Borocourt altogether. There were endless meetings to be had: with hospital staff, with social services staff, and with any number of representatives of local authorities (for both health and social services and – through a quirk of geography – for both Oxfordshire and Berkshire). There were questions to be resolved about his future medical care, about his financial entitlements, and about our ability to provide care to a standard that the authorities deemed acceptable – all discussed in the shadow of our ongoing complaint against Borocourt. But at least we were moving, slowly, in the right direction.

In due course our aspiration to give Giles a future outside Borocourt crystallised into a firm plan. We would install him permanently at Redcot, while maintaining a formal but reduced link with the hospital, on which we could fall back in emergencies. This required further months of fraught negotiations, but, in the meantime, we took the crucial step of hiring Phil Bunce to be Giles's full-time, live-in carer. We did so with trepidation. Ideally, my son's carer would have been less coarse in his language and less fond of pubs, and perhaps a bit more educated too. Yet in some obscure way Derek and I both knew that it would work. We had seen Phil's faults at Borocourt, but we had also seen his strengths. A big, strong, plain-spoken man, he had – unlike many of his colleagues – seemed unafraid of the residents, talking to them as if they were human beings. He might not have been the model professional, but he was caring, relaxed and respectful, and he had a kind of charisma that patients responded to. We felt sure that this was what Giles needed most.

Phil agreed to work for us full-time and to use his professional connections to hire other carers to work shifts when he was off-duty, so that Giles would have someone keeping an eye on him 24 hours a day. I tried not to think too much about the financial implications. The money I had realised through my sale of shares would not support such an arrangement for long – but with a bit of luck we would be able to recover from the state some of the money it was currently paying to keep Giles at Borocourt. The aforementioned discussions with the relevant local authorities led us to believe that such funding should eventually be forthcoming, but it was clear that it could take many months to jump through all the necessary bureaucratic hoops. In the meantime, every week that Giles remained in Borocourt felt like a week stolen from his life.

We decided to remove him as soon as we practically could – and sort out the finer details later.

It was September 1987 by then, and the hospital management remained implacably opposed to the idea. We were told in no uncertain terms by Dr Shepherd, the consultant in charge of Giles's case, that he did not consider it to be in his patient's best interest to be taken out of the professionally run facility in which he had spent the previous 11 years. Everyone agreed that it was "highly irregular" for a patient to be discharged into the care of a privately hired nurse with a blot on his CV. There was no legal reason to prevent us from discharging Giles: unlike most of Borocourt's patients, he had never been sectioned. But the professional disapproval was overwhelming. Local GPs were discouraged from getting involved with Giles, and it was some time before we could find a practice that would take him on.

It is hard to maintain your confidence, as a layperson, in the face of such robust expert insistence that you are wrong. But Derek and I kept reminding ourselves that things could hardly be any worse for Giles than they were already. At least our plan gave him a chance.

And so it was that, one sunny autumn morning, we led Giles away for the last time from the asylum and moved him into Redcot.

It was one of the most frightening steps we had ever taken, and there were many moments in the next few months when we wondered if we had made a terrible mistake. (If an asylum is a place of safety then, by definition, those who leave an asylum are exposed to danger.) But we never actually regretted it, and would eventually come to think of it as one of the best decisions we had ever taken.

And if we ever had had serious regrets, we would have needed only to look at the subsequent history of Borocourt to reassure ourselves that we had done the right thing. The ward team there was replaced in 1988; then, perhaps as a result of our complaint, the hospital was investigated in 1989 by the National Development Team (NDT), a government-funded advisory board specialising in services for the mentally handicapped. The NDT's report, published in 1990, was scathing. Conditions were described as "very poor", while patients' needs were said to be being neglected. Derek Thomas, director of the NDT, described parts of the hospital as "as bad as any I've seen in my 32 years in the service" and recommended that the hospital be "closed down as soon as possible". It finally closed in February 1992.

16: Big Ideas

It was not just Giles who was about to enter a new phase in his life. The wheels of change were in motion at F International as well.

The key year was 1985. With dizzying speed, landmarks were reached and passed. For example: we disposed (as previously mentioned) of our US subsidiary, Heights, freeing up both time and cash for more profitable activities at home; we set up a new UK subsidiary, Systematix, to develop microcomputer business systems for small companies, with help from my old friend and supporter Kit Grindley; we moved the last remnants of our head office operations into the Berkhamsted HQ; we developed a range of unmanned regional work-centres – positioned close to key motorway junctions and open night and day, seven days a week – for the benefit of home-workers who wanted or needed more direct interaction with their colleagues; we appointed our first group finance director; and we began to roll out our first rudimentary system of electronic mail, linking all our staff on our own purpose-built network. This last step is, with hindsight, such an obvious one to have taken that it is hard to believe that a distributed, IT-based company such as ours could have flourished for 23 years without it. But microcomputers (as personal computers were then known) were still a rarity, and only the most forward-thinking among us had even begun to think about the potential for linking large numbers of such computers together. Our first internal email network – which was fully functional by the end of 1986 – linked into people's homes via their television sets. (This was not, by the way, a popular innovation.)

We had about 1,000 people working for us by then, handling an average of 150 projects a month; getting on for 200 of these people – mainly managers and administrative staff – were salaried employees, largely based in Berkhamsted. Annual revenues that year were £7.6m, with pre-tax profits of about £340,000. Our clients – around 100 at any one time – were more blue-chip than ever: Unilever, IBM, Avis, Exxon, Midland Bank, Scottish Equitable, Coopers & Lybrand, Tesco, the BBC, the Treasury; and the work we did for them was growing more sophisticated. Yet in financial terms we were still only the 20th largest software company in the UK and had barely begun to make an impact globally. Our shares – mainly my shares – had a price-to-earnings ratio of just 7.7 (roughly half the industry average). We were simultaneously a huge success story and a tantalising case of yet-to-be-realised potential.

A survey of all our panel workers, conducted with the help of City Business School at the end of 1984, had revealed an unmistakable thirst for change. People were generally happy with the company, although many would have been happier had they been earning more. Most considered that they "worked for" F International, even though they had no guarantee that we would have any future use for them. Many had been with us for a long time. (I had lost count of the gold watches and bracelets I had handed out in recognition of 10 years' service, and now we had set up a 20 Year Club as well.) And most of them hoped to carry on working for us.

But there was one overwhelming dissatisfaction: people wanted more training, more involvement in decision-making and planning, more scope for personal development. We were already investing large amounts of time and money in training – much more than most companies – and devolving large amounts of responsibility to ordinary panel members. But our people still wanted to contribute more. They knew that the world was changing, and they wanted to be in the vanguard of the gathering global IT revolution. This eagerness represented a huge opportunity for the company. The challenge was finding a way to harness it.

With this as background, in July 1985, we had appointed a new chief executive for our UK operations: Hilary Cropper. I flatter myself that I am reasonably good at spotting, recruiting and developing talent, but I don't think I have ever made a more inspired appointment than Hilary. Headhunters had brought several possible candidates to our attention, but she stood out immediately as someone who might have been tailor-made for F International's needs.

Born and raised near Macclesfield, Cheshire, and educated at convent school and Salford University (where she studied mathematics), Hilary had begun her working life as an apprentice in a large engineering factory in Trafford Park. She did her early computer programming there as well, observing later that, in that overwhelmingly male environment, "you had to prove yourself over and over again. If you weren't better than the average guy you weren't going to get on. You had to prove your worth the whole time." This had left her with ingrained habits of high achievement that seemed to me to make her ideal chief executive material.

Now 44, she had spent much of the past 15 years with ICL, at one point running a big home-working software division for them and more recently heading their Professional Services business. So she had plenty of relevant expertise and experience. She was also at a stage in her life where taking charge of a medium-sized business success story and turning it into a global force to be reckoned with was precisely the sort of challenge she was ready for. Insiders felt that, had she been a man, she would have been on ICL's board by then. As so often in F International's history, a prejudiced workplace's loss was our gain.

The impact of her arrival was felt instantly, right across the organisation. Tough, brash, driven and demanding, Hilary buzzed with a terrier-like energy that made any form of professional complacency unthinkable in her presence. Perhaps more importantly, her ambitions for herself and for the company knew no bounds.

Even I found this a bit of a shock. She made no secret of the fact that she thought the company was underperforming – and that she saw the chief executive's position as an opportunity to make her fortune in financial terms as well as career terms. She insisted on a big salary, a big car and generous share options – with similar deals for other senior management. The options meant little at the time, since our shares were not publicly traded and we had never yet paid a dividend. But Hilary had ideas about that; and, in the meantime, it seemed reasonable to accede to the demands of a chief executive who had such a clear vision of how to unlock F International's unrealised potential. Also, of course, such options represented one more way of – ultimately – getting some of the ownership of the company into the hands of those who worked for it.

I remained group managing director of the F International Group (which at that point still included our Dutch, American and Danish subsidiaries, as well as an overseas operating company called FI Services and a small telecommunications venture called Sprint Telecoms), although over the next three years we would dispose of the foreign subsidiaries one by one (starting, later that year, with Heights). I stepped up my involvement in public life, serving (for example) six years on the Council of the Industrial Society (1984-90) and three years on the newly formed National Council for Vocational Qualifications (1986-89). I also acted as our external ambassador and, at board level, as an arbiter of last resort. But to a large extent I tried simply to keep out of the way, alternately congratulating myself on an inspired appointment and worrying that I might have unleashed a monster.

I needn't, on the whole, have worried. Hilary brought to the company an outsider's clarity of vision, which enabled her to spot and slaughter sacred cows with a detachment and ruthlessness that would have been impossible for an internally promoted chief executive. Yet she left intact the things that really mattered: our flexibility, our trust and empowerment of our staff, our ethics, our team spirit, and our collective belief that we could and should be the very best.

The full story of Hilary's 17-year involvement with the company deserves a book of its own, and I will relate only the highlights here. From my point of view, her tenure as chief executive was significant in three ways. It led, gradually, to my almost complete disengagement from the company (culminating in my retirement in 1993). It allowed me to take my dreams of staff ownership as far as they could practically be taken. And it did much (thanks to some spectacular successes in the 1990s) to empower me to begin the next – and arguably most important – chapter of my life. But all these outcomes were still some way off.

In the short term, Hilary's main strategic innovation was to insist that we focused all our efforts on the three market sectors that were most profitable for us: commercial, financial and public. Other markets – including the various foreign ones that I had been exploring – were, as she saw it, more trouble than they were worth. Perhaps I should have felt threatened or affronted by her forthright expression of these views, but on balance I felt that she was correct. In any case, it was only right that she should lead the company as she saw fit.

I continued to provide advice, guidance and symbolic oversight, but Hilary had little need for such things. She sensed, correctly, that our origins as a female-friendly company (and by implication as my brainchild) were no longer relevant to what we had to offer. As she put it – when urging me to make less of the "woman thing" in my public appearances – we were in danger of being known for who we were rather than what we did.

For similar reasons, she urged us to cut free from our cottage industry roots, which were betrayed both by our constant retelling of the story of our origins and by such amateur habits as our collective use of the term "sales" to refer to what anyone else in the business world would call "orders", and "revenue" to denote what others would call "sales". Our amateurism had been a virtue in the early days: we had worked for Freelance Programmers partly because we loved it, we had broken new ground because we didn't know any better, and we had survived and thrived partly because we adopted the low-cost, no-debt model of an amateur enterprise. Now, however, we were in a new kind of game, and a new mind-set was called for. We needed to think of ourselves as a blue-chip service company, providing top-of-the-range services for blue-chip clients (or "customers", as Hilary insisted on calling them).

I had always run the company on the basis of minimum cost – spending as little as possible on everything to reduce the danger of our outgoings outstripping our income. Hilary argued (and in retrospect I can see that she was right) that this approach was holding the company back, and that it was better to spend more in order to achieve maximum efficiency. In other words, we needed to think big.

All this was disconcerting, but it was backed up by convincing market research showing that potential clients now saw such ideas as "freelance" and "home-working" as suggesting a lack of professionalism. And so, before long, the background briefings about the company issued by our press officers ceased to make any mention of the company's origins as a flexible, home-based, female-friendly enterprise started with next to no capital on my dining-room table. Instead, it became simply "a leading computer systems company committed to delivering high quality, managed projects. It offers its clients exceptional flexibility through its use of its nationwide network of industry-experienced IT professionals."

I cannot pretend that this didn't hurt. Sometimes I felt as though I was being airbrushed out of history: as though I was an embarrassment to the company. (I felt this much later, as well, when Hilary was being fêted for her spectacular success with the company, and no one seemed interested in the golden legacy she had started out with.) But I also knew that my feelings were irrelevant. I wanted to pass on control, I had identified Hilary as the best person to whom to pass it, and it was up to me to deal with the emotional consequences.

In any case, for all the upheaval, I never really felt that Hilary lost sight of what the company stood for. I was uncomfortable with her personal style: unlike me, she rarely seemed to be troubled by self-doubt, and at times I felt that she was domineering. But she left the essence of the company intact, while her vision for its future had much in common with mine.

And one change that it was impossible to find fault with was the difference she made to the balance sheet. This had been her big selling-point when we appointed her. She had marked her arrival with a public pledge to double turnover within three years, and she achieved this comfortably. Turnover was £7.6m in 1985, £9.1m in 1986, £10.6m in 1987 and £15.5m in 1988. Profits increased even more impressively, from £340,000 in 1985 to £1m in 1988. And that was just the beginning of her ambitions (and, it turned out, of her achievements).

Hilary's analysis – which seems obvious now but was farsighted at the time – was that we had to expand or die. If the IT industry as a whole was growing at breakneck speed, we would rapidly become an insignificant player unless we grew with it; and an insignificant player would struggle to retain and attract not just top-drawer clients but also the bright, ambitious workforce who were our main asset and selling-point. Comfortable as it might be to carry on as a contented, medium-sized enterprise, that wasn't an option. The choice was between, on the one hand, breakneck growth as a world leader – and, on the other, rapid decline.

Hilary also saw growth as the key to improving our profit margins, which in 1985 were just 4.4 per cent, compared with an industry average of between 7 and 10 per cent. At Contract Professional Services, the home-working network that she had been running at ICL, the margin was 11 per cent (although that did not include the infrastructure costs of the main company). The bigger the business, she argued, the easier it was to spread and absorb the inevitable costs of training, research and development. So she focused her efforts – with my support – on doing bigger, more profitable jobs for bigger clients. One of her proudest early boasts was that the number of projects we did with a value of £500,000 or more tripled between 1986 and 1988. Another was that, between

1985 and 1988, earnings per share quadrupled, while the value of our net assets tripled in the same period.

She also looked to expand, eventually, through acquisitions and mergers, and did not rule out the idea that we should become a publicly quoted company. This was first mooted by our new outside shareholders, and would later be embraced – with rather shocking alacrity – by the very staff members to whom I was in the process of transferring my shares. It was, however, an idea that made me uneasy. If the company's shares were freely traded, it could easily become controlled by outside shareholders, and then anything might happen to it. Nothing would remain to anchor it to its values, and it could all too easily become just another corporation, committed only to the pursuit of profit at all costs.

Yet there were limits to what I could do to keep back the tide of change. There were other shareholders, including the FI Shareholders' Trust, who had views on the matter, and they were all keen for the company to be floated as soon as possible. Hilary's projections for future growth made many people feel that they were sitting on a goldmine; and even I, with my growing commitment to paying for a better life for Giles, was attracted by the idea of increasing the company's value. So I focused instead on trying to get as much of the company as possible into the hands of the workforce before we floated.

It all seemed to happen surprisingly fast. In August 1985 F International re-registered as a public limited company. This was partly a symbolic change: we did not become publicly quoted (as PLCs usually are). But, just as had happened when we became a limited company in 1964, the effect was to impart a new sense of seriousness and urgency to the enterprise. If we were a proper PLC – like ICI, BA, BT and all our other blue-chip clients – we needed to start thinking big.

The change also made it easier to introduce proper corporate governance. We resolved to conduct ourselves according to the "Blue Book" of company law for public companies (actually called the Butterworths Company Law Handbook), just as if we were publicly quoted. Within two years Harvard Business Review was writing admiringly about our corporate structure, which it described as "a classic but flat pyramid", with "seven layers of management" separating me – the group managing director – from the ordinary panel members. The different layers reported upwards formally, through board meetings and executive committees, and proper boundaries were observed between strategic responsibilities at board level and the operational issues that were the remit of the lower echelons of management. This was a big adjustment for me: I still found it hard not to think of the company as a huge extended family. But, by the same token, it was clearly what the company needed if it was to compete at the top of the global marketplace. It also made it more attractive to potential investors.

But the main point of our new status, as far as I was concerned, was that it allowed us to make share offers directly to the staff. Shares had been transferred to the FI Shareholders' Trust on an annual basis since 1981, and by 1985 the Trust had a stake of more than 17 per cent of the company; but I think it's fair to say that only a tiny handful of staff members had any more sense of owning the company then than they had done before the transfers began (even though the Trust balloted them from time to time for instructions on how to vote at general meetings). Now, however, they had the opportunity to own shares directly, purchased with their own money. Perhaps that would make a difference.

Later that year, shares equal to 11.2 per cent of issued plus new share capital were offered to F International's workforce. Just over half were taken up, as around 24 per cent of the staff bought shares under this offer.

This was a significant development. Derek and I had owned 81.9 per cent of the company at the beginning of 1985. By the end of the year we owned just 66.4 per cent of it. Around 13 per cent was owned by two institutional investors, Baronsmead Venture Capital and New Court Trust (from the distress sale mentioned in Chapter 15), and 16.8 per cent was owned by the FI Shareholders' Trust (whose holding – 17.9 per cent at the beginning of the year – had been diluted by the new rights issue), leaving nearly three per cent owned directly by individual workforce shareholders. So it was still effectively my company. But the sense of my being a remote proprietor whose interests were quite distinct from those of the workforce was greatly reduced. Those staff who were actively interested in owning part of the company now did so in a much more direct way. And the combined holding of the trust and the individual staff shareholders, equivalent to nearly a fifth of the company, gave them a weight at board level that could not be ignored.

There was, of course, no way for staff to sell their shares on the open market, but we operated a surprisingly successful internal market. Twice a year, two independent valuers would help us to determine the price of the shares, and shareholders declared their intention to buy or sell as they saw fit. (Such decisions were as likely to reflect personal financial circumstances as changing views about the company's prospects.) If buyers and sellers could not be matched, I would act as purchaser or seller of last resort.

Whatever the limitations of the arrangement, it was a significant improvement on how things had been before. Holders of the staff-owned shares now had more than a theoretical interest in the company's success. If the company thrived and increased in value, their own personal wealth would grow with it; conversely, a bad year for the company could have direct personal consequences.

Even then, there remained a majority of the workforce to whom the idea of co-ownership appeared to mean nothing (even though they were all beneficiaries, indirectly, of the FI Shareholders' Trust). Yet it was plain that, little by little, significant numbers of key employees were starting to think of F International as their company, and the idea was sinking in that, for those who wanted to enjoy the fruits of their labours, a rich harvest might be in prospect. I have no doubt that this played a significant role in the company's continued success and growth over the next few years.

17: Losing My Grip

In 1987 we celebrated our silver jubilee. Several hundred past and current members of our workforce gathered at the National Exhibition Centre in Birmingham for a big party. It was an emotional day, on which the formal speeches and presentations mattered less than the sheer warmth of the reunion. As the shrieks of recognition gave way to a hum of animated catching-up, I found it hard to keep the tears from my eyes. It felt as though a large part of my life was passing before me, and it was disconcerting to be reminded of how lucky I had been, of just how much time had passed, and of just how many people had given the best of themselves to bring F International to a successful maturity. And it was positively overwhelming to realise that, whatever mistakes I had made over the previous 25 years, most of the people whose lives my company had touched still seemed to feel warmly towards me.

Few of the party-goers were unscarred by the passage of time, but we had come through it all, and we could look back on what we had achieved with justifiable pride. We all knew how sceptical the world had been about our chances of making the company work. But we had not only survived: we had remained rather fond of one another. Obviously, not everyone saw eye-to-eye about everything, but, on the whole, we rather enjoyed each other's company, as we were now reminded. And that, of course, had been one of the secrets of our success.

We also paid our first ever dividend that year. I suppose it was remarkable that we had come so far without having done so, but as the main shareholder I had never really seen the company as a mechanism for generating cash. Rather, it had been an end in itself, which needed to make money in order to secure its own future. Now, suddenly, all the shareholders, including the individual workforce shareholders, could see that "profit" was not just an abstract idea.

Nor was it just those who had bought shares who made this discovery. Earlier in the year I had taken the unusual step of giving each member of our workforce a single share in the company as a "jubilee gift". These were of minimal value in themselves (about 25p each), but giving them meant that, as and when we issued new share

*In 1987 we had a big party at the National Exhibition Centre,
Birmingham to celebrate the company's Silver Jubilee.*

capital, every member of the workforce would have the legal right (as an existing shareholder) to buy new shares if they wished to do so. The dividend was too small for most of them to notice, but no one could now be unaware of the fact that they were being actively encouraged to participate in the company's future success.

To further this process, I now made my biggest transfer so far of my own shares to the FI Shareholders' Trust, bringing its stake up from 17 per cent (which it had climbed back up to again in 1986) to 24 per cent.

Hilary, whom we had promoted in May 1987 to be group chief executive in my stead, was determined that this should be the ceiling for the Trust's shareholding; otherwise, she insisted, potential investors would be deterred. So I began to explore instead the possibility of simply selling most of Derek's and my shareholding (now just 51.4 per cent between us) to whichever staff members were interested in buying it. To this end I began to cast around for additional board members with specialist knowledge of such proceedings.

Meanwhile, we prepared a prospectus for what everyone assumed would be an imminent float. (This took me by surprise. I had naïvely assumed that co-ownership would be seen as a goal in itself – but most people were more interested in converting their shareholdings into cash.) The main thing I remember about this prospectus was that the editor charged with preparing it insisted on using the word "he" in contexts where "he or she" was clearly required. When I challenged this, he explained that this was "merely a convention" and that, furthermore, a tiny footnote at the bottom of one of the inside pages explained that this convention was being used. Very well, I said: let's change both the footnote and the convention. And so it was that our prospectus went out, notwithstanding Hilary's reservations, with the word "she" used to stand for both masculine and feminine personal pronouns, and a small footnote somewhere explaining that this convention was being used.

As it happened, the prospectus had to be redone anyway, because in 1988 we changed the company's name again, at an Extraordinary General Meeting. Research had indicated that the "F" in F International was generating both confusion (did it stand for "Freelance"? "Flexible"? "Female"? Or something else?) and ambivalence (people were as likely to be put off by those f-words as to be enthused by them). Our new

There's something exhilarating about co-ownership when things are going well. This was at the Hemel Hempstead office.

name, FI Group, didn't seem to elicit such negative reactions, yet remained close enough to previous names to prevent doubts as to who we were.

We certainly didn't want to jeopardise the goodwill that already existed for us in the corporate world. A study of The Times' 1987 Top 500 Companies list had found that fully 25 per cent of the companies listed were FI Group clients. More impressively still, 50 of the list's top 100 were our clients – and eight of its top 10. From Sun Alliance to Allied Breweries, BICC to Fiat Auto UK, corporate big-hitters clearly felt that we had a service worth buying, and it was this, rather than any clever wording in our prospectus, that made us such an appetising prospect for the markets. The 1980s had seen a transformation in the relationship between business and IT: when the decade began, most companies still considered computers a marginal specialism; when it ended, there was scarcely a boardroom in the land that did not see IT-based strategies as the key to future prosperity. FI Group was both a cause and a beneficiary of this shift in attitudes. The main challenge now was to reap the harvest – and Hilary ensured that we did so with energy and enthusiasm.

I was also gratified to note that, in 1987, the quality standard that we had written some time earlier for the Ministry of Defence – based on quality standards created by Freelance Programmers in 1962 – was upgraded to be the NATO standard. It would be hard to imagine a more overwhelming riposte to the sexist machismo that we had fought in our early years. If even the military-industrial complex used us as a benchmark for quality, we really had conquered the world.

In fact, the dizzying rate of our growth – and that of the IT industry generally – slowed markedly at the end of the decade, in an early sign of what the wider economy would experience as the recession of 1990-92. (If you want to spot a recession in advance, keep an eye on the IT industry.) Our figures were on the mend again by 1991, but it did not seem a propitious time to be going to the market, and plans for a float were put on hold.

Instead, Hilary's ambitions to expand found expression in a series of strategic acquisitions, of which the most significant were AMP Computer Recruitment (in 1990) and Kernel Group (in 1991). These not only increased the company's size and scope but made it better balanced – allowing us, for example, to provide clients with staffing solutions that would help them run the IT systems we had set up for them. Those two acquisitions would in due course form the raw material for, respectively, FI Recruitment and FI Training.

Meanwhile, I was determined to press on with my plans for shared ownership, and the board saw that my desire to sell at the bottom of the market gave a good opportunity for effecting such a transfer. I persuaded Sir Peter Thompson, who in 1982 had successfully led a management buy-out when he was chief executive of the National Freight Corporation, to take over from Leighton Davies as chairman of FI Group in October 1990. Peter was also chairman of the CBI's Wider Share Ownership Task Force, and was seen by many as a leading authority on the transfer of company ownership into staff hands.

Peter insisted that, if we wanted to achieve a real change of culture and persuade the workforce to think of the company as their company, it was no good making piecemeal transfers of shares year by year. No matter how many shares I gave away (and by the end of 1990 a third of the workforce held shares), everyone still thought of it as my company. If we wanted them to think of it as their company, we needed to transform the company's ownership structure in a single dramatic swoop: what he called "Big Bang".

So: under Peter's guidance, the board gave the go-ahead for the sale to the workforce, in the autumn of 1991, of "a substantial proportion of the Founder's shares". A prospectus was prepared, the necessary legal and financial hoops were jumped through, and we began an internal publicity campaign to stir up enthusiasm. We also amended our articles of association to give double voting rights to shares held by those who currently worked for the company. Finally, just over 1,000 of our staff (319 employees and 690 self-employed associates) were invited to buy shares in the company in September 1991. Shares equivalent to 30 per cent of my remaining holding were offered at £2.70 each, and the minimum subscription was 50 shares for £135. My only stipulation was that the workforce had to be keen enough to invest at least £1m in the shares between them.

Around three-quarters of the employees, and a third of the self-employed contractors, took up the offer. The price was a generous one, capitalising the company modestly at about £6.2m, and those who took up the offer could theoretically have sold at a profit on almost any day thereafter. But most hung on in hope of the big payday that public flotation would bring.

It was not quite the John Lewis-style partnership that I had dreamed about. I continued to have my own private stake in the company. And a significant stake – which might easily grow in future – was held by outside investors whose overwhelming priority was profit. None the less, the sale represented a significant piece of empowerment. From the end of 1991, F International was controlled on major issues by the combined voting power of the staff shareholders and the Shareholders' Trust, who between them had a 43 per cent interest and (because of double voting) 62 per cent of the voting rights, while a substantial majority of those who worked for the company had a direct financial stake in its future.

Employee participation was no longer just a buzzword. This workforce actually owned the company.

And I didn't.

18: A Second Childhood

Losing control of the company that had dominated my life for nearly three decades was never going to be easy, even though it had been my choice to let it go. But some of the consequences were immediately welcome. I was, for the first time since 1962, financially independent of the business. Hitherto, my general intention to cede control to a new regime had been frustrated in practice by the fact that any notional assets I had were tied up in FI Group. Now, although I retained a substantial shareholding in the company (just under 36 per cent), my voice and views were no longer of major significance. For better or worse, the company was going to manage without me.

I thus found myself freer than I had been for years. I was still employed by FI, and gave them good value for my salary (which finished up at £100,000 a year). But my enthusiastic pursuit of the company's interests no longer involved sleepless nights. I was free from responsibility for the running of the business, free from the need to pour large quantities of time and effort into FI-related duties, and even free – thanks to my sale of shares – from short-term financial worry.

I had other, public duties (of which more later) to take up much of the slack. But the biggest benefit for me was that I was free to devote more attention – more emotional energy – to Giles.

The timing could hardly have been better. Caring for Giles "in the community" had been proving even more demanding than I had anticipated.

The initial transition from Borocourt to Redcot had, predictably, been traumatic. A young man who felt threatened and distressed even by minor changes of routine had suddenly to take on board a complete transformation in his lifestyle. He was living in a different place, with different people and, above all, in a different way. From being locked away in an institution which rarely aspired to anything more than damage limitation, he was suddenly at the centre of his world again, cared for by people whose priority was to maximise his quality of life. Anxiety and anger were the perverse but predictable short-term consequences.

The initial challenge was, in effect, to make Giles human again. He was not only profoundly vulnerable but had become profoundly institutionalised. Many of the obvious attractions of Redcot – the freedom, the one-to-one care – must, at first, have terrified him. But Phil Bunce rose to the challenge heroically, calmly containing tantrums, keeping damage to patient, carer and property to a minimum, and, all the time, encouraging Giles to believe in himself. It helped that Phil was physically huge and strong and seemed unperturbed by violent rages that most of us found terrifying. He also had the patience and good humour to communicate to Giles, eventually, the idea that he was loved, valued and respected again. He seemed to see Giles as a friend rather than a problem to be solved.

On the plus side, Giles's epilepsy was largely under control by now, subject to careful medication. But his behaviour remained highly challenging. An underlying norm of being "difficult" – roaring and refusing to do as he was asked – would be punctuated irregularly by interludes of frightening anger. Then he would thump and bang things, including his head, and, sometimes, lash out at people. We tried to take all this in our stride, but it wasn't always easy, especially when we remembered that we had, to all intents and purposes, forgone the safety net of the health and social services. One of my most vivid memories of this period is of the weekend ritual of the post-lunch walk. If we timed it right, it could be the highlight of our and Giles's week: a shared stroll through the countryside which combined fresh air, exercise, togetherness and, usually, a bit of laughter as well. But if we tried to leave a moment too late, or too soon, or failed to guess the precise amount of time that Giles considered appropriate for getting ready, it would all end – and indeed begin – in tears. Giles would not just refuse to come out with us but would rage, roar, lie on the floor and bang his head with frustration and fury. I cannot convey how traumatic this was for all of us, and it was tempting to abandon the idea of walks altogether. But we could not bring ourselves to deprive Giles of one of the happier features of his circumscribed life; and, in any case, tantrums could also result if Giles felt that we weren't going for a walk when we should have been doing so.

For Phil and his fellow-carers, such dilemmas arose every day. I am full of admiration and gratitude for the fact that they didn't just give up in despair. But it was more stressful than it might sound for me to try to manage all this from a distance – liaising with Phil by telephone while making any necessary arrangements for, for example, visits to the doctor to have self-inflicted injuries seen to, in between doing my work and trying to make sure that the necessary finance was in place. I remember at least one tearful telephone conversation with Giles's GP, at some point in his first year outside Borocourt, when I confessed that I simply didn't feel able to deal with the situation any more. The proximity of Borocourt and its specialist staff merely exacerbated my misery: we were, unfortunately, at odds with the very bureaucracies and institutions that had been put in place to help people like Giles.

But things gradually improved. Giles's moodiness, we realised, stemmed less from a dislike of being at Redcot than from the fact that he had to a large degree forgotten how to feel contented. The key was thus to increase his contentment. This was where Phil's unconventional gifts came into their own. He fussed less than he should have done about keeping the cottage clean and tidy, or about Giles's diet or personal hygiene. But he did treat Giles as a human being, taking him on long walks and talking to him as an adult and an equal. He took him on bus trips and shopping trips and trips to the pub, and even invited him back to his own run-down bedsit. He gave him jigsaws to do, and art materials to run riot with; and, perhaps most important of all, he never betrayed the least sign of having been upset by any of Giles's outbursts, tantrums and physical attacks.

Bit by bit, Giles was eased into a new life. The outbursts continued, but grew milder and rarer. He learnt to accept his new routines, and learnt to think of Phil as a friend. Derek and I continued our visiting routine. And Phil built up a roster of other carers to provide 24-hour cover – some of whom were clearly not up to the job but others of whom shared Phil's determination to inject some human warmth into Giles's life. Paul Moran – another rather rough diamond, though less so than Phil – fell firmly into the latter category. He was lovely with Giles, taking him off on walks and expeditions (to the local shop, for example) as if they were brothers or best mates. Paul would play a big part in Giles's life for more than a dozen years.

But for all these positive developments, it was also clear that this ad hoc arrangement was flawed. Giles remained highly volatile, and Redcot remained no more than an old-fashioned, rickety cottage, with two tiny bedrooms, no upstairs toilet and a steep, narrow staircase. It was far from ideal either as a place for three or four people to be in at once or as a place for containing tantrums and seizures.

Within a year, we had taken a deep financial breath and bought another house. It was a bungalow, about a mile from the hospital, on the other side of Kingwood Common. Called The Cuddy, it was bigger and more modern than Redcot (which we sold soon afterwards to help finance the purchase), with a wide, empty garden. We spent quite a lot of money on modernising it further, making it as suitable as possible for an unpredictable, epileptic, autistic young man. By the end, there was scarcely a breakable thing in the house, let alone a sharp corner or a vulnerable electrical outlet. There was also room for both us and a carer to be there comfortably alongside Giles.

Giles and Phil moved in as soon as it was ready, and, although this meant more upheaval for Giles, it was worth it. Slowly but surely, we all settled into a different way of living. Looking back on it now, I tend to remember the next few years as almost idyllic. Yet I know that this is inaccurate.

The true story is preserved in the conscientious case notes that his various carers kept for much of the next decade. Leafing through these today, I can find scarcely a page that does not contain some report of tantrums, rages and destructive behaviour. The following examples, selected at random from a few consecutive pages, give a flavour of the relentless challenge Giles posed to those charged with looking after him:

"4 May: The furniture in Giles's room has been quite damaged... The door, too, which was re-hung, needs mending following incidents..." "20 July: Whilst having a bath Giles completely lost control and became in danger of significant self-injury... Later in the day Giles... proceeded to his room where he started to throw furniture about; he smashed a small chest of drawers in this incident..." "11 August: Giles was heard to be shouting and roaring. He appeared to have been disturbed by a bad dream or hallucination... He then lost control and began to throw furniture before attempting to attack staff members in the corridor, upon which Giles was restrained using minimum necessary force." "1 November: Giles had a violent tantrum in the bathroom, he ripped the mirror from the wall and flung the toiletries from the shelves to the floor..." "11 November: Giles roared and head-butted his door... Loud bangs were also heard from his room during the evening/night." "27 February: Giles hit himself in the genitals whilst on a walk..." "24 April: Giles... acted in a threatening posture towards some children playing in the lane." "5 May: Giles...appeared highly agitated, having already punched his door. He arrived in the kitchen where he made manic requests for tea, which staff denied; following this he punched Martin [a carer] in the face, and then was immediately restrained using minimum necessary force [i.e., within the bounds of approved social services practice] ..."

I could cite scores, if not hundreds, of such instances but will not do so. No amount of habituation lessens the pain that a mother feels on witnessing, or even being told about, such episodes in her son's life; and the stabs of sympathetic misery seem scarcely less intense when I read about them now. What agonies lay behind these inscrutable outbursts? I can only wonder – and weep.

I have before me several years' worth of monthly reports. Each concludes with a monthly "behavioural chart", listing such behaviour in tabular form. For example (randomly selecting November 1996):

> "... Anxious words: 83
> Exposing himself: 20
> Gesticulating: 14
> Grimacing: 2
> Head-butting: 1
> Hitting himself: 4
> Holding fist to chin: 1
> Increase in volume: 70
> Knocking or tapping on windows: 10
> Need to restrain: 1
> Punching or hitting things: 16
> Self-restraint: 1
> Shoulder-barging: -
> Shouting and roaring: 22
> Throwing objects: 8
> Trance-like states: 2 ..."

That gives you an idea of the scale and range of the challenge that Giles's behaviour posed. But what strikes me about such statistics now is not how depressing they are but, rather, the improvement they show. They remind me how much more manageable his behaviour gradually became (by November 1996 he had been in The Cuddy for eight years), compared with the very blackest days just before he went into Borocourt and immediately after he came out. The incidents remained distressing, but their frequency and gravity had declined.

In the same way, what strikes me about the daily notes is not their tireless instancing of unruly, destructive or dangerous behaviour but the fact that such behaviour begins after a while to be punctuated by other things: "Giles seemed reasonably friendly to visitors..."; "He has shown some interest in art and produced a couple of colourful drawings..."; "Giles has... shown some interest of his own volition in gardening, and now frequently goes outside to pick up laurel leaves, putting them in the bonfire pit."; "Giles interacted fairly well with staff and visitors throughout November."; "Giles enjoyed and participated well in his new activity of trampolining."; "Giles... has participated in cake-making, bread-making and cooking..."; "Giles has been involved in choosing some new clothes..."

This is why my memories of this period are – as I mentioned earlier – fond. We were thrilled by such little examples of progress, in the same way that parents of "normal" children are thrilled by their offspring's more glamorous achievements. But what really mattered about such developments was their significance for Giles himself. Bit by bit, he was discovering stepping-stones that might lead him a little way out of his own closed world. And while no one imagined that they would lead him very far, at least he was finally getting a little bit of stimulation and variety in his life. I can see him there now, engrossed in his painting, still strangely handsome (despite the facial scars that he had accumulated from years of tantrums, accidents and seizures), a holy innocent glowing with the secret beauties of his own private world...

I must not exaggerate. I must not rewrite the past by pretending that these days were happier than they were. Giles's problems remained profound and intractable; time spent with him was still usually, at some level, heart-breaking. The good moments were good, and often profoundly beautiful, but they were rare. A creative activity such as preparing food might engage him utterly for five to ten minutes, creating an irresistible sense that here was a well-adjusted young man absorbed in a satisfying and fulfilling task; then his attention would wander, and the clouds of confusion and frustration would descend again. Yet these post-Borocourt years were, in one crucial respect,

Giles was a strong man and it was good to see him take a positive part in day-to-day activities.

quite different from any previous stage in Giles's life. For the first time, we felt that we could reasonably hope that things might, as time passed, get better: not much better, perhaps, nor very quickly; but still, to some tiny but perceptible degree, better. And that simple flicker of hope made all the pain, exhaustion and worry significantly easier to bear.

But that, as it turned out, was only part of the story. What began as a simple attempt to increase Giles's quality of life became, in due course, something much bigger.

The initial catalyst for expansion was our realisation that, once Giles had settled into The Cuddy, his standard of living was almost embarrassingly high – and certainly a lot higher than mine and Derek's. We laughed at this when it first occurred to us, but before long I had begun to wonder if it wasn't rather extravagant for so much care and money to be lavished on one young man, no matter how beloved. I have never been comfortable with waste, and have spent much of my life imagining ways of achieving efficiencies. So perhaps it was hardly surprising that, early in the 1990s, I found myself floating the idea that this bungalow and this team could with very little extra investment provide a similar standard of care for two people rather than one. I began to make discreet inquiries as to whether or not there was another disabled young man in the area who might benefit from joining Giles in The Cuddy.

This train of thought was soon joined by another one. After more than five years of caring for Giles in the community, our finances were close to meltdown. (Derek was slower than me to pick up on this problem, which caused us to have several heated arguments. He was never much good with money. We'd been sharing a bank account for well over 20 years before he realised that "O/D" on a bank statement stood for "overdrawn".) Providing this level of care was cripplingly expensive – more than £90,000 a year, excluding the capital cost of buying The Cuddy – and the proceeds of my share sale had been all but wiped out. This meant that the cost was increasingly being met from my own £100,000-a-year salary – after I had paid nearly half of it to the state in tax. This was terrifying. I had no objection to spending whatever wealth I had on Giles's well-being, but expenditure at a rate of nearly £1m of taxed income per decade was simply suicidal, especially since I was approaching retirement age (in 1993). And, in any case, Giles had a statutory entitlement to support from the state.

When we took Giles out of Borocourt in 1987 we were assured – orally – that he would not thereby lose his entitlement to assistance from the state (which had been paying to keep him in Borocourt). But the precise details had been complex, partly because of changes that were then in motion to do with the care of the learning disabled, and partly because of a disagreement between Berkshire and Oxfordshire County Councils as to which of them was responsible for Giles's case. (Borocourt was right on the border between the two counties, and had been founded jointly by the two councils in 1930; Giles was for some reason deemed to have been admitted from Berkshire but discharged into Oxfordshire.) Our concern back then had simply been to get Giles out of Borocourt as quickly as possible, and we had taken it on trust that the financial details would be sorted out in due course.

It would take several chapters to describe the subsequent saga in detail, but the long and the short of it was that, six years later, despite innumerable letters and meetings, the sorting-out had yet to be completed, and Giles's care had, in the meantime, been funded almost entirely by us. (A large annual grant from the Independent Living Fund, set up in 1988, had taken up some of the burden. This was much appreciated but nothing like enough to reduce our own contribution to a sustainable level.) So we devoted an increasing amount of time to putting pressure on the relevant authorities to resolve the situation; and, in the course of these indescribably protracted and frustrating negotiations, the idea arose that it might be more cost-effective, in several ways, to make The Cuddy's activities charitable.

Like many of my ideas, this one took time to gestate. The general concept was that the Cuddy would take in an extra resident or two, so achieving considerable economies of scale with overheads, staff, etc. The Cuddy would at the same time become a charitable concern, whose activities (providing residential care for young men with autism) would be financed both with payments from the relevant local authorities (e.g., Residential Care Allowance) and with top-up payments from a charitable trust that I set up around that time (1993) for that purpose. I could then pay for the Cuddy out of gross rather than net income, and the whole project would become significantly more sustainable – while the extra resident or residents might see their quality of life improve dramatically.

It turned out to be a lot more complicated than that. I won't go into all the regulatory and procedural details. But one point that soon became clear was that we would need two extra residents, not one, before we could be considered for charitable status. There was no question of rushing the process of finding new residents whose needs matched what the Cuddy and its staff could offer, and so in the short term we contented ourselves with step one in the process: finding one extra resident and seeing where that led to.

Some months later, Giles was introduced to his new housemate. James Beville was a wild, slightly elfin teenager who liked to run around the garden emitting inarticulate shrieks of what sounded like joy. His schooldays so far had, by the sound of things, been extremely difficult, for him and his parents, for much the same reasons that Giles's had been; and it was wonderful to feel that we could put the fruits of our painful journey to good use beyond our own family. Giles himself, though initially disconcerted when this new companion appeared in his life, would ultimately respond positively to the experience of sharing his world with another difficult and unpredictable young man.

The only people who never learnt to accept the new arrival were the neighbours, who unleashed a series of petty and, to my mind, disgraceful complaints. I think it might have been the rough language of some of the carers that disturbed them as much as the "shame" of having such young men in the neighbourhood. I replied politely to their complaints, seething with inner contempt. There were also two little girls living nearby, who used to mock James. We hoped he did not notice overmuch.

Generally, though, the Cuddy and its residents thrived. Giles, in particular, became unrecognisable as the distressed young man we had liberated from Borocourt. You would never have imagined that he was anything but handicapped; but the aura of wild, frustrated rage had dissipated, and he began to seem less like a threatening monster and more like a charming innocent. The outbursts and tantrums never stopped, but they became almost rare, and we learnt to recognise in their place that peculiar hum, or "severation", by which people with autism often indicate contentment.

Phil Bunce moved on after a few years, and so, much later, did Paul Moran. But Giles was able to form attachments to several of those who came after, as he matured into his thirties in the 1990s: Stephen and Carol Bradley, who began to manage The Cuddy as if it were a proper care-home business ; David Williams, who succeeded them in 1994; and staff such as Martin Beek, Mary-Jane Sheridan (on whom Giles clearly had a romantic crush), Carol Kelly, Jane Henderson and many others – all employed with the proceeds of FI Group's success. There were several non-speaking roles, too, played by the carers' pets, including a succession of dogs – Tess, Rusty, Amy, Eric, Sasha – who helped Giles to overcome completely the fear of dogs that he had developed during his Borocourt years, and, most notably, Daisy the Cat, whose saintly patience even extended to allowing Giles to trim her whiskers with scissors. (Daisy initially arrived with her mother, the princess-like Woolly, who found the household a little too lively for her tastes and before long took herself elsewhere.)

As time passed, the range of stimulation to which Giles could safely be exposed grew broader. He went on day-trips – shopping in Oxford or Reading, for example – and, eventually, on longer breaks: to Norfolk, to Bognor Regis, to Somerset, to Ireland, even to Disneyland in Paris. He remained suspicious of the unusual, with volatile emotions and a short attention span, and he needed even closer supervision than usual when he was on his travels. But there was no doubt that, on balance, sustained, supervised exposure to suitable new experiences improved his quality of life significantly. He became, in a sense, a changed person. After five years or so in The Cuddy he was doing things of his own accord that would have been unthinkable when he was in Borocourt. He would come out and greet us when we arrived to see him. He liked to get involved in unpacking the shopping. Sometimes, without prompting, he would help to wash up or lay the table; he would also choose to initiate a range of constructive activities, from painting to gardening to hitting tennis balls (which he liked to do with Derek). He enjoyed doing jigsaws, too, and learnt to complete them without looking at the pictures.

He would also – up to a point – speak. It is hard to know to what extent this was a development on his part or on that of his family and carers. Perhaps it was partly that we had learnt to understand his vocalisations better; but I have no doubt that it was also a question of his becoming more interested in the possibilities of communication. I don't suppose a stranger would have been able to interpret many of the sounds, but for those who knew him Giles's vocabulary would ultimately grow to include: "bee", "bunny", "butter", "button", "cake", "cat", "chips", "Daddy", "Daisy", "duck", "fan", "Giles", "hen", "home", "hello", "mate", "mind", "more", "orange", "owl", "pain", "Paul", "pie", "pin", "tea", "toast", "toilet", "tired", "vet", "what", "you". It wasn't much, for a grown man who was 24 when he came out of Borocourt and about 30 when that list of words was noted down. But it represented several huge strides out of the darkness that had engulfed his life during his years in the asylum.

It was much the same with my plans to make the Cuddy a charitable concern. Progress was slow but, over time, unmistakable. I endowed my new charitable trust (mentioned on the previous page) with cash and FI shares that I would otherwise have used for looking after Giles. My (justified) hope was that, by the time the shares came to be sold, they would be worth considerably more. The staff decided on the trust's name: The Kingwood Trust – after the area in which the Cuddy was situated. It was registered as a charity in 1994.

The management of the Cuddy became more professional and, as a result, more confident. Eventually, as my wealth from FI Group increased, we found ourselves able to expand. In 1994 we acquired a second home, White Barn, in Reading, which we developed to provide supervised accommodation for (eventually) three more handicapped young people. When the first of these moved in, our care provision activities became charitable. A third property, Conchiglia (near Abingdon), followed some months later.

Somehow, without my ever quite noticing the point of transition, my vague thought that there might be a more efficient way of organising and funding the Cuddy had turned into a solid, well-run enterprise that was changing several lives for the better and would soon be capable of running itself without much supervision – or even involvement – from me.

I am getting ahead of myself here, condensing years of sometimes fraught evolution into a few quick pages. There are other strands of my story to tie up before we go any further.

For the time being the point to note is simply this: almost without noticing it, I had taken the first step on what would turn out to be a thrilling new adventure – taking the wealth I had built up over the previous 30 years or so and using it to do good in the world.

For the first time in years – the first time since I had given up my leading role at FI Group – I felt as though I had important work to do: work at which I was skilled, the prospect of which filled me with excitement.

19: Steve Who?

The Kingwood Trust was born at a time when my career at FI Group was dying. The two processes were not connected, but the timing was convenient. I was due to reach retirement age in 1993. I had generally assumed that I would carry on with the company rather longer than that, but, the way things worked out, I was glad for the exit route that retirement provided.

It was not that there was anything dramatically wrong with my final years with FI Group: it was just that they felt somehow unsatisfactory. The little cottage enterprise I had founded in 1962 had become an unqualified triumph, providing work for around 1,000 people (by the early 1990s) and making well over £1m of profit every year. Yet it all seemed strangely hollow. Our personal lifestyle had barely changed, except in so far as we had been able to channel our wealth into Giles's care. We had no mansion, no fast car, no yacht – and, indeed, I don't think Derek would ever have allowed us to indulge in such gratuitous consumption. I'm glad of this, in retrospect, although I suspect that, without Derek's steadying influence, I might, as my wealth continued to grow, have acquired more of a taste for luxury and extravagance. But the odd thing back then was that, without such superficial trappings of success, it sometimes felt as though I had nothing to show for all those decades of struggle – as if I had simply imagined the whole thing.

It certainly felt like that sometimes when I went into work. FI Group was Hilary's company now, enjoying the spectacular success that, it seemed, Hilary had brought to it unaided. Or rather – because I have only to write that sentence to realise how embittered it sounds – the company was driving itself forward partly through Hilary's clear-sighted strategic vision and partly under its own steam. From 1991 onwards, hundreds of newly empowered shareholder executives were striving with every ounce of their energy and intelligence to improve their company's performance; and, in a thousand different ways, they were succeeding. Even Hilary had only a limited influence on this extraordinary collective drive. As for me: what I said and did was irrelevant. I was part of the company's history. What excited people was the company's future.

Voting at one of our Annual General Meetings. Chief Executive Hilary Cropper is on my right. Sir Peter Thompson (invited for his success in taking the National Freight Corporation into co-ownership) in the chair.

I don't think I was entirely useless. I gave Hilary advice when she asked for it (rarely) and provided her with introductions to valuable contacts (on which she seemed keener). I suggested and sometimes oversaw specific projects, found new market openings and, occasionally, gave a helping hand to new talent – although I began to wonder, later on, how helpful an ambitious young person at FI Group would find it to be seen as my protégé. I don't think anyone could dispute that I earned my salary.

But it was painfully obvious, all the time, that I was not indispensable. I still had an office and a seat on the board as Founder Director, but no one saw any need to consult me about anything beyond what the formalities required, and Hilary made little attempt to disguise the fact that she didn't really care what I thought about her plans for the company.

In the outside world, I still seemed to be the "go to" person for any kind of advice, analysis or commentary on matters relating to IT, flexible working or the changing nature of the modern workplace. (Perhaps Hilary felt pangs of jealousy about this, just as I felt pangs about her successes within the company.) My public fame was nourished both by FI Group's visible success and by the increasing number of public roles that I found myself performing. In 1989 and 1990 I was the first female president of the British Computer Society (which had finally achieved chartered status in 1984). In 1992 I was Master of the Worshipful Company of Information Technologists, which I had helped to set up in 1986 and which had just become the City of London's 100th livery company (attaining chartered status in 2010). I was also a trustee of Help the Aged, a Council member of the Industrial Society and Patron since 1987 of the Disablement Income Group.

Such activities nurtured my growing sense that pro bono activities could be as rewarding as profit-driven ones. They also gave me a prominence that led to a growing number of media appearances; to a series of honours – I was appointed a chartered engineer in 1990, while in November 1991 I became the first woman to win the British Institute of Management's Gold Medal for "outstanding achievement" (with particular reference to FI Group's pioneering of the "distributed office"); and to a number of non-executive directorships – for example, at AEA Technology (formerly the UK Atomic Energy Authority) from

1992 to 2000; and with Tandem Computers, in the US, from 1992 to 1997. I was even honoured, in 1995, with election to the US National Women's Hall of Fame; and with a Presidential Pin, awarded by former president Ronald Reagan, for "services to Anglo-American relations".

All this helped to shore up my fragile self-belief. Inside FI Group, however, it was almost as if I had never contributed to the company's success at all. Never mind the decades of sacrifice and drive, carving out market share through low profit-margins and building our reputation as a market-leading brand. I represented our humble origins and, as such, was little better than an embarrassment. Bit by bit I came to acknowledge that I wasn't wanted.

I was particularly hurt in 1991, when I was quietly informed – by Peter Thompson, the chairman I had brought in to oversee our share offer to staff – that the board wanted me to take early retirement. Their proposal was that I would remain on the board but would lose my executive role. I found this very upsetting and pointed out indignantly that I was more than earning my keep with all the business leads I was bringing in. Peter's response (and I appreciate that he was acting as a conduit for other people's views) was that they could get someone else to do all that for much less money. But the real reason was plainly that Hilary, in particular, would simply prefer it if I wasn't around.

It looks trivial and mundane in cold print. But back then I felt bitterly betrayed – like King Lear when, having given his kingdom to his two oldest daughters, he discovers to his horror and naïve surprise that they no longer treat him like a king. No doubt I was being oversensitive, but I felt absolutely rejected by my company – by people who I had always imagined had cause to feel grateful to me. This rejection seemed simultaneously hurtful and preposterous. This company that I had nurtured from infancy and nursed through countless crises and given to the people who now ran it – how could it imagine that it could ever exist without me? It was like a child rejecting its parent. (Had this perhaps been how my mother had felt, 50 years earlier, when I had insisted that I would rather live with Auntie?)

I was on my way to Paris that day, to give a speech. Later on, I was photographed on a barge on the Seine, with Penny Tutt. Even in black-and-white, you can see how red my eyes are. I understood the realities of the matter: the fact that Hilary and the board had every right, if they chose, to decide that I was dispensable. But that didn't make it any easier to bear.

Eventually, encouraged by Penny (and a little inspired by the thought that it had been from Paris that Margaret Thatcher, just a year earlier, had returned for one glorious last stand against those who had decided that her party no longer needed her), I went back and negotiated a compromise whereby I would remain in my current role until my 60th birthday and then leave the company completely. That seemed slightly less humiliating, and I was glad to have stood my ground to that extent. But my final two years at the company, up until July 1993, were overshadowed by the knowledge that I was only there on sufferance.

Perhaps you need to have founded your own company, and built it up through decades of life-defining effort and commitment, to appreciate how personal such rejection can feel. Obviously, none of us is indispensable in any job; and, equally, most of us will be replaced at some point by a younger, less experienced person who is more attuned to the particular challenges of the moment. I had considered myself reasonably aware of such truths and indeed was proud of my success in managing succession. But there was something about the haste with which the directors I had brought in had tried to bundle me out of the door that got under my skin. It felt like a challenge to my sense of self-worth; just as it felt like a challenge to my sense of self-worth when I heard Hilary spoken of as the sole begetter of FI Group's success. "What about the company she started off with?" I found myself saying, noiselessly, on more than one occasion. "What about the client book, the personnel, the culture, the goodwill, the freehold headquarters and the paid-up pension scheme?"

But I knew that no one was listening and, in fairness to myself, I had enough self-knowledge to realise that no one else was interested either. When you give away control of an organisation, as I had deliberately done, then, clearly, it is no longer in your control. Its behaviour will be determined by factors that have nothing whatever to do with you or your agenda. Individual members of the organisation may retain warm feelings towards you; but to the organisation itself you will at best be an irrelevance and at worst a nuisance. That is what giving away control means.

So: I wiped my eyes, got over it, and moved on.

There was plenty to keep me busy. My non-executive directorships took up an increasing amount of time; especially that with Tandem Computers (now part of Hewlett Packard), which required regular travel to sunny California. My general verdict on non-executive directorships is that, when all is going well, it is hard to imagine more stimulating and constructive employment. When times are hard, the imbalance between responsibility and power can make them feel like a hateful burden. (After Tandem and AEA, which I gave up in 1997 and 2000 respectively, I only ever took on one further non-executive directorship, with John Lewis, from 1999 to 2001.) But it was good for me at the time to try looking at the world from the perspective of companies other than FI Group, and to move among people who considered that what I had achieved with FI Group was worthy of admiration. I was the first commercial person to sit on AEA's board, and I was able to introduce a number of marketing concepts that made a big difference to the company's future. Similarly, I was the first non-American – and the first woman – to sit on the board of Tandem, who seemed grateful for my knowledge of the European market when the company subsequently expanded.

The British Computer Society and the Worshipful Company of Information Technologists were both fairly demanding, too. Each, in its different way, represented something I believed in. The former stood for the idea that information technology is not just some narrow specialism but, on the contrary, one of the key industries upon which the UK's future prosperity depends. (This idea seems more obvious now than it did 20 years ago.) The latter stood for the principle that, like any thriving industry, the IT industry has a responsibility to give something back to society; and that that "something" can as usefully be expertise as cash. I subscribe to both ideas as fervently today as I did then.

There was also Giles to be dealt with, and the Cuddy and, later, the Kingwood Trust, as well as the paid speeches and other activities that I continued to do for FI Group. So I was never less than busy, and retirement came round pretty quickly. Although I viewed my main career's approaching end with trepidation, it all concluded surprisingly amicably. At the final FI Group AGM that I attended I was presented with the biggest bunch of flowers that I have ever seen – bigger, I think, than me – while a month or so later they gave me a lovely party on board HQS Wellington (the "Head Quarters Ship" permanently moored on the north bank of the Thames near Cleopatra's Needle), where so many of my old colleagues, contacts, clients and suppliers had been rounded up that I felt as though I was on This Is Your Life.

By the next morning I was at peace with myself. I felt quite certain that, whatever unpleasantnesses there had been, I could look back on my career at FI Group with warmth and satisfaction. I had achieved my three main ambitions – to establish a successful and soundly based company; to hand over control of the company to the workforce; and to ensure highly competent leadership succession. It had, beyond doubt, been worth the effort and the pain; and, now that those objectives had been achieved, what would have been the point of continuing?

20: Starting Over

Derek and I spent much of the next year adjusting to a new kind of life. Derek had grown used to retirement; I had not. I tried for a while to do less with my days, and even treated myself to a visit to Australia, where I spent a few precious weeks with Renate, whom I had not seen for nearly a decade. But when I got back I felt uncomfortable having so much time on my hands – and worried that, having devoted so much energy and attention to providing for Giles, I had neglected to provide myself with a pension that would allow me to enjoy my retirement.

So I carried on working conscientiously at my non-executive directorships and my paid speaking engagements, and continued to network as though I had never retired. This networking had no conscious objective; it was just a way of living that I had grown used to. I liked mixing with the movers and shakers of business and politics, not because of any personal advantage they could bring me but simply because I enjoyed (and enjoy) their company. They interested me. In the IT industry, the most powerful, influential and innovative people were, in many cases, my friends. Once I had sought their company in the hope that it might produce business for me. Now I did so primarily for pleasure – although, who knew, maybe something might come of it anyway?

Derek and I also threw ourselves, with renewed enthusiasm, into managing the Cuddy and the Kingwood Trust, which I hoped could be established as stable, self-sustaining organisations. We had, unfortunately, developed over the decades a fairly encyclopaedic knowledge of issues relating to the care of children with autism (Derek had even joined a committee devoted to improving education legislation for disabled teenagers) and it seemed a waste not to make good use of this expertise. I also devoted a ludicrous amount of time to dealing with the fact – mentioned in chapter 18 – that Giles had not been receiving the financial support to which he was entitled from the state.

This anomaly was eventually resolved – not entirely satisfactorily – in March 1995, with the outstanding payments (backdated to August 1994 but not, unfortunately, to September 1987) made to the Kingwood Trust, which by then had been registered as a charity.

There were drawbacks to this re-engagement with the state: both The Cuddy and the Trust were subsequently plagued with visitations from representatives of the various relevant authorities. Boxes of all kinds were constantly having to be ticked, and many of the demands that were made of us didn't seem to be founded in the slightest understanding of autism.

At one point we were told that Giles had to start attending the local Training Centre. My warnings that they would not be able to handle him there were ignored. So along he went and, within a week or so, they began to insist that he be accompanied by one of our carers. A week or so after that, they insisted that he shouldn't come at all – which was fine by us but seemed a rather painful way of arriving at a conclusion that we could easily have reached in advance through informed, open-minded discussion.

But any such irritations were far outweighed by the lifting of the financial burden, over which I had been losing serious amounts of sleep since my salary from FI Group had stopped. These new local authority contributions, combined with the grant from the Disabled Living Foundation, covered most of the costs incurred by the Kingwood Trust in caring for Giles. Additional charitable donations from us were also needed, which was daunting, but at least the required level now seemed more manageable. There was also the crucial comfort of knowing that this financial relationship between the state and Giles had nothing to do with Derek or me and could thus be expected to continue after we were dead.

To ease the financial strain further, in 1995 we sold the Old Schoolhouse in Amersham – our home for the past 25 years – and bought instead a modest duplex in Henley-on-Thames. It was rather more compact, if not cramped, than I would have liked, but Derek was convinced that it was what we needed, and it did have the advantage of requiring minimal care and maintenance. The fact that there was no room there for most of our furniture from the Old Schoolhouse was a boon for the Kingwood Trust. Conchiglia, the new care home that we were in the process of opening in Radley (outside Abingdon in Oxfordshire), needed lots of furniture, so we gave it whatever we didn't have room for.

The net result was that our lives were suddenly simpler. There was less home to be cared for, no gardening to be done, less distance to be travelled in order to get to The Cuddy. There were also fewer calls on our time from The Cuddy, whose management had moved on from the inspired amateurism with which Phil and Paul had made it work in the early years. We now had an experienced manager, David Williams, who ran the Trust, the Cuddy, White Barn and Conchiglia with such professionalism that I was beginning to sense that here, too, I might soon be surplus to requirements.

Sometimes I wondered if we had simply reached a stage in life where there was nothing much left for us to do. Perhaps I no longer needed to be pushing myself to exhaustion every day; perhaps we could now settle down and prepare for a quiet, contented retirement.

But not yet. Two things happened in the spring of 1996 that changed the way I looked at the world. One, in March, was the death of my sister, Renate. We had seen sadly little of one another over the previous 25 years, but she had remained a big part of my world, and it was a shock to lose her. Her life had been messier than mine, and in material terms less successful, but to me she was always the same strong, reassuring older sister who had held my hand when we arrived in England and helped me settle safely into our new world. She had had a failed marriage and a knack of falling for unsuitable men; she was overweight; she ate all the wrong things; she had heart trouble and diabetes and I hate to think what else. But she always had a tremendous life-force, generating warmth and a sense of humanity whoever she was with. She had successfully fostered three boys, in addition to her adopted daughter. And one thing I discovered after her death (I flew to Australia for the funeral) was that, in her chosen field of social work, she was considered by many Australians to be a heroine: a tireless, compassionate champion of disadvantaged children who had changed many young lives for the better.

We had kept in touch mainly by post, sending each other letters and gifts several times a year; but the price and inconvenience of international telephone calls in the early days meant that we often went years without speaking. The last time I had seen her was that visit to Australia three years earlier; I was grateful to have had that chance, which by our standards was recent. I mourned her sadly, and, inevitably, reflected more frankly than usual on how much time I had left and how I would best use it.

The other significant event, just a few weeks after Renate's death, was that, after years of anticipation and delay, FI Group was finally floated on the Stock Exchange. It was six times oversubscribed, and within three months its shares were trading at 409p per share, from an offer price (in April) of 235p. This capitalised the group at £121.5m (up from £69.8m at flotation) and made many of the staff rich beyond their wildest dreams. (By this stage the workforce controlled 54 per cent of the equity, through a combination of individual shareholdings, the Shareholders Trust, and a Qualifying Employee Share Trust into which I had been selling shares – qualifying for roll-over tax relief – since June 1995.)

Hilary and several other directors became instant millionaires, while hundreds more found themselves sitting on substantial fortunes. More than a third of the company's shares were owned directly by its workforce – more than 70 of whom would become millionaires within a decade. When you take into account all the others who amassed smaller – but still substantial – windfalls, that is an awful lot of lives dramatically changed by the simple mechanism of being handed a part of the company they worked for.

I don't know what most of them did with the money. I don't know how many of them made or make any connection in their minds between their financial good fortune and the fact that, in many cases, I "gave" them my shares (and in other cases allowed them to buy them at a favourable rate). To be honest, I don't really see those transfers as gifts: it was their work that made the company's wealth, and they had a right to a share of it. I was fair, not generous. But every now and then, even now, I run into someone whose life was changed as a result of those shares, and the cumulative effect of such people's stories can be quite moving. "It was thanks to you that I was able to care for my father at home..."; "I used the money to start my own business...."; "I was able to take a year off when my husband was sick"; "I retrained to do the job I'd always wanted to do"; and so on. One long-time colleague told me recently that the sale of the shares had "enabled me to retire at 55 and undertake considerable pro bono work with charities and not-for-profit organisations... I have established my two children on the property ladder and have been able to make significant – in my terms – donations to the Worshipful Company of Information Technologists, my local hospice and church, and other charities. I have also established a scholarship at the University of Hertfordshire for a local female student to study IT..." Perhaps there were people who put the money to bad use, but I like to think that, on the whole, the ripples of that transfer of ownership have been benign.

Meanwhile, I needed to come to terms with the fact that my own remaining shareholding in FI Group now had a value (three months after flotation) of about £21.5m. I knew that this was only paper wealth, but, even so, it was considerably more wealth than I had ever imagined that I could possess. Perhaps I should have seen it coming. Instead, it was a shock. From lying awake at night wondering how I would be able to finance both my retirement and the Kingwood Trust, I abruptly found myself faced with a quite different problem: how could I make constructive and sensible use of this huge fortune?

In theory there was nothing to stop me from converting the shares into cash there and then. I saw no reason to do so, however, and I am glad that I didn't, because that was only the beginning. These were the early years of the dotcom boom, the great speculative bubble that saw the price of technology shares increase nearly six fold (as measured by the Nasdaq Composite Index) between 1995 and 2000. FI Group was one of the prime beneficiaries of this boom. On the one hand, it was at the cutting edge of technological and organisational innovation, which appealed to the market's greed; on the other, it was (unlike most other dotcom ventures) a solid company with a sound business model that was already generating consistent and substantial profits – which appealed to the market's conservatism. To me, it still seemed a highly attractive investment, and the financial community clearly felt likewise. Over the next few years, the share price soared, and soared, and soared – and by 2000 had more or less quadrupled from the offer price.

Even in 1996, it was clear that there was a good chance that my wealth would now increase by many millions of pounds a year without my having to lift a finger. Having spent half my life working 70- or 80-hour weeks trying to keep alive a young company that was paying me only a minimal salary, I found this prospect odd, and faintly obscene. Wealth as a reward for hard work, I could understand; wealth simply as a reward for wealth seemed wrong.

But I soon realised that, in joining the ranks of the super-rich, I was entering a world in which normal values don't always apply. I particularly remember a series of meetings with a financial adviser who was determined that he could make sufficiently dramatic inroads on my tax liabilities to justify a large fee for himself. My initial scepticism – why should I object to paying a reasonable amount of tax? – turned to contempt when he suggested that Derek and I should get divorced. Why? "Because it would be more tax-efficient." I dispensed with his services soon afterwards. (This episode reminded me of the previous time I had been advised on managing my wealth, a few years earlier. That "expert" invited me to become a Lloyd's Name: a lucrative-sounding arrangement whereby I could make a fortune from the insurance industry merely by signing up for a share of the profit of policies written at Lloyd's. When I pointed out that this sounded too good to be true and insisted on seeing the small print, I was scorned for my unsophisticated timidity. Luckily, I stuck to my guns: the small print showed that I would also be signing up for a share of the risk, and I declined to have anything to do with it. Scores of other self-made people were ruined in the 1990s after signing up as Names without applying common-sense scepticism to the proposition.)

Such experiences encouraged me to reflect with some detachment about what my wealth really meant. Did I value it? Yes: it was nice to feel that I would never again have to worry myself sick about how I was going to pay the bills. Did I want to keep it? Unquestionably, up to a point. If you have ever been poor, as I had, you tend to vow, as soon as you are in a position to do so, that you will never be poor again. I had no intention of ever again not knowing how our retirements would be paid for, or how Giles would be provided for after we were dead.

But £2m or £3m would be enough for that. What about the rest? There is, after all, a limit to the number of fine dinners you can eat, and as for yachts, jets and multiple homes, I've never really felt the urge. I have already mentioned that Derek was unenthusiastic about the idea of a life of luxury. He objected not so much out of reasoned principle as through a visceral sense that extravagant self-indulgence was simply wrong. My own instincts are less puritanical, but within a few months of being a multi-millionaire I had begun to feel grateful for Derek's restraining influence. Left to myself, I might well have succumbed to the invisible forces that encourage rich people to increase their living costs until they are no more free from financial pressures than anybody else. As it was, I found myself stopping and thinking about what I really wanted.

I realised that I could get pleasure from nice clothes, and perhaps from a few works of art. Apart from that, however, there was, when I thought about it, little appeal in luxury for luxury's sake. The advantage of being rich was not the possessions it could provide but the security and freedom. That was all that really mattered to me: to know that Giles's future was assured, and to be free, otherwise, to spend my time as I chose.

Once those two things were secure, it seemed ridiculous not to do something useful with whatever millions were left. My experiences with the Kingwood Trust had given me a taste for putting my wealth to good use. There were now three people living relatively happily at The Cuddy, with five more at White Barn and three just settling into Conchiglia. Our expertise as an organisation seemed to grow with our ambitions, and with a highly professional management in place there was every reason to believe that the wealth I had settled on the Trust would continue to be well spent. When I thought about this, I realised that I could derive far more satisfaction from spending my money in this kind of way than from spending it on luxuries for Derek and me that we didn't really want.

The appearance of these extra millions was an opportunity to do more of the same, on a more ambitious scale. With this in mind, in late 1996 I established a new charitable foundation, The Shirley Foundation, which I endowed with a substantial trust fund.

21: The Bitterest Pill

Perhaps it seems odd that I should have found it necessary to start the Shirley Foundation, when the Kingwood Trust had already been established, with some difficulty, and was already contributing positively to many lives that had been affected by autism. One reason was that the tax situation had become very complicated with Kingwood (because Giles was a beneficiary, and because of the combination of private and public funding), whereas with the Shirley Foundation I could simply transfer FI Group shares directly to the Foundation, without tax. But there was, unfortunately, another reason. Problems had arisen with the Kingwood Trust that were making it difficult for me to continue with it.

These problems had little to do with the functioning of the Trust itself. Instead, they were related to Derek.

It is difficult for me to describe this strange episode in our lives. To a large extent it is part of Derek's story rather than mine, and I feel uncomfortable describing it from my perspective. But I cannot tell my own story coherently without mentioning it.

The origins of the problem went back many years, almost to Giles's birth. Derek was a passionate father, who was devastated by Giles's autism and transcended his grief by vowing to do everything within his power to be the best possible parent to him. This admirable attitude had much to commend it, and was entirely in keeping with Derek's character. He stuck to his vow heroically, and I admire him greatly for it. But his approach also had drawbacks. Whenever there was any question of taking a step whose effects would include making life easier for us as Giles's parents – for example, by sedating him, or by putting him in some kind of institution – Derek's conscience would kick in. Such steps were impossible, he would insist: they would constitute a betrayal.

In fact, this wasn't always true. In some situations, helping the carer can be the best way to help the cared-for. But you can see where Derek was coming from and perhaps understand how, over the years, Derek's attitude to Giles became ever more fiercely protective – until it was almost paranoid. Whatever anyone else proposed for Giles – medication, restraint, isolation, professional supervision – Derek would suspect the motives of those involved. Were they trying to short-change Giles? Were they putting their needs before his? Was his quality of life suffering so that their lives could be easier?

These suspicions would have been easier to dismiss if he hadn't from time to time been demonstrably right. With Borocourt, for example, it had been Derek who had first insisted that Giles was not being treated with the care and respect he deserved. I dismissed his suspicions at first, and was proved wrong.

The subsequent long-drawn-out saga of our complaint against the hospital – which we made in 1985 and which was finally declared resolved by the Health Ombudsman (with a frustrating ruling in which only two of our nine complaints were fully upheld) in 1987 – fanned the flames of his paranoia; as did our long drawn-out struggle to secure for Giles the state funding to which he was entitled. It sometimes seemed that every organisation we dealt with wanted to sacrifice Giles's wellbeing to suit its own private interests, while bureaucrats and health professionals alike seemed to be trying to pull the wool over our anxious eyes. It was hardly surprising that Derek should feel that, without his ceaseless vigilance, suspicion and stubbornness, Giles would be lost.

Later, however, when the Kingwood Trust was up and running, Derek's protective attitude began to impinge on his duties as one of the charity's trustees – and would eventually cause us to fall out badly. He would come to trustee meetings and be intelligent and involved – his knowledge of autism and the care needs of people with autism was encyclopaedic by this stage – but essentially his concerns always involved Giles. The Trust was responsible for three houses and 10 beneficiaries by then, but for Derek it was always "Giles needs this" or "Giles needs that" or (often) "Giles is being given too much medication." (There was one medication, a strong anti-psychotic drug called Haloperidol, that bothered him particularly.)

These really weren't issues that a trustee should have been talking about. They were personal issues, not strategic ones. But Derek was being a parent rather than a proper trustee. He couldn't help it; and the trustees, paradoxically, were obliged to take his views into account.

The board of trustees tolerated the eccentricity. It was hard not to sympathise with such a devoted father. But then the difficulties multiplied – and one incident in particular caused an enormous amount of tension. Derek became suspicious of one of the carers who was working shifts at The Cuddy. It was hard to know why: the man seemed pleasant and competent and indeed charming. But Derek insisted that something was wrong, eventually homing in on the accusation that the man was locking Giles into his room at night – bad practice from a safety point of view and also a major infringement of Giles's autonomy. Derek was unable to substantiate this accusation, and did not even suggest an explanation as to why this might be happening, but he none the less made a formal complaint about it. The social services were forced to investigate, once the complaint had been made, and in due course it was rejected. (Some time later, however, a woman wrote to us, saying that she had been regularly "entertained" at night in the Cuddy's sitting-room by the man in question – which suggested that, while the allegation of wrongdoing remained unsupported by evidence, Derek's suspicions might have had slightly more basis in reality than I had assumed.)

By early 1997, the Trust had developed a life of its own, and the tensions were getting worse. I was still chairman of the trustees, but my significance as founder was becoming irrelevant, just as it had at FI Group. The Trust had acquired a new chief executive, Mary McGuire, who tried to organise things in a far more professional way and, in the process, fell out with Paul Moran, the longest-serving member of our original band of "amateur" carers at both Redcot and The Cuddy and, as such, one of the nearest things Giles had to a friend. Derek always said that Paul understood Giles's moods better than anyone, and when Paul left – which was sad but not improper – Derek never forgave Mary for it.

The ill-feeling became embarrassing. At trustees' meetings, it began to feel as though Derek was looking for ways to catch Mary and her team out. The idea that the Trust was inherently a good thing – perhaps the best thing that we had ever been able to do for Giles – was forgotten. In Derek's mind it had joined all those other sinister forces – doctors, local authorities, asylum administrators – that conspired to deprive our son of the love and happiness that we longed for him to have.

Eventually, the board of trustees had no alternative but to ask Derek to stand down as a trustee – especially when he threatened to get the Trust closed down. Yet I had no alternative in the short-term but to carry on as chairman, because the Trust was not yet ready to run without me – and, not least, because I believed in it. This meant that, in Derek's eyes, I had joined the ranks of the enemy. We quarrelled openly about this once or twice, then lapsed into a far deadlier silence, distant and resentful. We had been drifting apart in many ways over the years, each dealing with our share of our common burden in our own fashion. Now, shockingly, the common ground seemed to have vanished.

I tried to distract myself from the unhappiness by focusing on other things. I had, after all, all this money at my disposal. If I couldn't enjoy doing good with it through the Kingwood Trust, I would do so through the Shirley Foundation. I had a keen sense of my own mortality at the time, precipitated both by Renate's death and by my recent retirement. So, remembering Andrew Carnegie's famous dictum ("The man who dies rich dies disgraced"), I began to give my fortune away.

The Shirley Foundation made a series of transfers of shares to the Kingwood Trust, in the hope that thereafter it would thrive without me. I then searched around for other projects and found myself looking into the Worshipful Company of Information Technologists. I have already mentioned that I was involved in the setting up of this company. It now struck me that it could be a perfect candidate for some serious financial support. I was still feeling my way as a philanthropist, but it had already occurred to me that I had more to contribute than mere cash. My whole career – my whole fortune – was based on my ability to find better ways of doing things, to turn efficiencies into profits and innovations into wealth. So why not apply the same principles to my philanthropy? In other words: why not select recipients that were not just worthy but capable of multiplying the value of the gift by combining it wisely with expertise and intelligent systems?

The WCIT seemed to meet these criteria perfectly.

It would be many months, including an extended period of anonymous research, before this idea became a financial reality; but eventually, in 1998, the Shirley Foundation would donate £5m to the Worshipful Company. The first £1m provided a small working Hall (the first new Hall in the City for 50 years). The other £4m went into the company's own charitable trust, from where it could be applied to a variety of good causes with the added value of the expertise of those applying it. For example, if the trust gave money to a struggling not-for-profit organisation, freemen and liverymen of the company – all IT experts – would also be actively involved in giving that organisation IT advice. Subsequent studies have shown that, if members' time contributions are taken into account (using commercially defined consultancy rates), the value of a gift is leveraged by at least 10 to one by passing through the WCIT. In other words, the Shirley Foundation's £4m could eventually be expected to result in benefits worth £40m.

Even back then, in the late 1990s, I was beginning to appreciate the dazzling potential of this sort of intelligent philanthropy. It made the idea of giving away my hard-earned wealth considerably more exciting.

Meanwhile, another project had captured my imagination. It began in September 1997, when Mary McGuire mentioned that she was planning a visit to the celebrated Higashi school in Boston, Massachusetts, during a trip to the US. I was due to be in the US as well, so I asked if I could come along. She agreed, and one bright New England autumn morning she and I arrived in the Boston suburb of Randolph for a day-long tour of the world-famous specialist school for children with autism.

What we saw there astonished me.

A large, important-looking red-brick building in flat, spacious grounds, the Boston Higashi School seemed as full of confidence, purpose and order as a high-achieving Ivy League private school. Everything was light and spacious and in good repair, with an approach to design and decor that combined minimalism with warmth. As for the pupils, they were so well-behaved, in and out of class, that it was easy to mistake some of them for staff (as I initially did when I saw a couple of young men laying the table in the dining-room). The contrast to the behaviour I was accustomed to in children with autism was dramatic. In fact, they seemed so well-adjusted and calm that I assumed that – obviously – they must have come from a much less challenging point on the autism spectrum than Giles. Then our guide told us what some of them had been like when they first arrived, and I realised that many of these children had once been every bit as challenged and challenging as Giles. But there had been something in their education here that they had responded to.

I'd been vaguely aware of Higashi for several years by this stage, but I understood it only in terms of the broadest brushstrokes. The original

Higashi school had been opened in Tokyo in 1964. Its founder, Dr Kiyo Kitahara, had developed an approach to autism that she called Daily Life Therapy – an approach that proved so successful that after 20 years or so an American offshoot was established, opening in Boston in 1987.

Daily Life Therapy aims to give children with autism the confidence and tools to live independently by immersing them in a regime that is at once very stimulating and very structured. The system has three "pillars" (Dr Kitahara's term): vigorous physical exercise, which allows them to work off their frustrations instead of expressing them through destructive behaviour; emotional stability (provided by large numbers of highly trained staff – usually one for every three pupils); and intellectual stimulation, provided through very repetitive, almost ritualistic group tuition that exploits the autistic love of routine to impart the basics of literacy, numeracy, science, the arts and IT, as well as teaching a range of social skills. Disruption is kept to a minimum by the high staffing ratio, and by the policy of defusing any incidents with a quick burst of vigorous exercise. Distractions are kept to a minimum by, among other methods, keeping all teaching materials out of sight, apart from those that are actually in use.

The ostensibly communal nature of this teaching has the paradoxical goal of allowing each child to find what Dr Kitahara (who died in 1989) called the "most precious bud of self-identity" – having first equipped them with the self-belief and "stability of emotions" that they need in order to be independent.

There is a profound optimism at the heart of the system. "Higashi" means "east" in Japanese and was chosen by Dr Kitahara because it symbolised the hope of each new day's dawn, and the foundation behind the Tokyo and Boston schools is called the Higashi Hope Foundation. By contrast, the experience of autistic children in Britain in the second half of the 20th century – and of Giles in particular – could almost have been defined by the lack of hope in those whose job it was to teach them.

Remarkably, Daily Life Therapy seems to work. The system doesn't "cure" autism, but it does ameliorate its effects, by equipping pupils with a range of social and intellectual skills that greatly increase their chances of living with some degree of independence and contentment as adults. Perhaps that sounds like a modest goal, but I can assure you that, compared with Giles's experience, it sounded to me like the Holy Grail.

Mary McGuire left Boston with a few good ideas for improving the support that the Kingwood Trust offered to those in its care. I left with a wilder dream. It would be several days before I dared articulate it even to myself, let alone to anyone else. (And there was no question, by then, of my sharing it with Derek.) But the thought kept nagging away at me: how different might Giles's life have been, if he had been to such a school? And why could there not be such a school in the UK?

After a week or so, I began to use my contacts to ask this second question in places where it might make a difference. I was rewarded with a meeting with some senior officials in the Department for Education and Employment (as it then was). Their message was not especially encouraging – but not overwhelmingly discouraging either. The Department would love to have such a school in the UK, it seemed; but there was no question of one coming into existence unless a group of parents or other concerned parties took it upon themselves to found it.

I could hardly leave it at that. Instead, over the next three months, I asked around; spoke to an educational consultant, John Woodhouse, whom the DfEE had recommended; commissioned research into likely demand for a Higashi school in the UK; made contact with the Higashi Hope Foundation in Japan to see if they would be interested in the creation of a European offshoot; made contact with some likeminded parents (a Higashi Parent Group); found (through the parent group) two trustees with relevant experience; employed one of them (Kate Luker) as project director; appointed both (the other was Alison Ainsworth) to a Steering Group which also included me and John Woodhouse; and commissioned an estate agent to look for a property in the Midlands (where autism-specific services were most lacking) that might provide suitable premises for a Higashi school.

The project almost immediately acquired a momentum of its own, as each new group member contributed drive and motivation as well as expertise. This was alarming. What exactly was I letting myself in for? Had I really considered how insanely ambitious this was? And yet, as Penny Tutt put it when I discussed it over a drink, "This one really does sound as though it's got your number on it."

I knew she was right, and I kept her words in mind when, in March 1998, our estate agent recommended that we view a Queen Anne manor house in Berkshire called Prior's Court. It wasn't what we'd been looking for: we'd wanted a modern, functional, easy-to-maintain building in the Midlands, rather than a 18th-century property in 55 acres of landscaped grounds near Newbury. But, having seen it, all the trustees agreed that it would provide the perfect environment for the school of our dreams. All sorts of work would be required to make it fit for purpose, but there was something about the place that simply felt right. We spent a few weeks talking it through and then, in April 1998, agreed to bid for the property.

The buying process was oddly complicated, involving a series of closed tenders, and it was not until September 1998 that our final bid, of £15m, was accepted. But by that stage we all knew that there was no going back. The Prior's Court Foundation was incorporated in June 1998, and its trustee board – including Paul Cann, then chief executive of the National Autistic Society; Sir Derek Hornby, former chairman of Rank Xerox UK (who has a grandson with autism); and two trustees of the Kingwood Trust – met for the first time in August.

We also recruited a volunteer headhunter to start looking for a Principal for the school. (I had already learnt to be quite shameless in persuading people to donate their time and skills to my good causes.) And we appointed an architect to start considering – rapidly – how this Grade II* listed manor house could be turned into the kind of school we needed.

It was clear that considerable extra investment would be needed. Prior's Court had been in recent use as a boys' prep school (called, coincidentally, Kingswood); but that had now been relocated (to Bath), and the school we now had in mind had much more rigorous requirements in terms of the relationship between structure and purpose. Every room had to be suitable in terms of safety (e.g., no sharp-edged fireplaces or steep, rickety staircases); in terms of child-protection issues (e.g., no closed-off rooms where no one could see in through the window); and in terms of providing an environment where the pupils we had in mind would feel comfortable about learning.

Yet the basic idea seemed sound. We had a product – a teaching system that we would operate under licence from Higashi – and we knew that there would be a demand for it. We had a business plan that suggested that the school could become self-financing within five years. I had every confidence in our personnel, who by September 1998 included a Principal, Robert Hubbard, a head teacher with many years of experience teaching pupils with special needs, especially those with autism and other profound learning difficulties. It would be four months before he could join us full-time: his existing employers were reluctant to lose him. But having him signed up meant that we finally had on board someone who understood properly the educational aspects of what we were trying to do. It also felt like a huge commitment – persuading a specialist at the top of his profession to give up his job to join us – that in some ways meant more than spending £15m on Prior's Court itself. Now we really had to make it work.

Prior's Court was occupying most of my time by now. Not all of it: I remained a non-executive director at AEA Technology, while Giles, The Cuddy and Kingwood all required considerable attention as well. But it was Prior's Court that felt like my main job: the one that kept me awake at night. We had set ourselves a target of opening in September 1999, and, however simple I have made it sound, that was a mountainous challenge. With less than a year to go, we still hadn't sorted out which Higashi specialist would be helping us to implement the educational system we had seen in Boston. We still didn't know who our pupils would be, and were nervous about doing so before a few more pieces of the jigsaw were in place. Yet we had now invested so much in the jigsaw pieces that were in place that it was impossible to entertain any possible outcome other than ultimate success.

It was a bit like my early attempts to make a go of Freelance Programmers, more than three decades earlier. Yes, it was all, in a sense, a fantasy. But it was also a reality – the focus of my waking hours as well as my dreams. And it became more real with each passing day.

The one crucial and distressing difference was that, back then, I had had Derek to support me: Derek as my sounding-board and back-stop and, above all, as the rock of certainty that gave me courage when doubts threatened to dissolve my vision. Now, apart from a few practical exchanges about Giles at weekends, the two of us barely spoke.

My dream of a Higashi school in the UK had germinated and begun to grow with barely a word of Derek's input, although I kept him informed. Meanwhile, the situation with Kingwood had become intolerable. Derek had been bombarding the trustees and the management with complaints, and I had been forced to stand down as chairman. I had done so resentfully, but there was no alternative, and it was Derek that I blamed. He had become, in effect, an enemy of the Kingwood Trust, which seemed to me both unfair and profoundly destructive.

Looking back, I think that Derek was going through a psychological or emotional crisis that was affecting his judgement. If so, it was hardly surprising. This brave, intelligent, modest man had endured 35 years of suffering, uncomplainingly; his dreams of family happiness had turned to ashes, along with any ambitions he might once have had for his career. He had been strong for his son, fighting his corner when the whole world seemed to be against him; and he had been strong for me too, most heroically at the time of my breakdown in 1976 and 1977. If the cracks were now beginning to show in him too, who can blame him? No human being is invulnerable, no matter how determined we are to be brave.

Looking back, I can see that this was a time when, more than ever, Derek needed me to be strong for him. At the time, it didn't seem like that. I felt betrayed by him, just as he felt betrayed by me. His hostility made me defensive. The idea that a charity I had created could in some way be conspiring against Giles was not just absurd but offensive. And now, just as a fresh dream for doing good was adding purpose to my life, Derek's imaginings were taking all the joy out of the adventure. No doubt my judgement was less than perfect as well, and in retrospect I wish that I had been more understanding. But everyone else that I was dealing with on a regular basis seemed amazingly upbeat about the challenges we faced; Derek, by contrast, could see only the worst in things. The whole world seemed to be darkened by his suspicions.

By the summer of 1998 I had reached an appalling conclusion: we could not continue to live like this. I was spending a lot of time away from home anyway, often in London, where my fund-raising and other activities often required me to stay overnight in hotels. Now, with a heavy heart, I began to look around for a permanent home where I could live separately.

I told no one about this, apart from two or three close friends, and for many weeks we kept up the façade of things being more or less normal. I would stay in a hotel all week – something that I could now afford to do, although it seemed ridiculously extravagant – and then come back to Henley at the weekend so that we could go and visit Giles at The Cuddy. Derek was aware of my plans, but, at the same time, I don't think he had necessarily accepted that they would come to anything. We never really discussed it; we never really discussed anything. We were, I should add, sleeping in separate bedrooms by now. Even Giles – the person who was keeping us together – was more or less a taboo subject, given our disagreements about his care and medication. But we must have talked about him a bit – in that numb, semi-automatic way that estranged parents have – because at some point we agreed that, once the purchase of Prior's Court had finally gone through, we would take him there. It was, if nothing else, a good safe spot for a picnic.

That visit was fixed for the weekend of 17-18 October. By then, I had found a place – a small barn conversion halfway between Henley and Marlow – that I thought would be both affordable and practical for my new separate existence. All that remained was for me to summon the resolve to put in an offer – at which point our marital bridges would have been well and truly burnt. It would break my heart to do it; yet if I didn't, I would go mad.

I was still agonising about this in the second week of October. It seemed such a huge step to be taking, after all that Derek and I had been through together. Had our shared life really all come to nothing? Or was there still an alternative?

I went back to Henley that Friday evening – 16 October – and lay awake for much of the night, going round in mental circles.

Then, at about 9am on Saturday, the phone rang. It was The Cuddy, telling us that Giles was dead.

22: Life After Death

The world changed instantly. It has never changed back. It was like a light going out. Nothing I can write can begin to convey the desolation. The beloved, mysterious, tormented, beautiful being who had been at the centre of my life for 35 years was suddenly and irrevocably absent; and, as WH Auden wrote, "Nothing now can ever come to any good."

Parents who have lost a child will have some understanding of what I mean: of the inner howl of despair that reverberates through the rest of your life; of the ache that bites and gnaws and never heals. I envy the rest of you your ignorance. For 35 years, every thought I had had, waking and sleeping, had been coloured in some way by my knowledge that my son needed me and by my longing for him to be happy and safe; every thought since has been coloured by the knowledge that he is dead.

There were, in Giles's case, all sorts of mitigating circumstances. None made his loss any easier to bear. It is not uncommon for people with autism to die young. His death, when it came, had been a merciful one: a seizure in his sleep, rather than anything long-drawn-out or agonising; he probably knew nothing about it. Derek and I had, in any case, spent most of our son's life wondering with dread how he would fare if we died before him. Now we could set our minds at rest on that score. We could console ourselves, too, with the thought that in his final decade he had enjoyed a quality of life that would have been unimaginable in his teens and early twenties; and with the thought that, in Kingwood and Prior's Court, he had inspired charitable projects that would continue to change many lives for the better for years to come. Such consolations were forgotten within minutes of being offered.

But one thing did change: our proposed separation came to nothing. We didn't even need to talk about it. Splitting up was simply out of the question. The issues that had driven us apart seemed suddenly petty, compared with what we had shared in the past and the great shared burden of grief that we now had to carry into the future. We had come this far together, and we would confront whatever lay ahead together. I'm not sure if either of us was much comfort to the other at the time: bereaved parents rarely are, when both parties are so overwhelmed by their own pain. But what remained of our family instinctively pulled together, and we have remained together ever since.

The reconciliation was uneasy at first. Giles's death propelled Derek into a pit of despair so profound that it was hard to reach him. After half-a-dozen fruitless attempts at collaboration, I made all the arrangements for the funeral myself. I am glad that I did so, and sorry for Derek that he could not. It was a humanist service, in Reading, where scores of people whose lives Giles had touched – care-workers, health professionals, a few who had lived at the various Kingwood homes, and a surprising number of family friends – turned out to celebrate his life. There was music by Mozart, Haydn and Bach. Messages from many well-wishers were read out. An address by a humanist minister emphasised the fact that Kingwood's work would be a lasting memorial to Giles. I gave my own reading, of Max Ehrmann's "Desiderata", trying to focus on the fact that my troubled son was now at peace.

He had, as several people remarked, had a great gift for inspiring affection: not just from his parents but from many who came into contact with him. In his calm moments he had a delicate handsomeness – like a film star of the black and white era – that touched hearts. He went through much of his innocent, vulnerable life cut off from the world, yet he had an extraordinary and lasting impact on it. People loved him; and his parents loved him more than words can say.

Somehow we got through the funeral. At the end, a young man who had lived for some time in White Barn approached me. We had often seen one another, but he had minimal speech, and his interactions with me had hitherto been confined to spitting, kicking and hostile glares. This time, he spoke: a quiet but quite distinct "Sorry." I don't think I have ever felt so moved – or so strengthened – by the empathy of a fellow human being.

Afterwards, mourners were invited back for refreshments at The Cuddy. Derek did not join us. He could not bear the thought of revisiting Giles's home. He has never been there since.

There then followed the long, bleak aftermath. The strange semi-euphoria of the funeral day evaporated, and the death-related chores that had to be dealt with (his estate; the future of The Cuddy; the disposal of his clothes and books) seemed to disappear from my "to do" list all too quickly. As each task was completed, it felt as if another

Giles was a handsome boy. The near-ethereal beauty of many children on the spectrum would merit research. Did autism inspire John Wyndham's sci-fi **The Midwich Cuckoos?**

link between me and my Gilesy was being severed. I was losing him, for ever, for the last time. (The very last link was broken two years later, when Daisy the cat died.)

I thought about him all the time, and dreamt about him every night. (He still appears in my dreams, a decade and a half on, but only two or three times a month now.) I was also constantly being ambushed by unexpected reminders of him: a children's song that he liked, for example; or – with remarkable frequency – someone in the street whose looks, bearing or gait suggested his. Such surprises regularly brought me to the brink of tears. (But I don't cry in public.) A decade and a half later, they are rarer but no less overpowering.

I will never recover from his loss. I have merely grown used to the pain, which recurs in many forms. Sometimes the thought of a tragic aspect of his life will stab me. (He never – not once – called me mother.) At others, it will be a positive memory that makes the tears well up. For example, the thought of his smile: that proper smile that he would occasionally give, oh so rarely, with his eyes. The smile would vanish as abruptly as it had appeared, but it would keep you going for months. There is, of course, joy in such memories as well. But it is a bitter joy. I will never see that smile again.

There is also one mysterious memory that still haunts and fascinates me. A few days before his death, I spoke to Giles on the telephone. I used to call him regularly at The Cuddy, just to see how he was, but the calls were not so much conversations as monologues. I would say things like "Hello, Giles. It's Mummy. How has your day been?", and so on; and he would either listen in silence or acknowledge me occasionally with grunts or with the noise that was his version of "all right" – a trademark response that seemed to indicate general comprehension and assent. But on this final call, for the space of less than a minute, he unleashed a long string of what sounded like sentences. It was so abrupt, and so utterly out of character, that I initially thought I had slipped into a dream – and the actual words he used never sank in. His enunciation was as blurred as ever: what was unusual was that he was stringing whole sequences of words together, rather than limiting himself to one-word utterances as he usually did. Afterwards, I asked the carer who had been supervising the call at Giles's end if my ears had been deceiving me, but she agreed that he had indeed been talking in an almost normal way. Yet neither of us could pin down what he had said. The words were too indistinct, and had taken us too much by surprise – and before we knew it the memory of them had melted away.

Years later, I am still tantalised by this incident. Was something happening in his brain, perhaps related to the seizure that would kill him? Was he saying goodbye? Was he trying to communicate something important to me? It is profitless to speculate; but, equally, it is almost impossible not to.

For a long time, Derek and I barely spoke about Giles. Each knew that the other was thinking about him, but for the first year or two it was simply too painful to discuss the subject. The best we could offer one another was simply to be there, slowly rebuilding the trust that had broken down between us. They say that the death of a child kills most marriages; I think ours survived precisely because, at the moment of bereavement, it was in trouble. Neither of us had any expectations of the other, and what half-comforts we were ultimately able derive from one another thus came as a welcome surprise rather than a disappointment.

But it was a painfully slow rebuilding process, putting back together not just our relationship but our two broken lives. Each of us adopted a quite different approach. Derek resolved that, having had his life poisoned by autism for 35 years, he was never again going to give the subject a moment's thought. Disillusioned by what had happened to Giles, he had long abandoned the Church of England Christianity that had sustained him through our early married life, and he now proceeded to spend several years in a state of existential despair from which he has only recently and partially emerged. I, by contrast, felt a new urge to explore life's spiritual dimensions, in the hope of giving meaning to what Giles had been through. Derek had lost faith in his religion; I lost faith in my atheism. I doubt, however, if either of us has finished our spiritual journey. We are still exploring, and may yet end up in the same place.

But I did draw one immediate spiritual conclusion from Giles's death that has remained an article of faith for me ever since. After all that suffering there had to be something I could do to redress the balance. And if there was any meaning to be found in what had happened, it was surely to be found by my throwing myself into the struggle against autism to a degree that I had never imagined before.

That way, at least, I might make some kind of sense of Giles's life and death.

It was hard, at first, to translate this conviction into practical deeds. Everything seemed so hopeless, it was hard to muster the energy to do anything. Gradually, however, the demands of existing projects began to prod me back into action.

My first major engagement, less than six weeks after the funeral, was a big lunch at the Mercers' Hall in the City of London, celebrating my £5m gift to the Worshipful Company of Information Technologists, which had been officially announced just a few days before Giles's death. Buzz Aldrin, the astronaut, was guest of honour. In normal circumstances, I would have been thrilled to meet him. As it was, I was mainly concerned to get through the day without losing my composure. I more or less managed it.

Thereafter, the challenges of Prior's Court reasserted themselves with a vengeance, clamouring for my attention. Robert Hubbard took up his position as Principal at the beginning of 1999 and, not unnaturally, was eager to speed up the recruitment of pupils and staff. Architects and builders were already worrying about completing the renovation works on time and on budget. It was all very well for me to have lost my enthusiasm for everything, but the project remained real. I had to find a way of making it work.

The crisis that really galvanised me back into action was a breakdown in our relationship with the Higashi Hope Foundation. I will not try to apportion blame for this; indeed, I am not even sure that I have ever properly understood what went wrong. But the central fact was simple enough: the deal had fallen through. And the resulting problem was stark: here we were, eight months before our projected opening date, with a huge question-mark over our ability to use the teaching system that was the project's raison-d'être.

I may momentarily have felt tempted to use this as a pretext for abandoning the whole idea. If so, the temptation was rapidly drowned by the enthusiasm of my colleagues, especially Robert, who had already run two specialist schools for autistic children (in Cambridgeshire) and was now simmering with enthusiasm at the prospect of creating such a school from scratch. As he saw it, the collapse of our arrangement for acting as a licensed Higashi franchise was an opportunity rather than a problem. After all, he argued, it was not as if there was nothing at all of value in the way the British educational system currently approached children with learning difficulties. Similarly, it would be dogmatic to insist that the Higashi system was perfect. What we really needed – and what we were now free to create – was an approach that combined the core ideas of Higashi (structure, high staff-to-pupil ratios, use of physical exercise as a behaviour-management tool) with the best aspects of British methodology. Robert could hardly wait to start recruiting and training staff with such an approach in mind. We tried to hire a former Higashi employee as a trainer, but this soon fell through too, and we all became progressively committed to what is now known as Prior Methodology – an eclectic, dynamic approach that is plainly Higashi-inspired but, at the same time, is very much a bespoke system in its own right, adhering to the best UK educational practices.

The challenge of getting the physical fabric of the school ready in time was as urgent as ever. The builders were now in situ, and the scaffolding was going up around the building, but the list of things to be done seemed to lengthen by the day. Parts of the property had simply fallen into disrepair. One wing – added in the 1960s – eventually had to be pulled down; asbestos was found under the dining-room floor; part of the roof was leaking; there were major problems with the drains; and so on. We also needed, among other things, to replace the steep main staircase with a wide, shallow one; to shut off another staircase altogether; to replace narrow, sharp stairway corners – which can result in anxiety and bad reactions to surprises – with broad, curving ones where children can see what is coming well in advance; to add or reposition windows and doors to meet child protection requirements; to install fire escapes that our pupils might reasonably be expected to use safely; to install a sensory swimming-pool in one half of the ugly modern sports hall; and to incorporate enormous amounts of storage space.

It didn't help that the building was listed. Every significant alteration had to be approved, and even ostensibly simple matters such as knocking down a derelict (and hazardous) glasshouse proved unexpectedly problematic. (The glasshouse turned out to be listed too: "the best 'Messenger' glasshouse I've ever seen", according to the National Trust-recommended specialist who eventually restored it for us.)

I could spend several chapters describing the obstacles and pitfalls we encountered in the course of the renovation, from structural and safety issues to heritage-related bureaucracy, building regulations and boundary issues to unwanted resident wildlife (including rooks, doves, hornets, moles and rabbits). Kate Luker eventually identified well over 1,000 snags that the builders had to be asked to deal with. Predictably, costs soared – the project, including start-up losses, would eventually cost the Shirley Foundation nearly £30m – but, none the less, it was happening, and Kate managed to keep the works more or less on schedule.

For me, the sheer volume of things to be done helped to fill the vacuum that Giles's death had left in my life. It was therapeutic to spend weekends – which for as long as I could remember had revolved around Giles – getting my hands dirty and my brow sweaty performing manual tasks in the house or, more often, the grounds. I don't suppose this labour made a great deal of difference in the overall scheme of things, but it was soothing to tire oneself out in practical challenges, knowing that, in this at least, determination and persistence would eventually achieve the desired goal. It also provided opportunities for starting to rebuild my fragile relationship with Derek, who occasionally joined in. I particularly remember three dusty, dangerous weekends when we painstakingly pruned a mess of overgrown arched pear-trees (complete with hornets' nest), which, like much of the garden, were protected by a heritage listing. The practical need for teamwork forced us to rediscover an element of mutual trust, and the shared frustrations and satisfactions reminded us that we might have something in common beyond our tragic experience as parents. (We didn't know whether to laugh or cry when, a year later, some professional gardeners, ignorant of the listing, simply uprooted the trees in question.)

And so life went on, and the months raced by, and before we knew it was late August, and the builders had finished, leaving our purchasing manager, Keith Hall, just three weeks in which to install all the furniture and equipment the school needed before our scheduled opening date of 13 September. The property now included a new two-storey residential building, capable of housing 60 students, with the bedrooms planned to afford the privacy required under the Childrens' Act. There was a small covered swimming pool, a renovated gym, and some new landscaped formal courtyards. The clocks in the two clock towers had been mended, and we had obtained an official charter and coat of arms, including the motto: "To learn to be" – which seemed to me to sum up what our pupils might hope to get out of Prior's Court.

We had at this stage only two pupils signed up, which was discouraging, especially since we had 28 staff. But Robert was confident that demand would pick up, and the opening went ahead, in a low-key way, on 13 September 1999. Eight months later, we held a more public event, when the school was officially opened by the Princess Royal, and already the number of pupils had increased to nine.

My main memories of that royal opening, I should add, are of torrential rain and of my unwise insistence that the princess should be served biscuits made by the children themselves. (I realised at the last minute that the batch they had prepared was too burnt and disgusting to be fit for consumption by any human being, let alone a princess, and we opened a shop-bought packet instead.) I also remember looking around me, at the animated pupils and the beautiful, friendly surroundings and the confident, motivated staff and knowing beyond doubt that Prior's Court would be a success.

So it proved. Like FI Group and Kingwood before it, Prior's Court rapidly acquired a life and momentum of its own. I was much quicker this time to accept that it could and should proceed without me. I have no educational expertise; Robert Hubbard and his staff had plenty. Under Robert's leadership, with intelligent management from the Prior's Court Foundation (now chaired by Sir Derek Hornby), the school achieved its target of financial independence by 2002, and I retired from the Foundation, as planned, in 2003. Since 2004, the school has had about 60 pupils, aged between five and 19, looked after by 360 staff. A Young Adult Centre opened in 2011.

The school's stated goals – to build communication, to reduce challenging behaviours, to develop appropriate sleeping, eating and toileting patterns and to equip students with a "toolbox" of transferable life skills (along with some appropriately modified knowledge of the National Curriculum) – are achieved with impressive regularity. Some pupils are able to move on after four or five years to local units (e.g., local authority schools or care provision); while the general aim is for students who stay till age 19 – especially those who started early – to find paid employment afterwards. (In the Young Adult Centre, students stay until 25.) It is, in short, a thriving organisation, with a worldwide reputation as a model of good practice in the care and education of children with autism.

I am immensely proud of this success story, yet my role in it has for many years been purely symbolic. I am Founding Patron, and that is all. But I love to visit the school and to see the pupils' progress. It reminds me that it is possible, through the good will of many people, to make a difference in the world; and perhaps in some way it reminds me of Giles and the life he might have had.

And there is one particular aspect of life at Prior's Court that remains my personal contribution: a collection of more than 300 works of contemporary art, scattered strategically around the house and grounds.

I acquired most of this collection – which includes paintings, sculptures and a variety of applied arts – between 1999 and 2002 (although I am still adding to it), and have loaned it to the school on a semi-permanent basis. (The original idea was to give it, but the responsibility of ownership would, it seems, have created too many headaches for the management.) The idea is for the art to meet the spiritual needs of pupils and staff, and to provide extra channels of communication for and between both.

I believe that art is not just decorative – and, sometimes, educational – but has enormous therapeutic value, especially for autistic children, who learn visually, not aurally. It is a steady, visible, enduring good that enhances the lives of those who come into contact with it; and children, including children with learning difficulties, have as much right to that good as anyone else.

I have, subsequently, made other artistic gifts. For example, I recently commissioned portraits of Tim Berners-Lee and Stephen Hawking for the Royal Society; and I have given a sculpture of Hawking, by Milein Cosman, to University College, Oxford (where the great physicist studied as an undergraduate); and a painting of HRH The Duke of Edinburgh (in 2012) for the Prince Philip House HQ of the Royal Academy of Engineering, of which I am a Fellow. But the art that means most to me is in the Prior's Court collection. Many of the artists chosen are my own personal favourites, but it is the artworks' collective relationship with the school – the way they imbue the whole environment with humanity, warmth and depth and create a sense of shared wonder between pupils and staff – that makes them magical. If

It was my privilege to commission a portrait of Tim Berners-Lee, father of the Internet, for The Royal Society.

the atmosphere of the school has some kind of "healing" effect, I am sure that the art has something to do with it.

The main linking idea is that the works should be inspirational, hopeful, developmental, calm and serene rather than stimulating or challenging. The palettes tend towards the quiet and pastel; the shapes are generally abstract; and materials and structures are selected on the basis that anything that can get broken will get broken. Artists are grouped to suggest different moods in different places, helping to give shape, focus and meaning to a landscape that might otherwise seem frighteningly vast. The art also helps pupils to find their way around, and gives them the confidence to explore.

I find it fascinating to see how, over and over again, across the years, these artworks can reach out to pupils, creating the human connections that are the essence of what the school is trying to achieve. Generally the tactile pieces are the most popular. The dog by Elizabeth Frink gets a lot of pats, while a water sculpture is arguably our most successful commission of all (not least with the local pigeons).

But pupil reactions can never be predicted. One very quiet John Miller painting appealed to one child to the point of obsession. He liked it so much that he kept licking it. Before long there was spittle all over it, and we had to move it higher up the wall. There was also a wooden bench (not strictly speaking an artwork) that proved so popular that someone kept biting chunks out of it. That one had to be removed altogether.

I am sure that there are people who see the Prior's Court art collection as an indulgence, but I have no doubt that it is integral to the school's most important characteristic: the simple fact that it is a cheerful, friendly, unthreatening place. The world tends to feel benign when you are at Prior's Court. Children feel safe there, and parents feel comfortable about letting them go there.

This last point is important. There are few things more pitiful than the sight of the parent or parents of a child with autism, handing them over to the care of a residential institution for the first time. Almost invariably, such parents will be tormented by guilt. They will feel that they have failed their child by not being able to care for him or her at home; feel that they are putting their own sanity before their child's; and fear that their child will be left feeling lonely, frightened, confused and abandoned when they drive away.

From time to time I see such parents, and, when I can, try to reassure them. I tell them, in all honesty and with total conviction, that Prior's Court is the school to which I would have been only too happy to entrust my own autistic son's physical, intellectual and spiritual development – if only such a school had existed at the time. I explain that I understand all too well the agony that a parent feels on entrusting such a child to an institution of any kind – but that half a lifetime of bitter experience has taught me beyond doubt that to leave a child with autism in a sympathetic specialist school whose regime may loosen the condition's grip on that child is the most loving thing that any parent could do for them.

And sometimes, after such an encounter, I am reminded of another parent who performed a similarly counter-instinctive act more than 70 years ago, sending her children away into the unknown from Nazi Vienna in order to give them a chance of life. And I wonder if, on balance, I may perhaps have been over-harsh in my judgement of my mother.

23: Fighting Back

Prior's Court was one of my proudest achievements – a source of even more satisfaction than being appointed a Dame at the beginning of 2000; or, for that matter, the Beacon Fellowship Prize that I was awarded ("for starting innovative charities in the fields of autism and IT") in 2003. But by the time I stood down from the Prior's Court Foundation, in 2003, the school was just one item in an increasingly complex portfolio of charitable activity that was occupying my time.

There were several reasons for this, of which perhaps the most pressing was the curious fact that, at precisely the time that I was pouring money into the development of the school and other causes, I was growing rapidly and spectacularly richer.

This was not the result of any new initiative on my part. Rather, it was caused by the continuing success of FI Group, in which I retained a shareholding of 5.1 per cent. I had had little to do with the company since its 1996 flotation, but it had flourished without me. It had also grown spectacularly, helped both by Hilary's dynamic leadership and by a continuing culture of staff ownership. Some 30 per cent of the company was directly or indirectly owned by the staff (compared with 25 per cent when I retired in 1993) – which was all the more impressive given that the original shareholding had been diluted by a series of major acquisitions. These included: IIS Infotech Limited, an Indian computer services company based in New Delhi, bought for £26m in 1997; OSI, a London based project management and IT consultancy group, bought for £100m in 1999; Druid, a Reading-based software consultancy, bought for £725m in 2000; and Synergy International Consulting, bought for £14m in 2001.

This breakneck expansion had, on the whole, worked well for the company. Taking over IIS Infotech allowed FI Group to offer the kind of managed, high-quality outsourcing to India that I had first envisaged 20 years earlier; OSI added further depth to the company's already impressive client base, bringing with it such prime customers as American Express, Prudential and Orange; Druid was more controversial but did at least turn a rival into a subsidiary, as well as making the group's gender balance more even, since Druid had a very male culture. (One analyst described the takeover as "like Bath rugby

INVESTITURE AT BUCKINGHAM PALACE

I received my dameship from HRH The Prince of Wales in 2000 (my OBE in 1980 was presented by HM Queen Elizabeth II).

club merging with Cheltenham Ladies' College lacrosse team", which led to various jokes about which company was which.)

Pre-tax profits in 1999-2000 were £27m (excluding goodwill amortisation relating to the Druid deal), up from £17m the previous year. Turnover had reached £307m a year (up 35 per cent), and the company was still growing. Right across the business world, anyone who aspired to be at the cutting edge of management was looking at the kind of efficiency solutions that FI Group offered, from IT systems to outsourcing. If a company was a household name, it was a fair bet that it would have a working relationship with FI: Barclays, Bank of Scotland, British Telecom, Diageo, Kingfisher, GlaxoSmithKline, AstraZeneca, Boots – they were all FI Group clients, and the projects they commissioned were bigger than ever (for example, a joint banking venture with Bank of Scotland – now part of Lloyds TSB – that was worth £150m).

The company was also poised to benefit from the start of a new millennium: a lot of IT investment worldwide was thought to have been postponed until after 1 January 2000, because of concern about the "Millennium bug" (the danger, more serious than some people now imagine, that the change of date from a year ending in "99" to one ending in "00" might cause expensive or even disastrous malfunctions in middle-aged computer systems). FI Group had already been doing a good trade helping clients to protect themselves against the threat, but its passing would be better still for business.

All of this had made the company more attractive than ever to investors, and the share price had rocketed. In early 2000, shares in the group reached an all-time peak of 885p per share, giving the company a market capitalisation of more than £2.5bn – and making paper millionaires, as previously mentioned, of at least 70 staff members. Hilary herself had cashed in her share options in 1999, at a £17m profit, making her Britain's best-paid female executive; she had also been appointed CBE that year. (She was appointed a Dame in 2004. I was on the Industry Honours Committee by then, and supported her appointment, although it was not me who nominated her.)

As for me, I was shocked to be told that I was listed in the 2000 edition of the Sunday Times Rich List as the UK's 11th richest women (three places below the Queen) and the second-richest self-made woman (after Ann Gloag of Stagecoach). My total wealth was calculated at £140m.

Given that I had already given away tens of millions of pounds by this stage (to Kingwood, to Prior's Court and to the Worshipful Company of Information Technologists), along with roughly a quarter of my FI Group shareholding, it was disconcerting – and faintly obscene – to find that I was now several times richer than I had been before I started. But such are the vagaries of capitalism. I took the news with a pinch of salt, knowing that paper wealth can go down as abruptly and arbitrarily as it goes up, and resolved to do as much giving as possible before my fortune shrank again.

I think it was this reasoning, combined with the realisation that I no longer needed to keep a big chunk of my wealth on one side to provide for Giles's care after my death, that led me to get involved in a flurry of charitable activities around the turn of the millennium. The most prominent of these was Autism 99, one of the very first virtual conferences of any kind – and the first ever such conference in the field of disability. The idea (which seems obvious now but didn't then) was that the worldwide web could be used to bring together people with specialist knowledge of autism from all over the planet, at a small fraction of the cost and inconvenience that a conventional international event would involve. The online event was a year in preparation and was, I think, a spectacular success. Some 65,000 people, from 114 countries, took part, from research scientists to ordinary people with first-hand experience of the condition. I say that it was a success partly because of the buzz it created and the numbers and names involved, but mainly because the connections it forged have continued to function and multiply ever since. The three-week "live" conference left a permanent online legacy (its archive can now be found at www.autismconnect.org.uk), as well as a living legacy of new relationships between experts on autism around the world.

There were dozens of other projects as well, all of which made demands on my time and attention as well as my wealth. Between 1998 and 2001, the Shirley Foundation gave support to 73 different causes, big and small, many but not all relating to autism. Their total value was about £20.5m. It would be tiresome to describe or even list them all, but a few stand out in my memory. One involved helping the Wirral Autistic Society to develop a community and IT centre with residential accommodation at Bromborough, Wirral. This was initially supposed to be a £15,000 upgrade to the society's computer systems, but I realised when I looked closely at the project that it really wasn't going to produce value for my money. Then I noticed a semi-derelict building near their headquarters, and discussed the idea of turning it into a proper computer centre – a bigger investment but a more strategic one. It ended up as a wonderfully rewarding £750,000 project, and I have remained involved with the society since. One of the things I liked about this little group was the way they used music to encourage self-expression. Some of the residents even formed a little band, The Beathovens. When I was a guest on BBC Radio 4's Desert Island Discs in 2010, one of my chosen records was a private tape of The Beathovens performing "Summer's Child", a song of their own composition.

Other significant support from the Shirley Foundation went to the Autism Research Centre of Cambridge University (for research into the prevalence of Asperger's Syndrome – a mild form of autism – among primary school children); to Birmingham University (for a web-based distance learning course on autism); to the Department of Child Psychiatry at Oxford University (for research into sleep disorders in children with autism and the efficacy of behavioural therapies in treating them); to the World Health Organisation (for autism research); to PACE (Parents Autism Campaign for Education); to Resources for Autism (for three years of support for a service helping parents to obtain statements of Special Educational Needs for their children); and to a year-long public awareness campaign called Autism Awareness 2002.

The Shirley Foundation also facilitated the formation of an All-Party Parliamentary Group on Autism, as well as similar all-party initiatives in the Scottish Parliament and the Welsh Assembly. This in turn stimulated my interest in autism in Wales, where more than 30,000 people are affected by the disorder. It occurred to me that, for non-communicating children, a bilingual country like Wales must be an even harder environment to grow up in than a monolingual one. Eventually, in partnership with an inspirational worker in the field called Hugh Morgan, I was instrumental in setting up Autism Cymru, a highly effective special interest group that started in May 2001 and has helped bring the needs of people with autism close to the top of the Welsh political agenda. (Autism Cymru worked with the Welsh Assembly to develop – and later on to help implement – the world's first government-led national strategy for autism.)

There was also one large donation that had nothing to do with autism. This was the Oxford Internet Institute, a project first suggested to me in 2000 by some fellow members of the Worshipful Company of Information Technologists who had been discussing the idea with Balliol College. The initial plan – once I had agreed to join them – was that the Shirley Foundation would contribute £100,000 seedcorn funding. Once everything was in place to go forward, however, I authorised a contribution of £10m, which (matched by £5m of core funding from the Higher Education Funding Council for England) allowed the Institute to open as a university department in 2001, with its own dedicated building becoming operative in July 2003.

The institute's raison-d'être is to be a centre of excellence for rigorous studies of the non-technical aspects of the internet – the social, legal, economic and ethical effects of a revolutionary communications tool – in the hope that its findings will inform government policies worldwide. I have supported it because I think such work is important: the internet is dismantling old certainties as rapidly as any innovation since the printing press. But I have also found it enormously rewarding to be involved in such a pioneering, strategic project so late in my career, working with bright academics in an area that is still close to being my special subject. I enjoy the meetings and discussions in which the Institute has involved me. It's not just that it's flattering (although I can't deny feeling gratified to have been made a foundation fellow at Balliol): it's the fact that I simply find it more stimulating to talk to academics about abstract concepts than talking to people about where they went on holiday and what car they drive. I also get great pleasure from seeing my money working to such good effect. To that extent, good philanthropy is like good business: the reward comes from seeing a system achieve what you wanted it to achieve.

The more I gave during these years, the more I realised that I didn't really want to be giving lots of little hand-outs to lots of piecemeal projects. I wanted to contribute my strategic insight as well as my wealth. So I began to be more discerning about what I supported, and to adopt a more conscious policy of investing rather than giving with no strings attached. I realised that the really empowering gifts are the ones that fund infrastructure rather than one-off projects; and that you get more bangs-per-buck (as the weapons industry puts it) from big donations than from little ones.

I also realised that what remained of my fortune would be more likely to make a difference to the world if I focused my giving on the specific areas that concerned me, rather than spreading it too thinly. One of these areas, information technology, now seemed well catered for by my donations to the Oxford Internet Institute and the Worshipful Company of Information Technologists. But autism – or, rather, the battle to understand, cure or ameliorate the effects of autism – was still a cause in desperate need of all the support it could get. The £35m I had given to the cause so far had merely scratched the surface.

I therefore put it to my fellow trustees at the Shirley Foundation that henceforward we should fund only causes relating to autism. Specifically, we resolved in 2002 that we would consider funding only projects that were innovative in nature, with the potential to have a strategic impact in the field of autism spectrum disorders.

Since then, we have made around 20 different donations, to a variety of different projects. In 2011, for example, £250,000 was pledged to the new Autism & Disability Loan Scheme with an interesting charity, Paintings in Hospitals (founded back in the 1950s and revitalised in recent years by a young New Zealander, Director Stuart Davie). Edinburgh University got £1m for a microscopy unit for its Patrick Wild Centre for Research into Autism, Fragile X Syndrome and intellectual disabilities. And about £500,000 went to an organisation called Autistica (www.autistica.org.uk), which I helped to set up between 2005 and 2007 and whose infrastructure we have been funding, to the tune of several million pounds, since then.

My declared strategic aim is a huge one: to determine the causes of autism by 2014, and to halve the global cost of this perplexing disorder by 2020. In my mind, the mission can be stated more simply still: I want to devote what remains of my wealth and my life to finding a cure for autism.

Ambitious? Certainly. Unrealistic? Not necessarily. Another thing my experience of life has taught me is that the only people who achieve on a grand scale are those who dream on a grand scale. And it struck me that, although many brilliant minds had been grappling with the problem for many years, they had tended to be brilliant specialist

Balliol College honoured me for my contributions (Oxford Internet Institute and St Cross church) by commissioning this portrait by Saïed Dai to hang in Hall. The image on the tablet in my lap is of the church's sundial; the geometric solid indicates mathematics and – subliminally – my heritage.

minds: biologists, chemists, neuroscientists, behaviouralists and so on. But what if I added to the mix my own talents as a generalist? What if I applied to the problem some of the entrepreneurial and strategic skills that I had developed during my decades in business?

One of the first things I did was to commission a literature review of the research on autism to date, so that I could get a sense of what the main areas of exploration were. I was surprised to find that this had never been done before – which just goes to show how an ignorant outsider can sometimes make a positive difference. Perhaps, I reasoned, I could make other such contributions. I hadn't needed to be an avionics engineer to design systems for Concorde, and, by the same token, I didn't necessarily need to be a neurologist to contribute to this fight.

Such thoughts in due course gave rise to a project called Kaspar, a kind of macro-study in which I tried (with the help of such eminent professors as Simon Baron-Cohen and Geri Dawson and of such eminent institutions as Oxford, Cambridge and Washington universities and the MIND Institute in California) to form an objective picture of what was needed to get at the causes of autism. I saw this as analogous to the US government trying to establish what needed to be done to get a man on the moon in the early 1960s.

The answer that eventually presented itself in this case was that a budget of at least £400m would be needed. This was clearly way out of my depth, and, as a result, I was forced to think more strategically still. Who else was working on this? How were they organised? And could their collective work be made more effective or efficient?

The two main organisations working in the field were both in the US: Cure Autism Now (CAN), on the west coast, and National Alliance for Autism Research (NAAR), on the east coast. I became involved with NAAR, which seemed the more strategic and science-based of the two, joining their board (in 2004) and helping them to make better use of IT in their fundraising. This eventually led to the establishment of a NAAR in the UK, which in due course evolved (at its third naming) into Autistica. Autistica is now the main vehicle for the Shirley Foundation's activities in this field. It is also the largest UK charity raising funds for medical research into autism. That, for me, is part of the attraction: it generates funds as well as dispensing them. I know that the challenge we face is so huge that my limited wealth

Autistica chose to study autism spectrum disorders in Saudi Arabia because of its concentrated gene pool. Eileen Hopkins and I signed the Memorandum of Understanding with the Prince Salman Centre for Disability Research in 2006. Throughout my visits it was very obvious that I was serving yet again as a female role model.

– even in its entirety – can do no more than facilitate a few scratches at the surface. But by injecting my money at the right strategic point, where it can be used to leverage more and bigger donations and to ensure that whatever money is raised goes to the projects with greatest potential, I can get the maximum possible benefit from what I give. Autistica provides grants for researchers, mentors fellowships to recruit new researchers to focus on autism and provides funding for larger, collaborative programmes. It also tries to draw together and coordinate the findings of experts in different disciplines (immunology, epidemiology, behavioural sciences, molecular and cellular biology, genetics and neuroscience) and different countries.

At the time of writing, Autistica's hopes of a breakthrough reside mainly in four encouraging areas: the study of susceptibility genes for autism led by the Autism Genome Project (the largest research collaboration ever assembled); research into the younger siblings of children diagnosed with autism, which may allow earlier detection, diagnosis and treatment; new forms of neuro-imaging clarifying structural and functional differences in the brain, to help diagnosis; and studies of human brain tissue – the world's most precious resource – looking for markers for autism at a cellular level. (I am proud to say that, since 2009, Giles's brain has been among those available to researchers via Oxford's Brain Bank for Autism.)

Will anything come of this? Who can say? All I know is that it is worth trying.

I know that money cannot guarantee scientific advances; I know that research cannot be rushed; I know that all my donations may ultimately come to nothing. But, equally, I know that there is nothing I would rather have done with the money. It is better to fight and fail than simply to shrug and declare that nothing can be done. There are about 130,000 children on the autistic spectrum in the UK today, out of perhaps 500,000 people altogether who have some aspect of the disorder – and, of course, there are many hundreds of thousands of parents and other relatives who experience daily the indirect agonies that this condition inflicts.

Leaving aside the financial implications – and the annual cost of autism to the UK economy has been estimated at £28bn – I believe that it is simply wrong to give up in the face of human misery on such a scale. To accept autism as something unavoidable, which cannot be eradicated and thus is not worth fighting, strikes me as on a par with saying, in the 1930s, that there was nothing that could be done about the thousands of Jewish children in Europe whose lives were at risk from Nazism.

There were plenty of people in Britain who did say that. But there were, luckily for me, others who took a less supine view.

24: For Richer, For Poorer

The flow of millions from FI Group always felt too good to be true, and, sure enough, as the new century unfolded the company's fortunes changed. The dot-com bubble burst in March 2000, and continued to deflate until late 2002. FI Group coped with the initial run on technology shares better than most; but the sector's continuing decline eventually took its toll.

It was, by now, a truly global business – a fact reflected by its announcement in March 2001 that it was going to change its name to the less parochial-sounding Xansa. (I approved of this change: global brands need brand names that resonate all over the globe. But I was hurt not to have been forewarned about it.) It was also a very substantial business, with a workforce of over 6,000 people, including about 1,200 in India; a market capitalisation of £1.2bn; and forecast sales for 2001-2002 of £515m. So it didn't seem to be in any immediate danger of collapse.

But its share-price slid, more slowly than many but downwards none the less, with obvious consequences for the balance sheet. At the same time, clients and potential clients came under pressure from the general downturn. Discretionary spending on consultancy, strategic IT and long-term "vision" projects was quickly cut back – especially by the blue-chip clients who now provided such a large part of the company's business. And although the market would no doubt recover soon, it was hard to see where short-term growth would come from.

Then the terrorist attacks of 11 September 2001 dealt a new blow to global business confidence, and the company's seemingly unstoppable upward momentum went into reverse. In 2000-2001, profits were down to £3.5m (from an underlying £27m – excluding acquisitions – the previous year). In 2001-2002 a staggering £507.8m loss was reported. (Some £497m of this was an impairment charge to write down the value of its £725m purchase of Druid, which now seemed seriously overpriced; but the underlying trend was unhealthy too.) To make matters worse, a major contract with HBOS (the First Banking Systems co-venture with what used to be Bank of Scotland) was terminated 18 months early in June 2002, leading to a loss of £91m of contracted revenue. The share price plummeted. At one point in September 2002 shares were trading at 37.5p, valuing the company at just £125m; they later settled at around 90p – still roughly 90 per cent down from their peak.

In August 2002, Hilary Cropper stood down as chief executive. Her 17 years in the post had seen the company's turnover rise from £7m to (at its 2000 peak) £450m – an increase of more than 6,000 per cent. For two of those years she had been the UK's highest-paid businesswoman, and few would have disputed that she deserved it. The final 12 months of her tenure had taken some of the gloss off her achievements, but she would, plainly, be a hard act to follow.

Hilary remained as chairman, working three days a week. Alistair Cox, recruited from the building materials group, Lafarge, replaced her as chief executive. Then, in 2003, Hilary stepped down as chairman as well – and shocked her many admirers with the announcement that she had been suffering from ovarian cancer since 2001. She had, it seemed, told no one at the company about her illness, undergoing chemotherapy at weekends and on short holidays. But no one, not even a superwoman, is indestructible, and she had finally had to admit defeat.

She died late the following year, aged 63. I was saddened by her death, despite the tensions in our relationship. She had been a formidable and positive force, principled and tireless, and in financial terms she had taken my company to heights that were, literally, beyond my wildest dreams for it.

Her successors were competent but lacked her Midas touch. The company performed respectably but uninspiringly, shrinking slowly in the face of economic forces beyond its control. The losses were stemmed and reversed: Xansa reported a £27.7m pre-tax profit in 2002-3, a £24m profit in 2003-4, a £12.5m profit in 2004-5 and a £13.3m profit in 2005-6. But the basic narrative, as these figures suggest, was one of contraction. Overheads were cut and sights were lowered. No one talked about conquering the world any more. The share price remained depressed.

I had hardly anything to do with Xansa at this stage in its history, but what I did see left me with the impression that it was no longer particularly different from any other multi-national, profit-driven, publicly quoted corporation. The ethos of employee ownership continued: there was a company broker to facilitate share-trading; a company banker who lent money against the company's shares; a company PEP, so that people could hold shares in a tax-effective way; loans to new staff to help them buy their first shares; and a variety of share option schemes. But the buzz of common enterprise had gone. It was as if the long-term downward trend of the share-price and revenues had taken the excitement out of shared ownership. Where once people had dreamed of making their fortunes by making the company's fortune, they now seemed more concerned with keeping a firm foothold on the corporate ladder.

Perhaps I am being unjust. I was, as I say, an outsider by this stage. But, at any rate, the great adventure was coming to an end.

Alistair Cox remained chief executive until 2007, when he moved on to Hays, the recruitment firm. Bill Alexander, the group chairman, took over as interim chief executive. Then, in July that year, it was announced that the company was in advanced talks regarding a possible takeover. The bidder was a French company, Groupe Steria SCA, which specialised, like Xansa, in IT-driven consultancy services, notably (unlike Xansa) in the European public sector.

Their offer, of 130p per share, was accepted, and my remaining shareholding – nearly three per cent of the company – was exchanged for cash. The purchase was completed, for £470m, via a scheme of arrangement on 17 October 2007. Xansa was delisted from the Stock Exchange, and the company that I had founded 45 years earlier ceased to exist.

I mourned its passing, naturally. But the financial aspects of the story left me relatively indifferent. Somehow, in the space of seven years, my notional unspent fortune had declined by at least £70m. I barely noticed. I had never really thought of that money as real, anyway, and at least now I knew where I stood. As for the company itself, it had been a remarkable story – from that first £6 investment in 1962 – and I was glad that it had ultimately been a success story. Much good had come from it, from the many staff members whose lives had been changed through shared ownership to the many millions of pounds that it had allowed me to use for the benefit of those less fortunate than me.

Meanwhile, the knowledge that my remaining stock of disposable wealth was finite and unlikely to grow significantly helped me to think more clearly about my philanthropic aims. (I say "philanthropic" rather than "charitable" because, increasingly, I am conscious of a difference. Charity repairs the immediate damage of social ills; philanthropy tries in a more preventive way to make society a better place to live in. For those who can afford to give large sums, philanthropy is a more productive investment.)

I knew that I wanted – and want – to give away all that remains of my wealth before I die. (Should I fail to do so, my will and the Shirley Foundation are set up to dispose of the rest within five years of my death.) But I do not want to scatter it thoughtlessly: the traumas of my early life have left me with a horror of waste. Instead, I want to combine everything left to me – money, time, business sense, connections, vision – and give it together, in such a way as to make the greatest possible difference.

I was 74 when Xansa ceased to exist, and my reserves of energy are, like my money, depleted. But I am happy to spend whatever time I have left working to make a few lives happier. I have worked hard all my life, and I see little point in changing my habits now.

My last non-executive directorship – as "general inspector" for John Lewis – finished in 2001; I had finished with AEA Technology the previous year. But there has rarely been a weekday since then when I have not ended the day feeling tired out by hard work. Until recently, this may have been a life-style choice as much as a necessity. Better to work myself to exhaustion than to sit quietly on long, empty evenings, thinking about Giles. But even now, when I can look back on the highs and lows of my life with slightly more equanimity, I see little attraction in just waiting limply for the clock of my life to run down. I would rather be doing my best to achieve something, trying to make a difference.

There was a point, at the beginning of 2009, when things appeared to be getting quieter. I stood down from the chair of Autistica – in keeping both with good corporate governance and with my policy of leaving the organisations I create to stand on their own feet – and noted with pleasure that my diary was looking empty. All my big projects were largely running themselves, and a number of lesser ones were either approaching their conclusions or were ticking along nicely with little ongoing contribution from me. These included: a book that I commissioned in 2007 – written by Adam Feinstein and recently published by Wiley/Blackwell as A History of Autism: Conversations with the Pioneers; a £1m challenge grant to Balliol in 2007 for a Historic Collections Centre in St Cross Church in Oxford (the architect made a super job of the conversion: a tiny part remained consecrated, and the first service in the beautifully restored space was held in 2012); some work in 2008 to bring the UK's autism charities closer together; and an attempt on behalf of Autistica to promote the study of autism in Saudi Arabia, where the frequency of marriage between close family members could yield priceless statistical information about autism's genetic components.

So I found myself looking forward to spending more time at home, seeing Derek, catching up with friends, going swimming, going to galleries and restaurants, and so on. It seemed a rather tempting (and novel) prospect.

Then, in March 2009, I received a telephone call from the Cabinet Office. The Office of the Third Sector (now the Office for Civil Society) was appointing the UK's first ever Ambassador for Philanthropy, and I had been suggested as a suitable candidate for the role. It took me all of five minutes to consider the matter before I agreed to take it on. I took up the post, for a one-year term, in May 2009.

It was a great honour. It was also a challenge, not least because the brief was open. My broad aim was to give philanthropists "a voice", and to encourage a culture of philanthropic giving both in and beyond the UK. I was given access to a room in Admiralty Arch and some office support staff. Apart from that it was up to me. I provided my own funding, and set my own agenda, committing myself in an early press release "to act as the voice of philanthropy as well as championing innovative and effective forms of giving; and to make recommendations to Government about how to encourage and facilitate giving".

The need for such a voice seemed self-evident. There are 26 million people in the UK who make charitable or philanthropic donations of one kind or another – by which measure we are Europe's most generous country, outstripped globally only by the US. But that is just one way of looking at it. An alternative analysis would be that we lag shamefully behind the US, particularly in terms of major donations. The average Briton gives £225 a year; the average American £600. And whereas the top 30 givers in the UK (as calculated by the Sunday Times Rich List) give just 1.2 per cent of their wealth, the equivalent top donors in the US give 13 per cent. So there is, plainly, room for improvement.

I set myself the mission of giving existing philanthropists a voice and a visible presence in national and international life – in the hope that others might discover, through them, the rewards of philanthropy.

Part of the problem, I was certain, was the old idea among well-off Britons that "We don't talk about money." I felt that the key to achieving American levels of generosity was to encourage American levels of openness: so that people are proud of giving, and enjoy giving, and are even – if they like – a little competitive about giving. I don't mean that competition should be the point of philanthropy: just that the wealthy should feel comfortable enthusing about their donations and the projects that they support, in the same way that many of them already enthuse happily about their yachts, cars, racehorses, fine wines and holiday homes.

With this in mind I focused on promoting the idea that it is a pleasure to give, not a duty. I appointed a chief of staff: a US entrepreneur with excellent connections in philanthropic circles called Roberta d'Eustachio. Heaven knows how I would have managed without her. We put a lot of effort into the creation of a website, www.ambassadorforphilanthropy.com, which allowed existing philanthropists a platform to talk about why they gave and what they got from it. And I published an Ambassador's Pledge:

"I pledge to inspire the idea that giving is a pleasurable act of desire and compassion to help, change or challenge any aspect of society by raising the bar on our capacity to be generous."

The website proved remarkably successful. Having tested out different models of how a global "social media" website might work, we developed it as a membership organisation along with sponsorship and advertising. The internet platform – mission driven – has a portfolio of benefits for members. The aim is for it to become self-supporting. Early contributors included James Caan, Stelio Stefanou, Simon Merchant, Alec Reed, Satish Modi, Frederick Mulder and many others. Each made a video presentation (still available on the website), discussing their philanthropic experiences and motives. What they had to say was, pretty much without exception, enlightening, thought-provoking and inspiring.

It was a natural extension of this to establish a network of British philanthropists to bring donors together on a regular basis to learn and share knowledge and put forward their views collectively to decision-makers in and beyond government. I also chaired a Philanthropy Advice Steering Group, to help develop a marketplace for philanthropic advice. And I participated in a number of events in the UK and abroad, from a policy forum on "Unleashing the Potential of e-Philanthropy" at the Oxford Internet Institute to meetings with the British Banking Association to help retail banks make giving easy, not to mention such exotic missions as an appearance at the 9th Commonwealth Women's Affairs Ministers' Meeting in Barbados (to persuade other nations of the benefits of promoting philanthropy).

A change of government in 2010 made relatively little difference to this work. After some early talk of "expanding the philanthropy ambassadors programme begun by the previous government", the new Coalition eventually decided not to renew state support (such as it was) for the experiment. My response was to carry on, privately and globally – with measurable effect. Ireland, Singapore, several eastern European countries and surprisingly, the United States were the earliest enthusiasts, but others have followed suit.

The over-riding objective in all this has been, simply, to encourage clearer thinking about what philanthropy is. It seems to me self-evident that any exercise that does this will inevitably encourage more philanthropy.

Human beings are born with an instinct to give. Our brains are hard-wired for sharing: brain scans show that the pleasure-centres in the brain are neurochemically stimulated when we act unselfishly. Yet although we are taught to share as children, most of us are somehow brainwashed later in life into thinking that sharing and giving are forms of self-harm: things to be practised, if at all, as painful duties.

I tried as Ambassador, and have tried since, to reverse this misconception. Giving may be a duty, but it is above all a pleasure. Look at the philanthropists' testimonies at www.ambassadorforphilanthropy. com, and you will find no mention of any of them having been altruistic. Instead, they enthuse about how rewarding philanthropy has been for them: about how much more they have got from their money by using it for someone else's benefit than they would have done by trying to enjoy it alone. This is a crucial concept. Philanthropy isn't about letting someone else take your money and spend it as they, rather than you, see fit. (We call that "tax".) Rather, it is about putting your money to uses you believe in, and taking pleasure from the process. Your money isn't lost, just because someone else has it. It is simply realising its potential: wealth as numbers on a bank statement transformed into wealth that enriches the world – and, as a result, enriches you.

My own philanthropy – from my personal contributions to the autism and IT sectors to my broader campaigning as an ambassador for philanthropy – has given my life a breadth that makes me feel truly fortunate. As a social entrepreneur, I meet more interesting people, travel purposefully to more interesting places (in 2012, for example, I made two fascinating trips to Israel, which I would never otherwise have visited), and feel more fulfilled than I ever did in the years spent making my fortune. I must have given away well over £65m by now – more, if you wish to assign a notional value to the 24 per cent shareholding, in a company that at one point would be worth £2.6bn, that I put into the hands of the staff of F International; and more still, I suppose, if you also wish to include the one per cent of pre-tax profits that the company gave to charity every year for the last 30 years of its existence. Since 1994 I have been involved in nearly 100 philanthropic projects, leaving me with less than a tenth of the wealth I once had. I have ring-fenced a little to ensure that Derek and I can live out the remainder of our lives without fear of poverty, but the rest I hope to give away, in my lifetime, to autism-related causes.

Perhaps it is a question of growing up. The older you get, the more you realise that the things that really matter in life are not the material things. In 1998, I had felt a frisson of slightly guilty pride when I was included for the first time on the Sunday Times Rich List (valued on that first appearance at £40m). I felt a much warmer glow of pride five years later when, as a result of my giving, I dropped off it again. Neither impulse was unselfish. It was merely a question of one form of pleasure being richer than the other.

This is what I have tried to emphasise in my work as an ambassador: giving is a pleasure, not a duty. It is also a social and cultural activity, not merely a financial transaction. I try always to remember how awful it was to accept charity and be expected to be grateful – grateful for not having been murdered like a million other Jewish children. So although I generally give in a business-like, strategic way, I try never to lose sight of the human side of the gift. I would never just write a cheque: that demeans both giver and recipient. Instead, I give with a warm heart – and a warm hand, too, because what's the fun in writing gifts into my last will and testament? I want to give in my lifetime. Giving is what I do. It connects me to the future.

And yet, just as I evolved from entrepreneur into philanthropist, so I think I may now be evolving into a fundraiser. There is a limit to the money I can give, but there is scarcely any limit to the money that other people can give. And if my work can persuade 50 people to give £1m each, that is a more worthwhile achievement than simply giving away £1m of my own money.

Philanthropy will, I think, be one of the key megatrends of the next 50 years. Governments everywhere are paring back the welfare state, and the societies that do not wither as a result will be those in which philanthropists step forward to contribute as they see fit. They cannot replace the state, but they can, if they choose, acquire a significance comparable to that which they had in Victorian times. If my current work – including this book – can help persuade those who have something to give that it is worth their while to give it, my ambassadorial efforts will not have been wasted.

25: Letting Go

It turned out that the story of Freelance Programmers didn't quite finish when Xansa was acquired by Groupe Steria in 2007. The soul of the company lives on.

I learnt this in February 2008, when I was invited to Evian, on the French shore of Lake Geneva, for a conference organised by the French company for 100 of its leading executives. The purpose of the conference was to celebrate Steria's distinctive corporate culture: a culture that takes pride in its inclusiveness, flexibility and corporate and social responsibility – and that bears a startling resemblance to the ethos I once tried to create for my own company.

I was vaguely aware of this already, but in Evian I realised for the first time just how close the resemblance was. Established in 1969 by a French telecom engineer and computer pioneer called Jean Carteron, Steria was founded, according to Carteron, "on my conviction that economic and ethical interests are not mutually exclusive, and that financial performance follows from employees' direction of and dedication to a company in whose future they have a stake." It listed its core principles as creativity, independence, international ambition – and employee ownership.

Like Xansa, Steria had been a technological and conceptual innovator, breaking new ground in such fields as word-processing, calculators, interactive information systems, flight simulation, cash-dispensing networks, Metro systems and identity cards. And Carteron, like me, was convinced that there was a relationship between such creativity and the fact that employees had a stake in the company.

Like Xansa, Steria has never achieved total employee ownership. It is a publicly quoted company, first listed on the Paris stock exchange in 1999. But 20 per cent of the company is still owned by or on behalf of staff shareholders, who not only share the benefits of the company's success but have the power to influence decision-making. Under French company law Steria is a "partnership limited by shares". Soderi, the company representing the employee shareholders, is the sole General Partner – with the right to "debate, approve and reject" strategic decisions (such as acquisitions) made by the chief executive.

Around 4,000 of the company's 20,000 employees (spread over 16 countries) own shares.

As with Xansa, Steria is an imperfect realisation of a noble ideal. But it seems to work well – the company had a turnover of €1.7bn in 2010 – and it is clear that this is an organisation with a sense of values as well as a profit motive. There is, for example, a Steria Foundation, which supports projects that use IT to benefit disadvantaged people (another cause close to my heart).

Jean Carteron is retired now, but he, like me, had been invited to the Evian conference, and I was moved beyond words when François Enaud, the chief executive, invited both of us on to the podium before explaining to those present that the unique culture they were celebrating was our creation. Perhaps he was merely being gracious (a habit that had been markedly absent from Xansa's boardroom in its later years), but I took his words to heart. It felt as though, for the first time since I had been edged out of FI Group as an irrelevance in the early 1990s, my original ideal for the company was being partially validated again. It also brought home to me that such ideals are often more resilient than we imagine. Xansa the corporate giant was dead; but the spirit of common enterprise that had animated F International was alive and well.

I returned to England full of hope. It is easy to look back on a life of material success and mourn the fact that so much of what once seemed solid has drifted away on the tides of time. But I realised clearly now that the things that matter are often more substantial than they seem.

The company that I began in 1962 generated, over the years, hundreds of millions of pounds: in sales, in revenue, in profits – however you like to measure it. That company no longer exists, and nearly all of that money has gone. What have endured are the good things: the friendships; the memories; the worthwhile projects that some of that money created (the Kingwood homes, Prior's Court, the Oxford Internet Institute); and, scarcely less important, the original ideal of the company: the idea that ownership, like money, is more effective and empowering if it is shared.

That idea is demonstrably true in material terms. Employee-owned companies consistently outperform listed companies, according to the UK Employee Ownership Index, which since 1992 has measured the performance of companies that are more than 10 per cent owned

The company that I set up in 1962 ceased to exist after 45 years when it was acquired by Steria. Early in 2008, together with Jean Carterton – Steria's founder in 1969 – I was invited to join Chief Executive Francois Enaud for its top management conference in Evian.

by employees. An investment of £100 in the FTSE All-Share Index in 1992 would at the end of June 2011 have been worth £242. The same investment in the EOI would have been worth £767.

What I cannot demonstrate with figures are the non-material advantages of shared ownership. Yet these are considerable too. It is fairer. It spreads the strains of work as well as its rewards. And when it works well it creates a sense of community that makes the whole business of earning a living more enjoyable and rewarding. I remember an auditor for the Ministry of Defence carrying out a quality audit at F International (as it then was) in 1985 and saying: "I have to tell you that this is one of the best software houses I have ever seen. But the other thing is, it is obvious that you all have such a lot of fun." The person who cannot look back on their career and remember a reasonable amount of fun is truly impoverished, irrespective of how much they have earned.

Shared ownership is not a universal panacea. Some employee-owned concerns work badly; many public or privately-owned companies work well. But the co-operative approach is not the cranky ideal that some boardroom "realists" like to make it out to be. It works. Few British retail companies have weathered the latest economic downturn so robustly as John Lewis. No wonder all three main political parties have talked recently about using "John Lewis style partnerships" to run key public services. In an age when capitalism is in danger of becoming as discredited as communism, the ideals of co-operatism have more to offer than many people assume.

But employee ownership is not just about sharing. It is also, in practice, often about giving. Such schemes depend on someone, usually the proprietor, deciding at some point to transfer ownership of some or all of a company to its employees. And it is this aspect of the ideal, I think, that has the greatest significance for my story.

Of all the things I have given, it is arguable that the shares in my company that I gave away had the greatest financial value. In fact, I have rarely thought of this transfer of ownership as a gift, and I would be wrong if I did. The staff had a right to share in the company. Without them, the company would not have been so prosperous (and I am certain that Xansa would never have reached anything like the financial heights it eventually did if it hadn't been powered by the fuel of staff ownership). But while I never doubted that aspect of the transfer, I did sometimes struggle with a more abstract issue: the fact that transferring ownership also means, ultimately, transferring control.

That was the real challenge: surrendering power. Anyone can adjust to having a bit less money; ceding control of an enterprise that really matters to you is, by contrast, painfully counterintuitive. Who in their right mind would entrust an organisation that they have built up against all the odds, through years of tears, toil and sweat, to someone else? What if they mess it up? What if they don't really understand what it is that you have created? What if they take it in some dangerous new direction, or manage it in a less idealistic way?

Yet without that surrender, the most important part of the transaction is lost. A feudal grandee can be as generous as he likes with his wealth and property, but as long as he remains the grandee then his dependants are not empowered: they are merely well-fed. Empowering them means letting go: in other words, ceasing to be the grandee.

I have struggled all my life with an instinct to hang on to the things that matter most to me, to control and protect them myself. Yet the art of surrender is, I am convinced, a key to many kinds of success – and fulfilment. And many lives are limited by a failure to master it.

There is a well-known (anonymous) saying in the world of emotional self-help literature: "If you love something, let it go. If it is yours, it will come back to you; if not, it never really belonged to you in the first place." It's a slightly glib formula, rendered trite by over-use; but it expresses a useful truth about love, jealousy and possessiveness. It could also be adapted, with a little distortion, to many other fields.

One of the reasons why Freelance Programmers thrived in its early days – where so many new enterprises fail – was that, simply by allowing our programmers and project managers to perform their duties when and where they pleased, I had surrendered a significant part of the control that employers traditionally exercise over those who work for them. Our competitors were still insisting that their staff worked for fixed hours, in fixed places, clocking in and clocking out and having to account for what they were doing throughout each shift. I trusted mine to manage their own time, as long as the work got done. The result? Not the anarchy and idleness that a traditionalist manager would have predicted but, instead, unrivalled productivity.

Later, my gradual, painful handover of the company to its workforce and my successors led first to a culture of sustained motivation and ultimately to a great leap in profitability that, paradoxically, generated far more wealth for me after I had let go of it than it ever had before. My instincts had told me that no one else could match my passion, perfectionism and strategic insights; my intellect told me otherwise, and was proved right.

I was quicker to manage succession with the Kingwood Trust, with Prior's Court, and with Autistica. None of the handovers was entirely painless, but I always knew, in each case, that letting go was the right thing to do. And each organisation has thrived without me – not despite my absence but because of it. Those running the organisations are empowered to give the best of themselves precisely because the organisations are theirs to run.

The older I get the clearer it becomes to me that empowerment is the key to business success: not the blind surrender of power and responsibility to whoever wants it, but targeted empowerment, where those to whom power and responsibility are given have been painstakingly selected and, where appropriate, nurtured. The wise manager or proprietor invests in that targeting above all else. It is people, not assets, that make the modern business world go round. It is their creative drive that sparks new enterprise and innovation, their professionalism and dedication that ensures quality, their energy that makes things happen – and, always, it is teamwork that carries forward the vision. Yes, by all means lead from the front, if that is your style, but always remember that leadership is nothing unless those who are led give the best of themselves. Like love, leadership is, at its best, about giving, not taking. The people you lead need to recognise that they too have power – and responsibility. And if this then causes them to claim credit for your collective successes, so what? What matters is that they are successes and not failures. Lao Tse observed more than 2,500 years ago that "When the best leader's work is done, the people say: 'We did it all ourselves.'" The best leaders enjoy hearing them do so, rather than worrying that "their" glory has been misappropriated.

But it is not just in business that the habit of letting go can yield dividends. It also works – or has worked for me – in more personal areas. I was only five when my weeping mother put me on a train full of 1,000 children and "let go", entrusting me to the kindness of strangers.

Her trust was repaid. I have seen many other mothers weep as they let their vulnerable children go, entrusting them to an unfamiliar environment – Prior's Court – where they could receive care, therapy and education on a scale that no individual family, no matter how loving, could provide. And, further down that road, I have shared the nervous excitement (and tears) of parents and carers as many of those same children, their education completed, have been "let go" again, to take their first steps towards semi-independent living.

No one thought of independence as a worthwhile goal for children with autism when Giles was growing up. People like him needed to be shut away, for their own safety and society's convenience. Yet such lack of trust in the world and its most vulnerable members can be corrosive and, often, counter-productive. The period of Giles's life when he had the greatest physical protection from the dangers of the outside world was the nightmare period he spent in the subnormality hospital at Borocourt: the time when he was least trusted and least able to make and learn from his own mistakes. The periods when he had the greatest quality of life were those when that safety-net had been replaced with a far looser one: in those happy early schooldays at The Walnuts, where he was given a degree of (supervised) freedom that no parent would have dared to allow at home; and, more visibly, in those last years at The Cuddy, when he was allowed (under supervision) to discover, by trial and error, his own version of adult life. Of course, he was never fully independent. But it was trust, not confinement, that allowed him to live.

It never occurred to me when I set out to write this book that "letting go" might be the connecting theme of my life. Yet the more I think about it, the more obvious it seems. So many of my landmark breakthroughs seem to have involved some form of counter-instinctive loosening of my grip on something. In early adulthood, with the help of psychoanalysis, I was eventually able to let go of the traumas of my early childhood – and immediately began to thrive as a result. When I left FI Group, it was letting go of my accumulated resentment that allowed me to discover a rewarding new phase of my life, when I could so easily have wasted my retirement in backward-looking bitterness.

Perhaps most significantly of all, learning to let go of my money has been absolutely central to what I now see as the most rewarding stage of my life. It would have been so easy to cling on to it: to subscribe to the old myth that looking after number one is all that matters, and that a fool and her money are soon parted. Yet it is hard from my current perspective to see how I could have gained anything like so much happiness and satisfaction from my wealth had I kept it for myself. What would I have done with it? Kept it in a bank? Frittered it away in shops? Spent it on racehorses and yachts?

I don't pretend to be totally indifferent to the comforts of wealth. Simply being free from financial worry is a luxury granted to few. I enjoy buying nice clothes, too, and occasional pieces of furniture or works of art for our apartment. But there is a limit to the number of possessions you can actually enjoy, or to the number of fine dinners you can eat or exotic holidays you can take; and there are drawbacks to extreme wealth (such as insincere would-be "friends") as well as advantages.

On balance, I have no doubt at all: the money I have let go has brought me infinitely more joy than the money I have hung on to. I say "let go" rather than "given away" because it is not, usually, a question of simply giving the money to someone as a present. Such gifts can be patronising and produce limited benefits. Rather, I have tried to release my money in the form of empowering investments which allow other people to achieve things that lack of capital had previously preventing them from doing.

That is when the process becomes truly rewarding for all concerned. The given money repays its value many times over. It is a bit like gardening, and, indeed, I have often thought of myself as a gardener: someone who "grows" people and enterprises. I have planted my financial gifts as seeds, renouncing my ownership of them as I did so; and, when I have planted wisely, they have been gloriously fruitful.

I know that we live in an imperfect world. I know that people sometimes let you down or take advantage of you. But sometimes – often – they don't; and I am grateful to have learnt this important truth, through force of circumstance, early in life. Most of us have well-developed instincts for fear, suspicion and cynicism. The instincts for trust and hope sometimes need a little encouragement.

Perhaps that is the single message with which I should end this book: have faith in other people. No one is faultless, but nearly everyone has virtues (often hidden) and potential (often unrealised). I don't think I have ever achieved anything of note that did not at some point require me to make a leap of faith in some other human being. If I have a talent, it is that: the ability to believe in what others can achieve. I recommend it. Trusting others is also about respecting yourself. The assumption that people will betray you or cheat you or let you down can all too often be self-fulfilling.

I don't know what else life has in store for me. But I believe more firmly than ever that I will get the most out of what remains to me by giving rather than receiving, and by having faith – in human nature, in my own nature, and in the world itself.

I came close to annihilation at the outset of my life, and deep down I remain a refugee. I know that nothing lasts for ever; I know that tomorrow may well be quite different from today. All the more reason, then, to welcome the uncertainties of the future – and to see each unknown tomorrow as an opportunity, not a threat. We waste too much time being afraid, when what we should really fear is wasting time.

I was the first woman Master of the IT livery company; the fifth woman overall, three having been royal.

I found the City an uncomfortably masculine environment though I joined in its many ceremonies. Here the IT livery company is making a presentation to the incoming Lord Mayor, Brian (now Sir Brian) Jenkins.

*I love to learn and would have loved to go to university. The academic world
has since much honoured me – here I am in 1991 receiving an honorary
Fellowship from what is now Staffordshire University.*

My interest in women's affairs has been ongoing. This portrait by Howard Neil Pugh was taken in 1993 when I chaired Women of Influence.

The school's dining room had originally been the billiard room when Prior's Court was the private home of the Palmer family. It was converted yet again in 2009 to provide a training facility. Quality buildings are amazingly flexible.

The 55 acres of parkland at Prior's Court were an exhilarating responsibility. This massive tree by the main door dates from the eighteenth century. The wild (that is, totally natural) wood is always cool and calming.

My Freedom of the City of London in 1987 is a matter of enormous pride.

The Royal Corps of Signals and the IT livery company have been affiliated since 1982. During my year as Master, yes Master, I presented this leopard skin which had been shot by my father in law in India when serving under the Raj. I also gave some of Uncle's things from the Great War to the Signals Museum in Blandford. My experience of donations to museums is 100% successful.

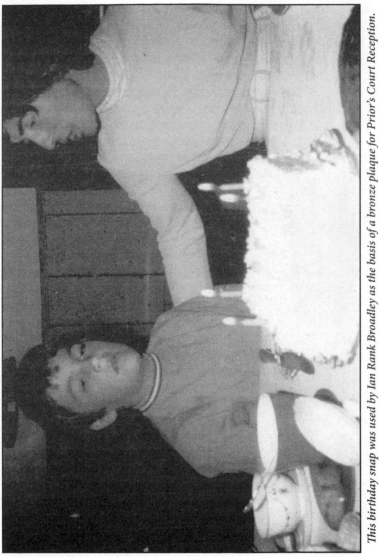

This birthday snap was used by Ian Rank Broadley as the basis of a bronze plaque for Prior's Court Reception.

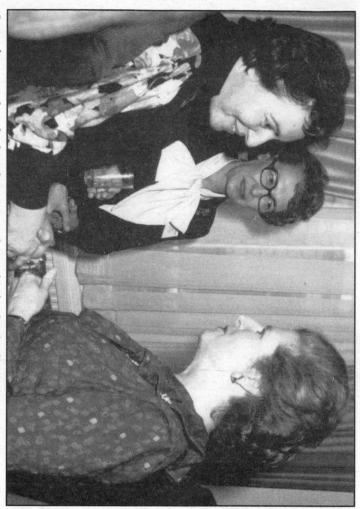

I served on a number of technical committees during the Thatcher (and Major) regimes. We met also when she was Chancellor of the University of Buckingham, and at the British Computer Society.

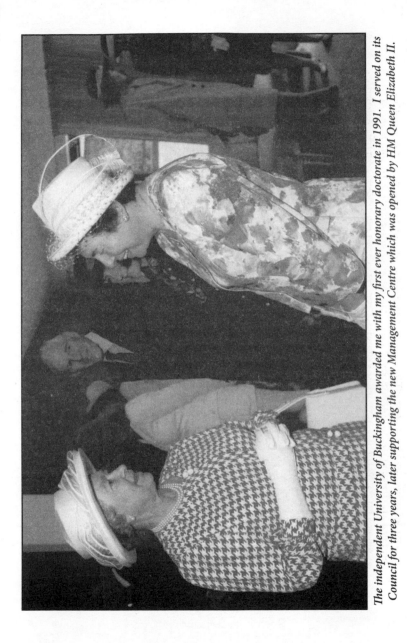

The independent University of Buckingham awarded me with my first ever honorary doctorate in 1991. I served on its Council for three years, later supporting the new Management Centre which was opened by HM Queen Elizabeth II.

My largest-ever philanthropic project was the Prior's Court Foundation. After 22 hectic months from inception to commencement, the residential school was formally opened by HRH the Princess Royal amidst torrential rain in the summer of 2000. An Adult Learning Centre opened in 2011.

I introduced Bill Gates to The City's captains of industry.

The celebrity photographer Baron took this picture for free after my OBE award in 1980. But the prints were exorbitantly expensive...

The Old Schoolhouse in Chesham Bois was a much larger version of our first home, Moss Cottage. We were there for 25 years, joined at various periods by friends and family. My company was also headquartered there at one time – until the neighbours complained!

The straight stretch of river at Henley on Thames is most beautiful. It is famous for its annual Regatta. We enjoyed occasional entertaining at the Phyllis Court Club.

HRH The Duke of Kent – whom I'd earlier met when I was the first woman President of the chartered British Computer Society – presented me with the Institute of Electrical Engineers' Mountbatten Medal in 1999.

My second cousin, the artist Milein Cosman, did some sketches of me in the 1960's, one of which I had laminated for Giles.

I always enjoy speaking with students and learn much from their bright comments and queries.

Derek and I are so different... my irresistible force meeting his immovable object... that people were surprised by our marriage and even more surprised that it lasted.

Another three tiered cake – but of ice cream –
was the dessert at our Golden Wedding party.

A happy picture at our Golden Wedding when 50 of us celebrated at Le Manoir aux Quat' Saisons. One guest had been at our wedding in 1959. I had the same flowers as on my wedding day.

Glammed up for an after-dinner speech in the City.

*Man on the Moon, Buzz Aldrin helped celebrate
my £5m gift to the IT livery company.*

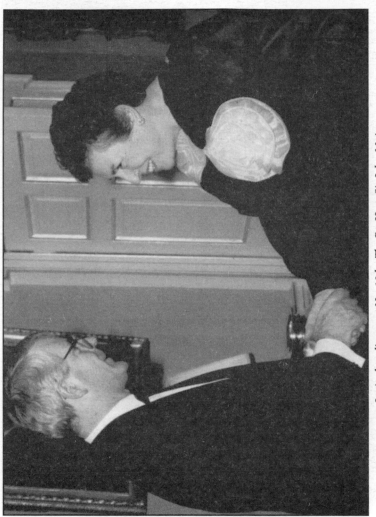

Invited to dinner at No. 10 by The Rt. Hon. Sir John Major.

As part of self-training, I organised a visit to a dying industry. There proved to be lots of jobs I would dislike more.